BOOK -
"GOD = THE GOD
MATRIX!~'"

PREVIOUS BOOKS:

1) The REAL PROPHET of DOOM!...(...!)
2) The REAL PROPHET of DOOM VOL.2 (...!)
3) The REAL PROPHET of DOOM VOL. 3 (...!)
4) The REAL PROPHET of DOOM (KISMET) (INTRODUCTION) PENDULUM FLOW
5) The REAL PROPHET of DOOM (KISMET) (INTRODUCTION) PENDULUM FLOW - (II)
6) The REAL PROPHET of DOOM (KISMET) (INTRODUCTION) PENDULUM FLOW - (III)
7) NEW BOOK - REAL MESSAGES of GOD I, II, & III-!!!~'
8) BOOK TITLE: GOD is The `-MATHEMATICIAN!!!~'
9) The `-GOD `-BOOK of `-NUMEROLOGY!~'
10) DEATH CIPHERS/CYPHERS for LIFE & DEATH!!!~'
11) DO `-YOU BELIEVE in `-GOD??? 'IS, `-DESTINY 'REAL???
12) "YOUR `-DAYS of ``-LIVING are `-NUMBERED!!!~'"
13) BOOK - "GOD = THE GOD MATRIX!~'"

BOOK - "GOD = THE GOD MATRIX!~'"

DWAYNE W. ANDERSON

BOOK - "GOD = THE GOD MATRIX!~'"

iUniverse books may be ordered through booksellers or by contacting:

iUniverse
1663 Liberty Drive
Bloomington, IN 47403
www.iuniverse.com
844-349-9409

ISBN: 978-1-6632-5327-9 (sc)
ISBN: 978-1-6632-5337-8 (hc)
ISBN: 978-1-6632-5328-6 (e)

Library of Congress Control Number: 2023909639

Print information available on the last page.

iUniverse rev. date: 03/06/2024

WITHOUT a '-DOUBT, OUR LIVES are '-ETCHED; and, '-ARTICULATED in '-TIME' to an '-EVENTUALITY; of '-GOD'S VERY OWN '-PURPOSE, to '-OUR '-VERY '-OWN PURPOSE of '-BEING; in the '-EXISTENCE/ EXPANSE of '-TIME!!!-' OUR '-time OF '-LIVES (BIRTHS, DEATHS, MARRIAGES, CHILDREN, etc.); are '-EXACTLY '-SET by '-GOD!!!-' ALREADY '-PROVEN through '-**R**ECIPROCAL-**S**EQUENCING **N**UMEROLOGY-**RSN**; and, **R**ECIPROCAL-**S**EQUENCED-**I**NVERSED-**R**EALITIES-**RSIR**!!!-' AGAIN; ENJOY the '-READS!!!-'

BULLET POINTS FOR: *BOOK - "GOD = THE GOD MATRIX!-"'*

- *THE LIFE AND DEATH OF CELEBRITIES –*
- *THE LIFE AND DEATH OF SCIENTISTS –*
- *THE LIFE AND DEATH OF COMMON PEOPLE –*
- *INTROSPECTION of GOD, the UNIVERSE; and, the MAN/WOMAN '-INSIDE –*
- *READING; and, UNDERSTANDING the '-SCIENCE of '-NUMBERS in the FOCUS of* Reciprocal-**S**equencing-**N**umerology-**RSN**-'
- *DISCOVERER & FOUNDER of RECIPROCAL SEQUENCING INVERSED REALITIES – EQUATIONS of '-REALITY in LIFE & DEATH - AUTHOR: DWAYNE W. ANDERSON -*

I've `-CREATED a NEW TYPE of PHILOSOPHY (**R**eciprocal-**S**equencing-**N**umerology)/ (*Reciprocal-Sequenced-Inversed-Realities*) that `-PROVES without `-QUESTION the `-PRESENCE of GOD'S EXISTENCE in our DAILY AFFAIRS!!!!!~'

GOD = The GOD MATRIX!!!~' What was before before the BIG BANG, etc.??? If GOD had a beginning WHAT was BEFORE BEFORE GOD, ETC. LOOK anywhere on EARTH 360 into SPACE & where does it END??? Is there a WALL of SPACE, what's on the OTHER SIDE... The CONTEMPLATION of GOD = FOREVER!!!~'

GOD = THE GOD MATRIX!!!~' ALL 27% DARK MATTER/ALL 68% DARK ENERGY = ALL of it IS GOD!!!~ HARRY LORAYNE died at AGE 96 = 9x6 = 54 = BIRTH/DAY = 5/4 = Was BORN in the MONTH of 5; and, DIED in the MONTH of 4!!!~' DEATH/DAY # NUMBER = 4+7+20+23 = 54 = BIRTH/DAY # NUMBER = 5+4+19+26 = 54!!!~'

HARRY LORAYNE (AMERICAN MAGICIAN & MEMORY-TRAINING SPECIALIST) died at the AGE of (`-96) = 9x6 = (`-54) = `-BIRTH/DAY = (5/4)!!!~' Was `-BORN in the `-MONTH of (`-5); and, `-DIED in the `-MONTH of (`-4)!!!~' `-DEATH/DAY # `-NUMBER = 4+7+20+23 = (`-54) = `-BIRTH/DAY = (`-5/4) = "SEE

2

`-BEFORE"!!!~' `-BIRTH/DAY # `-NUMBER = 5+4+19+26 = (`-54) = `-BIRTH/DAY = (`-5/4) = "WAS `-BORN in the `-MONTH of (`-5); and, `-DIED in the `-MONTH of (`-4)!!!~' `-BIRTH/DAY # `-NUMBER = (`-54) = `-DEATH/ DAY # `-NUMBER = (`-54)!!!~' `-AGE of `-DEATH = (`-96) = 9x6 = (`-54) = "SEE `-BEFORE"!!!~' `-BIRTH/ YEAR = 1926 = 19+26 = (`-45) = RECIPROCAL = (`-54) = "SEE `-BEFORE"!!!~' FRAGMENTED `-BIRTH/DAY # `-NUMBER = 5+4+1+9+2+6 = (`-27)!!!~' FRAGMENTED `-DEATH/DAY # `-NUMBER = 4+7+2+0+2+3 = (`-18)!!!~' FRAG `-BIRTH (`-27) (+) FRAG `-DEATH (`-18) = (`-45) = RECIPROCAL = (`-54) = `-ALL `-AROUND # `-NUMBER for HARRY LORAYNE (AMERICAN MAGICIAN & MEMORY-TRAINING SPECIALIST)!!!~'

FRAGMENTED `-BIRTH/DAY # `-NUMBER = 5+4+1+9+2+6 = (`-27) = `-DIED this `-MANY `-DAYS before `-HIS `-NEXT `-BIRTH/DAY = (`-27) = FROM `-DEATH-to-BIRTH!!!~' (27x2) = (`-54) = `-BIRTH/DAY & `-ALL `-OTHER `-LINKAGES!!!~'

THOMAS EDWARD SIZEMORE JR. died at the AGE of (`-61); WHILE, being `-BORN in the `-YEAR of (`-61)!!!~' WAS `-BORN in the `-MONTH of (`-11); and, `-DIED in the `-MONTH of (`-3) = 11/3 = 11x3 = (`-33) = 3/3 = `-DEATH/DAY!!!~'

`-DIED (`-94) `-DAYS from `-BIRTH/DAY-to-DEATH/ DAY = RECIPROCAL = (`-49) = `-DEATH/DAY # `-NUMBER = 3+3+20+23 = (`-49) = RECIPROCAL = (`-94)!!!~'

ACTOR CHRISTOPHER D'OLIER REEVE (MOVIE/ SUPERMAN) died at the AGE of (`-52)!!!~'

BIRTH/YEAR = (`-52) = WHILE having an AGE of DEATH of = 52 for ACTOR CHRISTOPHER D'OLIER REEVE (MOVIE/SUPERMAN)!!!~'

DAY of `-BIRTH = (`-25th) = RECIPROCAL = 52 = AGE of DEATH = (`-52) for ACTOR CHRISTOPHER D'OLIER REEVE (MOVIE/SUPERMAN)!!!~'

ACTOR GEORGE REEVES (SUPERMAN) died at the AGE of (`-45)!!!~'

`-DEATH/YEAR = (`-59) = 5x9 = (`-45) = `-AGE of `-DEATH!!!~'

WAS `-MARRIED to ELLANORA NEEDLES from 19(40) to 19(50) = 40/50 = (45 + 0 + 0) = (`-45) = AGE of DEATH for ACTOR GEORGE REEVES (SUPERMAN)!!!~'

AMERICAN ACTOR ROBERT BLAKE died at the AGE of (`-89) = RECIPROCAL = `-BIRTH/DAY = 9/18 = RECIPROCAL = 81/9 = 8x1/9 = (`-89) = `-AGE of `-DEATH from `-BIRTH/DAY!!!~' `-DEATH/DAY = 3/9 = FLIP 3 to 8 = 8/9 = `-AGE of `-DEATH from `-DEATH/DAY!!!~' `-BIRTH/DAY # `-NUMBER = 9+18+19+33 = 79 = 7x9 = (`-63) = RECIPROCAL = (`-36) = FLIP 3 to 8; FLIP 6 to 9 = (`-89) = `-AGE of `-DEATH from `-BIRTH/DAY # `-NUMBER!!!~' `-BIRTH/DAY = 9+18 = (`-27) = `-DEATH/DAY = 3x9 = (`-27)!!!~' 27+27 = (`-54) = WAS 5' 4" in `-HEIGHT!!!~' `-DIED in the `-MONTH of (`-3); and, was `-BORN in the `-MONTH of (`-9) = (`-3/9) = `-DEATH/DAY for AMERICAN ACTOR ROBERT BLAKE!!!~' `-BORN in the `-MONTH of (`-9); and, `-DIED in the `-MONTH of (`-3) = (`-9/3) = RECIPROCAL = (`-3/9) = `-DEATH/DAY for AMERICAN ACTOR ROBERT BLAKE!!!~'

`-DIED (`-193) `-DAYS from `-BIRTH-to-DEATH = 1(93) = `-WAS `-BORN in the `-MONTH of (`-9); and, `-DIED in the `-MONTH of (`-3)!!!~'

`-BIRTH/YEAR = 1933 = 1(93)3 = `-DIED (`-193) `-DAYS from `-BIRTH-to-DEATH = 1(93) = `-WAS `-BORN in the `-MONTH of (`-9); and, `-DIED in the `-MONTH of (`-3)!!!~' (9 `-DIVIDED by (`-3)) = (`-3) = `-WHAT's `-LEFT!!!~'

(365 (-) 193) = (`-172) = 1x72 = (`-72) = 8x9 = (`-89) = `-AGE of `-DEATH for AMERICAN ACTOR ROBERT BLAKE!!!~'

AMERICAN BUSINESSMAN GORDON EARLE MOORE died at the AGE of (`-94) = 9+4 = (`-13) = `-BIRTH/DAY = 1/3!!!~' Was `-BORN in the `-MONTH of (`-1); and, `-DIED in the `-MONTH of (`-3) = `-BIRTH/DAY; `-AGAIN!!!~' `-AGE of `-DEATH = (`-94) = 9x4 = (`-36) = `-DEATH/DAY = 3/24 = 3/2+4 = (`-36)!!!~'

`-BIRTH/DAY # `-NUMBER = 1+3+19+29 = (`-52)!!!~'
`-DEATH/DAY # `-NUMBER = 3+24+20+23 = (`-70)!!!~'
(70(-)52) = (`-18) = 6x3 = (`-63) = RECIPROCAL = (`-36) = 9x4 = (`-94) = `-AGE of `-DEATH for AMERICAN BUSINESSMAN GORDON EARLE MOORE!!!~'

`-BIRTH/DAY # `-NUMBER = 1+3+19+29 = (`-52)!!!~'
`-DEATH/DAY # `-NUMBER = 3+24+20+23 = (`-70)!!!~'
(70(-)52) = (`-18) = FLIP 8 to 3 = (`-13) = `-BIRTH/DAY = (`-1/3); `-AGAIN!!!~'

`-DIED (`-80) `-DAYS from `-BIRTH-to-DEATH = 8x10 = 8+10 = (`-18) = "SEE `-ABOVE" = & = FLIP 8 to 3 = (`-1/3) = `-BIRTH/DAY; `-AGAIN!!!~'

AMERICAN SINGER, GUITARIST, DRUMMER CLARENCE EUGENE "FUZZY" HASKINS died at the AGE of (`-81)!!!~' BIRTH/DAY # `-NUMBER = 6+8+19+41 = 74 = `-DEATH/DAY = 3/17 = 3+1/7 = (`-47) = RECIPROCAL = (`-74) = `-BIRTH/DAY # `-NUMBER!!!~' BIRTH/DAY # `-NUMBER = 6+8+19+41 = 74 = `-DEATH/DAY = 3/17 = RECIPROCAL = 71/3 = 71+3 = (`-74) = `-BIRTH/DAY # `-NUMBER!!!~'

`-DEATH/DAY # `-NUMBER = 3+17+20+23 – (`-63) = `-WAS `-BORN in the `-MONTH of (`-6); and, `-DIED in the `-MONTH of (`-3) = 6x3 = (`-18) = RECIPROCAL = (`-81) = `-AGE of `-DEATH for AMERICAN SINGER, GUITARIST, DRUMMER CLARENCE EUGENE "FUZZY" HASKINS!!!~'

`-DEATH/DAY # `-NUMBER; `-AGAIN = 3+17+20+23 = (`-63) = 6x3 = (`-18) = RECIPROCAL = (`-81) = `-AGE of `-DEATH for AMERICAN SINGER, GUITARIST, DRUMMER CLARENCE EUGENE "FUZZY" HASKINS!!!~' `-DEATH/DAY # `-NUMBER = 3+17+20+23 = (`-63) = `-BIRTH/DAY = 6/8 = FLIP 8 to 3 = (`-6/3) = `-DEATH/DAY # `-NUMBER!!!~'

FRAGMENTED `-BIRTH/DAY # `-NUMBER = 6+8+1+9+4+1 = (`-29) = 2x9 = (`-18) = RECIPROCAL = (`-81) = `-AGE of `-DEATH for AMERICAN SINGER, GUITARIST, DRUMMER CLARENCE EUGENE "FUZZY" HASKINS!!!~' FRAGMENTED `-DEATH/DAY # `-NUMBER = 3+1+7+2+0+2+3 = (`-18) = RECIPROCAL

= (`-81) = `-AGE of `-DEATH for AMERICAN SINGER, GUITARIST, DRUMMER CLARENCE EUGENE "FUZZY" HASKINS!!!~'

`-DEATH/DAY = 3/17 = HALF/RECIPROCAL = 3/71 = 3(-)71 = (`-68) = `-BIRTH/DAY = (`-6/8)!!!~' `-BIRTH/DAY = 6x8 = (`-48) = 4x8 = (`-32) = RECIPROCAL = (`-23) = `-DEATH/YEAR!!!~'

GARY ROBERT ROSSINGTON died at the AGE of (`-71)!!!~' `-BIRTH/YEAR was (`-51); and, `-DEATH/DAY # `-NUMBER = 3+5+20+23 = (`-51)!!!~' `-BIRTH/DAY = 12/4/19/51 = `-REMOVE (`-51) from the `-FRAGMENTED `-BIRTH/DAY # `-NUMBER = 1+2+4+1+9 = (`-17) = RECIPROCAL= (`-71) = `-AGE of `-DEATH for GUITARIST GARY ROBERT ROSSINGTON!!!~' FRAGMENTED `-DEATH/DAY # `-NUMBER = 3+5+2+0+2+3 = (`-15) = RECIPROCAL = (`-51) = `-BIRTH/YEAR for GUITARIST GARY ROBERT ROSSINGTON!!!~' `-WAS `-BORN in the `-MONTH of (`-12); and, `-DIED in the `-MONTH of (`-3) = 12/3 = 1x23 = (`-23) = `-DEATH/YEAR = (`-23) = 1x23 = 12/3 = 12+3 = (`-15) = RECIPROCAL = (`-51) = `-BIRTH/YEAR!!!~' `-DEATH/DAY = 3/5 = 3x5 = (`-15) = RECIPROCAL = (`-51) = `-BIRTH/YEAR = 1951 = 19(-)51 = (`-32) = RECIPROCAL = (`-23) = `-DEATH/YEAR for GUITARIST GARY ROBERT ROSSINGTON!!!~' `-BIRTH/DAY = (`-12/4) = HALF RECIPROCAL = 21/4 = 21(-)4 = (`-17) = RECIPROCAL = (`-71) = `-AGE of `-DEATH for GUITARIST GARY ROBERT ROSSINGTON from LYNYRD SKYNYRD!!!~'

RONALD WAYNE VAN ZANT died at the AGE of ('-29)!!!~' '-**FRAGMENTED** '-**BIRTH/DAY # '-NUMBER = 1+1+5+1+9+4+8 = ('-29) = '-AGE of '-DEATH for ORIGINAL LEAD VOCALIST of LYNYRD SKYNYRD!!!~'** '-DEATH/DAY # '-NUMBER = 10+20+19+77 = 126 = FLIP 6 to 9 = ('-129) = 1x29 = ('-29) = '-AGE of '-DEATH for ORIGINAL LEAD VOCALIST of LYNYRD SKYNYRD!!!~' '-BIRTH/YEAR = 1948 = 19(-)48 = ('-29) = '-AGE of '-DEATH for ORIGINAL LEAD VOCALIST of LYNYRD SKYNYRD!!!~' '-DEATH/YEAR = 1977 = 19(-)77 = ('-58) / DIVIDED by ('-2) = ('-29) = '-AGE of '-DEATH for ORIGINAL LEAD VOCALIST of LYNYRD SKYNYRD!!!~' '-MARRIED NADINE INSCOE in 1967 = 19(-)67 = ('-48) = '-BIRTH/YEAR for RONALD WAYNE VAN ZANT = ('-1948) = 19+48 = ('-67) = '-YEAR '-FIRST '-MARRIED!!!~' '-BIRTH/DAY = ('-1/15) = HALF RECIPROCAL = 1/51 = 1+51 = 52 / '-DIVIDED by ('-2) = ('-26) = FLIP 6 to 9 = ('-29) = AGE of '-DEATH for ORIGINAL LEAD VOCALIST of LYNYRD SKYNYRD!!!~' '-PARTIAL '-DEATH/DAY # '-NUMBER = 10(-)20+19 = ('-29) = AGE of '-DEATH for ORIGINAL LEAD VOCALIST of LYNYRD SKYNYRD RONALD WAYNE VAN ZANT!!!~'

SINGER/SONGWRITER KURT COBAIN (NIRVANA) `-**DIED** at the `-**AGE** of (`-**27**)!!!~'

/|\ FRAGMENTED `-**BIRTH/DAY** # `-**NUMBER** = (2 + 2 + 0 + 1 + 9 + 6 + 7) = (`-**27**) = `-**AGE of** `-**DEATH for SINGER/SONGWRITER KURT COBAIN** (`-**27**)"!!!~' /|\

AMERICAN ACTOR JAMES DEAN `-**DIED** at the `-**AGE** of (`-**24**)!!!~'

/|\ FRAGMENTED `-**BIRTH/DAY** # `-**NUMBER** = (2 + 8 + 1 + 9 + 3 + 1) = (`-**24**) = `-**AGE of** `-**DEATH for AMERICAN ACTOR JAMES DEAN** (`-**24**)"!!!~' /|\

AMERICAN ACTOR (JANSEN RAYNE PANETTIERE) died at the `-AGE of (`-28)!!!~' `-DEATH/DAY = 2/19 = 2/1(-)9 = (`-28) = `-AGE of `-DEATH = (`-28) = FLIP 8 to 3 = (`-23) = `-DEATH/YEAR!!!~' `-BIRTH/DAY # `-NUMBER = 9+25+19+94 = (`-147)!!!~' DAYS from `-BIRTH-to-DEATH = (`-147) `-DAYS!!!~' CALENDAR `-YEAR (`-365) (-) (`-147) = (`-218) = 28x1 = (`-28) = `-AGE of `-DEATH!!!~' (`-147) = RECIPROCAL = (`-741) = 74(-)1 = (`-73) = FLIP 7 to 2; FLIP 3 to 8 = (`-28) = `-AGE of `-DEATH!!!~' `-DEATH/DAY # `-NUMBER = 2+19+20+23 = (`-64) = TIMES X (`-2) = (`-128) = 1x28 = (`-28) = `-AGE of `-DEATH!!!~' `-BIRTH/YEAR = 1994 = 1+9+9+4 = (`-23) = `-DEATH/YEAR = (`-23) = FLIP 3 to 8 = (`-28) = `-AGE of `-DEATH!!!~' WAS

`-BORN in the `-MONTH of (`-9); and, `-DIED in the `-MONTH of (`-2) = (`-9/2) = RECIPROCAL = (`-29) = `-DIED within `-HIS (`-29th) `-YEAR of `-EXISTENCE!!!~' HEIGHT = 5' 7" = (`-57) / `-DIVIDED by (`-2) = (`-28.5) = `-AGE of `-DEATH!!!~'

AMERICAN ACTOR (RICHARD JAY BELZER) died at the AGE of (`-78)!!!~' (`-78) = FLIP 7 to 2; FLIP 8 to 3 = (`-23) = `-DEATH/YEAR!!!~' `-AGE of `-DEATH = (`-78) = `-DIVORCED DALIA DANOCH in (`-78) = "A (COMMON) PATTERN of (LIFE)"!!!~' WAS `-BORN in the `-MONTH of (`-8); and, `-DIED in the `-MONTH of (`-2) = (`-82) = FLIP 2 to 7 = (`-87) = RECIPROCAL = (`-78) = `-AGE of `-DEATH!!!~' `-DEATH/DAY = 2/19 = FLIP 2 to 7 = 7/19 = 7/1(-)9 = (`-78) = `-AGE of `-DEATH!!!~' `-BIRTH/DAY = 8/4 = 8x4 = 32 = FLIP 3 to 8; FLIP 2 to 7 = (`-87) = RECIPROCAL = (`-78) = `-AGE of `-DEATH!!!~' PORTRAYED the CHARACTER "JOHN MUNCH" for (`-23) YEARS = `-DEATH/YEAR = (`-23) = FLIP 2 to 7; FLIP 3 to 8 = (`-78) = `-AGE of `-DEATH!!!~'

AMERICAN ACTOR & FILMMAKER (OLIVER BURGESS MEREDITH) died at the AGE of (`-89)!!!~' `-BIRTH/DAY = 11/16 = 11+16 = (`-27) = RECIPROCAL = (`-72) = 8x9 = (`-89) = `-AGE of `-DEATH!!!~' `-BIRTH/ YEAR = 1907 = (97x1+0) = (`-97) = `-DEATH/YEAR!!!~'

`-BIRTH/DAY # `-NUMBER = 11+16+19+07 = (`-53)!!!~'
`-DEATH/DAY # `-NUMBER = 9+9+19+97 = 134 = 1x34
= (`-34) x 2 = (`-68) = RECIPROCAL = (`-86) = FLIP 6
to 9 = (`-89) = `-AGE of `-DEATH!!!~' `-DEATH # (`-134)
(-) `-BIRTH # (`-53) = (`-81) = 9x9 = 9/9 = `-DEATH/
DAY!!!~' FROM `-BIRTH-to-DEATH there are (`-68)
DAYS = RECIPROCAL = (`-86) = FLIP 6 to 9 = (`-89) =
`-AGE of `-DEATH!!!~' CALENDAR `-YEAR (`-365) (-)
(`-68) = (`-297) = "TWO 97's" in `-BIRTH & in `-DEATH
= 1907/1997!!!~' `-DEATH/YEAR = 1997 = (1+9+7)(9) =
17/9 = 1+7/9 = (`-89) = `-AGE of `-DEATH!!!~' `-BIRTH/
YEAR = 1907 = 19(-)7 = 12 = FLIP 2 to 7 = (`-17) = 8+9
= (`-89) = `-AGE of `-DEATH!!!~' FRAGMENTED
`-BIRTH/DAY # `-NUMBER = 1+1+1+6+1+9+0+7 = (`-
26)!!!~' FRAGMENTED `-DEATH/DAY # `-NUMBER =
9+9+1+9+9+7 = (`-44)!!!~' FRAG `-BIRTH (`-26) (+) FRAG
`-DEATH (`-44) = (`-70) / `-DIVIDED by (`-2) = (`-35) =
RECIPROCAL = (`-53) = `-BIRTH/DAY # `-NUMBER!!!~'
`-MARRIED to KAJA SUNDSTEN in 1951 = 19+51 = (`-
70) = "SEE `-PREVIOUS `-ILLUSTRATION"!!!~' FRAG
`-DEATH (`-44) (-) FRAG `-BIRTH (`-26) = (`-18) = 9+9 =
9/9 = `-DEATH/DAY!!!~' `-DEATH = 9/9/19/97 = 4(9's) =
4x9 = (`-36) = FLIP 3 to 8; FLIP 6 to 9 = (`-89) = `-AGE of
`-DEATH!!!~' `-WHAT'S `-LEFT = (`-17) = 8+9 = (`-89) =
`-AGE of `-DEATH!!!~' WAS `-BORN in the `-MONTH
of (`-11); and, `-DIED in the `-MONTH of (`-9) = 11/9 =
11x9 = (`-99) = 9/9 = `-DEATH/DAY!!!~' `-DEATH/YEAR
= 1997 = 19(-)97 = 78 = 7x8 = (`-56) = 5' 6" = `-HEIGHT

for AMERICAN ACTOR & FILMMAKER (OLIVER BURGESS MEREDITH)!!!~'

AMERICAN COMPOSER (GERALD FRIED) died at the AGE of 95!!!~' **BIRTH/DAY = 2/13 = 23x1 = (`-23) = `-DEATH/YEAR!!!~'** BIRTH/DAY # `-NUMBER = 2+13+19+28 = (`-62)!!!~' DEATH/DAY # `-NUMBER = 2+17+20+23 = 62!!!~' `-BIRTH/DAY # `-NUMBER = (`-62) = `-DEATH/DAY # `-NUMBER!!!~' 62+62 = 124 = 1to4 = 9(+)5 = (`-14) = `-DIED (`-4) DAYS after `-HIS `-LAST `-BIRTH/DAY = 9(-)5 = (`-4)!!!~' `-WAS `-BORN in (`-2); and, `-DIED in (`-2) = (2+2) = (`-4) = `-DIED this `-MANY `-DAYS from `-BIRTH-to-DEATH!!!~' `-PARTIAL `-BIRTH/DAY # `-NUMBER = 2+13+19 = (`-34)!!!~' `-DEATH/DAY = 2/17 = 2x17 = (`-34)!!!~' `-BIRTH/ YEAR = 1928 = 9(8(-)2(-)1) = (`-95) = `-AGE of `-DEATH!!!~' FRAGMENTED `-BIRTH/DAY = 2+1+3+1+9+2+8 = (`-26) = RECIPROCAL = (`-62) = `-BIRTH #/`-DEATH # = (`-62)!!!~' FRAGMENTED `-DEATH/DAY = 2+1+7+2+0+2+3 = (`-17)!!!~' FRAG `-BIRTH (`-26) (+) FRAG `-DEATH (`-17) = (`-43) = RECIPROCAL = (`-34) = "SEE `-ABOVE"!!!~' FRAG # `-BIRTH (`-26) (-) FRAG `-DEATH (`-17) = (`-9) = 4+5 = (`-45) = 9x5 = (`-**95**) = `-AGE of `-DEATH for AMERICAN COMPOSER (GERALD FRIED)!!!~'

OAKLAND A'S (SALVATORE LEONARD BANDO) BIRTHDAY # NUMBER = 2+13+19+44 = 78 = AGE of DEATH!!!~' **BIRTH = 2/13 = 23 = YEAR of DEATH!!!~'** OAKLAND A'S RAY FOSSE BIRTHDAY # NUMBER = 4+4+19+47 = 74 = AGE of DEATH!!!~' This is a RESOUNDING PATTERN of over 100 TIMES in MY 12 BOOKS!!!~' DWA

AMERICAN ACTRESS (JO RAQUEL WELCH) BIRTH/DAY # = 9+5+19+40 = 73 = FLIP 7 to 2 = 23 = DEATH/YEAR!!!~' 40(-)19 = 21(5) = `-DEATH/DAY = FEBRUARY 15th!!!~' REVERSE `-LOOKUP on `-BIRTH/ DAY # `-NUMBER = 40(-)19(-)5(-)9 = (`-7) = DEATH/ YEAR = 2+0+2+3 = (7)!!!~' HEIGHT 5' 6" = 5x6 = 30 = DEATH/DAY = 2x15 = 30!!!~' 30+30 = 60 = `-DEATH/ DAY # `-NUMBER = 2+15+20+23 = 60!!!~' PARTIAL DEATH/DAY # = 2+15+20 = 37 = RECIPROCAL = 73 = `-BIRTH/DAY # `-NUMBER!!!~' DEATH/YEAR = 23 = RECIPROCAL = 32 = FLIP 3 to 8 = (`-82) = `-AGE of `-DEATH for AMERICAN ACTRESS (JO RAQUEL WELCH)!!!~' FRAGMENTED `-BIRTH/DAY # `-NUMBER = 9+5+1+9+4+0 = 28 = RECIPROCAL = 82 = `-AGE of `-DEATH!!!~' FROM `-BIRTH-to-DEATH there are (`-163) days = (1+6)3 = 73 = `-BIRTH/DAY # `-NUMBER!!!~' (`-163) = 16x3 = 48 = 4x8 = 32 = FLIP 3 to 8 = (`-82) = `-AGE of `-DEATH!!!~' (`-163) = 16x3 = 48 = 4x8 = 32 = RECIPROCAL = 23 = DEATH/YEAR!!!~'

FRAGMENTED `-DEATH/DAY # `-NUMBER = 2+1+5+2+0+2+3 = 15!!!~' FRAG `-BIRTH (`-28) (+) FRAG `-DEATH (`-15) = 43 = 20+23 = `-DEATH/YEAR!!!~' `-BORN in the `-MONTH of (`-9); and, `-DIED in the `-MONTH of (`-2) = (`-92) / `-DIVIDED by (`-4) = (`-23) = DEATH/YEAR!!!~'

AMERICAN ACTOR RAYMOND THOMAS BAILEY "CHARACTER = WEALTHY BANKER MILBURN DRYSDALE of THE BEVERLY HILLBILLIES" died at the AGE of 75!~' FRAG BIRTHDAY # = 5+6+1+9+0+4 = 25 = FLIP 2 to 7 = 75 = AGE of DEATH!~' BIRTHYEAR = 1904 = 19x4 = 76 = DIED within HIS 76th YEAR of EXISTENCE!~' BIRTHDAY = 5/6 = 5x6 = 30 = FLIP 3 to 8 = 80 = DEATH/YEAR!~' BIRTHDAY # = 5+6+19+04 = 34 = FLIP 3 to 8 = 84 / (DIVIDED by) (`-2) = 42!!!~' DEATHDAY # in REVERSE = 80(-)19(-)15(-)4 = 42!!!~' FRAG DEATHDAY # = 4+1+5+1+9+8+0 = 28 (X TIMES) (`-2) = 56 = BIRTH/DAY!!!~' BIRTHYEAR = 1904 = 19(04) = 19(-)4 = 15 = (4/15) = DEATH/DAY!!!~'

BOTH CYNTHIA JANE WILLIAMS & CAROLE PENNY MARSHALL (LAVERNE & SHIRLEY) died at the AGE of (`-75)!!!~' CYNTHIA JANE WILLIAMS BIRTH/DAY # `-NUMBER = 8+22+19+47 = 96 =

RECIPROCAL = 69 = 1+25+20+23 = `-DEATH/DAY # `-NUMBER!!!~'

AMERICAN ACTRESS LISA LORING started acting as the ORIGINAL WEDNESDAY ADDAMS in 19(64)!!!~' SHE died at the AGE of (`-64)!!!~' (64+64) = 128 = HER `-DEATH/DAY!!!~' BIRTHDAY = 2+16 = 18 = DEATH/ DAY = 1to8!!!~' FRAG BIRTH # = 2+1+6+1+9+5+8 = 32 x TIMES 2 = 64!!!~' A RUDE AWAKENING!!!~'

ACTRESS (ANNIE WERSCHING) FRAG BIRTH # = 3+2+8+1+9+7+7 = 37!!!~' DEATH/DAY # NUMBER for ACTRESS ANNE WERSCHING = 1+29+20+23 = 73!!!~'

`-BIRTH/DAY = 3/28 = HALF RECIPROCAL = 3/82 = 3+82 = (`-85) = RECIPROCAL = (`-58)!!!~'

ACTRESS ANNIE WERSCHING `-DIED (`-58) DAYS from `-BIRTH-to-DEATH = `-BIRTH/YEAR = 19(-)77 = (`-58)!!!~'

`-BIRTH/YEAR = 19/77 = 19+77 = (`-96) = 9x6 = (`-54) = RECIPROCAL = (`-45) = `-AGE of `-DEATH for ACTRESS ANNIE WERSCHING!!!~'

MOTOWN'S (BARRETT STRONG) FRAG BIRTH # = 2+5+1+9+4+1 = 22 = 2x11 = 21 = 3x7!!!~' DEATH/DAY

NUMBER for MOTOWN'S BARRETT STRONG = 1+29+20+23 = 73!!!~' WAS '-BORN in the '-MONTH of ('-2); and, '-DIED in the '-MONTH of ('-1) = ('-21) = (7x3)!!!~'

'-RECIPROCALS = CREATED by DWA!!!~'

HOCKEY PLAYER (ROBERT MARVIN HULL) DEATH/DAY = 1/30 = 1+30 = 31 = RECIPROCAL = 1/3 = '-BIRTH/DAY!!!~' FRAGMENTED BIRTH/DAY # for HOCKEY PLAYER ROBERT MARVIN HULL = 1+3+1+9+3+9 = 26 / DIVIDED by 2 = 1/3 = '-BIRTH/DAY = ('-ALSO) DEATH/DAY = 1/30 = "JUST '-ADD A '-ZERO"!!!~'

'-AGE of '-DEATH for HOCKEY PLAYER ROBERT MARVIN HULL was ('-84) = 8x4 = ('-32) = RECIPROCAL = ('-23) = '-DEATH/YEAR!!!~'

AMERICAN SINGER & DRUMMER (KAREN ANNE CARPENTER) had a '-BIRTH/DAY of (3/2)!!!~' SHE was BORN in the MONTH of (3) & DIED in the MONTH of (2); while, DYING at the AGE of (32)!!!~' IN MY 12 BOOKS; if I SHOWED YOU THIS OVER 100 TIMES; what, would YOU SCARILY THINK??? (DWA)

DAREDEVIL (ROBERT EDWARD KNIEVEL II) died on (1+13+20+23) = (`-57) = `-HIS VERY OWN BIRTH/DAY = (MAY 7ᵗʰ)!!!~' THIS has been seen ALL THROUGHOUT my 12 BOOKS including HIS FATHER'S DEATH!!!~' NOW, a RE-RELEASE of my 12ᵗʰ BOOK (YOUR `-DAYS of `-LIVING are `-NUMBERED!!!~') just for the ELVIS/ LISA MARIE PRESLEY FAMILY!!!~' (DWA)

HARRY LORAYNE (AMERICAN MAGICIAN & MEMORY-TRAINING SPECIALIST) died at the AGE of (`-96) = 9x6 = (`-54) = `-BIRTH/DAY = (5/4)!!!~' Was `-BORN in the `-MONTH of (`-5); and, `-DIED in the `-MONTH of (`-4)!!!~' `-DEATH/DAY # `-NUMBER = 4+7+20+23 = (`-54) = `-BIRTH/DAY = (`-5/4) = "SEE `-ABOVE & `-BEFORE"!!!~'

When YOU think of a `-BEING talking to YOU; and, guiding you THROUGH EVERYTHING; that has `-CREATED; and, is in `-CONTROL of `-EVERY SINGLE micro-ATOM and ATOM in the `-UNIVERSE; there is a LOSS of WORDS!!!~' There ISN'T ANY KIND of EXCLAMATION in CREATION that CAN DESCRIBE IT!!!~'

When `-YOU think OF being the ARCHITECT of a BUILDING; or, an ENGINEER of a `-PROJECT; you have the `-deepest APPRECIATION of ALL of WHAT GOD has done in HIS `-Creating of ALL LIFE, ALL THOUGHTS;

and, ALL MATTERS of FORCE to INCLUDE energy & matter!!!~' TAKE a RIDE on the WILD SIDE!!!~'

BRITISH AUTHOR ANNE PERRY was `-BORN in the `-MONTH of (`-10); and, `-DIED in the `-MONTH of (`-4) = 10/4 = RECIPROCAL = 4/10 = `-DEATH/DAY!!!~'

AGE of `-DEATH for BRITISH AUTHOR ANNE PERRY = 84 = 8x4 = (`-32) = RECIPROCAL = (`-23) = `-DEATH/ YEAR!!!~'

`-BIRTH/YEAR = 1938 = RECIPROCAL = 8391 = (8) (3+9+1) = 8(13) = 8(1+3) = (`-84) = `-AGE of `-DEATH for BRITISH AUTHOR ANNE PERRY!!!~'

AMERICAN PHOTOJOURNALIST & ACTIVIST KWAME BRATHWAITE was `-BORN in the `-MONTH of (`-1); and, `-DIED in the `-MONTH of (`-4) = (`-1/4) = RECIPROCAL = (`-4/1) = `-DEATH/DAY!!!~'

`-BIRTH/YEAR = 1938 = RECIPROCAL = 8391 = (8) (3(-)9(-)1) = (`-85) = `-AGE of `-DEATH for AMERICAN PHOTOJOURNALIST & ACTIVIST KWAME BRATHWAITE!!!~'

AMERICAN CARTOONIST ALLAN JAFFEE `-DIED at the `-AGE of (`-102)!!!~'

FRAGMENTED `-DEATH/DAY # `-NUMBER = 4+1+0+2+0+2+3 = (`-12) = "JUST INSERT a `-ZERO" = (`-102) = `-AGE of `-DEATH for AMERICAN CARTOONIST ALLAN JAFFEE!!!~'

AMERICAN CARTOONIST ALLAN JAFFEE was `-BORN in the `-MONTH of (`-3); and, `-DIED in the `-MONTH of (`-4) = 3/4 = 3x4 = (`-12) = "JUST INSERT a `-ZERO" = (`-102) = `-AGE of `-DEATH for AMERICAN CARTOONIST ALLAN JAFFEE!!!~'

`-BIRTH/DAY # `-NUMBER = 3+13+19+21 = (`-56) = RECIPROCAL = (`-65)!!!~'

Was A REGULAR CONTRIBUTOR to MAD MAGAZINE for (`-65) `-YEARS; and, `-ITS LONGEST RUNNING CONTRIBUTOR!!!~'

`-DEATH/DAY # `-NUMBER = 4+10+20+23 = (`-57) = 5+7 = (`-12) = "JUST INSERT a `-ZERO" = (`-102) = `-AGE of `-DEATH for AMERICAN CARTOONIST ALLAN JAFFEE!!!~'

(56 + 57) = 113 = 11x3 = (`-33) = `-BIRTH/DAY = (`-3/13) = 33x1 = (`-33)!!!~'

'-DEATH/YEAR = 2023 = RECIPROCAL = 3202 = 3(-)2 (02) = ('-102) = '-AGE of '-DEATH for AMERICAN CARTOONIST ALLAN JAFFEE!!!~'

THINK, of ALL the PEOPLE in MY ('-13) BOOKS; and, '-SEEING '-THEM '-RESURRECTED!!!~' '-THINK of THESE '-INDIVIDUALS in THEIR '-GREATEST of '-TIMES; and, '-REALIZE that '-YOU will be '-TALKING to '-THEM; and, ALSO '-SEEING them '-AGAIN; in the '-FLESH!!!~' YOUR '-FAMILY '-MEMBERS, '-too!!!~'

FOR the '-SOON '-RESURRECTION/; could '-YOU '-imagine the '-GREATEST of OUR TIMES walking among US in their YOUTHFUL VIGOR; while, WE; are of the CURRENT '-AGES that WE ARE??? '-IMAGINE playing BALL or MUSIC with the GREATEST of ALL TIME!!!~' '-IMAGINE your GREATEST WORLD LEADERS '-too, '-NOW!!!~'

CHRISTINE ANNE MCVIE (MUSICAL GROUP / FLEETWOOD MAC) died at the '-AGE of ('-79)!!!~'

'-WAS '-BORN in the '-MONTH of ('-7); and, '-DIED in the '-MONTH of ('-11) = 7/11 = 7(1+1) = 7/2 = '-BIRTH/DAY = 7/12 = 72x1 = ('-72)!!!~'

CHRISTINE ANNE MCVIE (MUSICAL GROUP / FLEETWOOD MAC) `-DIED (`-141) DAYS from `-BIRTH-to-DEATH = `-DEATH/DAY = 11+30 = (`-41)!!!~'

(365 (-) 141) = (`-224) = 2x24 = (`-48) = RECIPROCAL = (`-84) = `-BIRTH/DAY = 7x12 = (`-84)!!!~'

(84 + 84) = (`-168) = 1x68 = (`-68) = `-MARRIED JOHN MCVIE (MUSICAL GROUP / FLEETWOOD MAC) in (`-68)!!!~'

`-AGE of `-DEATH for CHRISTINE ANNE MCVIE (MUSICAL GROUP / FLEETWOOD MAC) = (`-79) = 7x9 = (`-63) = FLIP 3 to 8 = (`-68)!!!~'

`-MARRIED JOHN MCVIE in (`-68) = RECIPROCAL = (`-86) = `-MARRIED EDDY QUINTELA!!!~'

MARRIED EDDY QUINTELA in 1986 = 19(-)86 = (`-67) = RECIPROCAL = (`-76) = `-DIVORCED JOHN MCVIE in (`-76)!!!~'

`-DIVORCED JOHN MCVIE in (`-76) = FLIP 6 to 9 = (`-79) = `-AGE of `-DEATH for CHRISTINE ANNE MCVIE (MUSICAL GROUP / FLEETWOOD MAC)!!!~'

`-MARRIED to EDDY QUINTELA for (`-17) `-YEARS!!!~'

`-MARRIED to JOHN MCVIE to (`-8) `-YEARS!!!~'

(17 / 8) = 7(1+8) = (`-79) = `-AGE of `-DEATH for CHRISTINE ANNE MCVIE (MUSICAL GROUP / FLEETWOOD MAC)!!!~'

`-BIRTH/DAY = 7/12 = BIRTH/MONTH (7) = BIRTH/ DAY 7+12 = (`-19) = 79x1 = (`-79) = `-AGE of `-DEATH for CHRISTINE ANNE MCVIE (MUSICAL GROUP / FLEETWOOD MAC)!!!~'

`-BIRTH/YEAR = 19+43 = (`-62) = RECIPROCAL = (`-26) = FLIP 2 to 7; FLIP 6 to 9 = (`-79) = `-AGE of `-DEATH for CHRISTINE ANNE MCVIE (MUSICAL GROUP / FLEETWOOD MAC)!!!~'

AMERICAN BROADCAST JOURNALIST BARBARA JILL WALTERS died at the `-AGE of (`-93)!!!~'

`-WAS `-BORN in the `-MONTH of (`-9); and, `-DIED in the `-MONTH of (`-12) = 9/12 = 9(1+2) = (`-93) = `-AGE of `-DEATH for AMERICAN BROADCAST JOURNALIST BARBARA JILL WALTERS!!!~'

`-BIRTH/YEAR = 1929 = RECIPROCAL = 9291 = 9(2+9+1) = 9(12) = `-WAS `-BORN in the `-MONTH of (`-9); and, `-DIED in the `-MONTH of (`-12)!!!~'

FRAGMENTED `-BIRTH/DAY # `-NUMBER = 9+2+5+1+9+2+9 = (`-37)!!!~'

FRAGMENTED `-DEATH/DAY # `-NUMBER = 1+2+3+0+2+0+2+2 = (`-12)!!!~'

(37 + 12) = (`-49) = 4x9 = (`-36) = RECIPROCAL = (`-63) = FLIP 6 to 9 = (`-93) = `-AGE of `-DEATH for AMERICAN BROADCAST JOURNALIST BARBARA JILL WALTERS!!!~'

`-MARRIED to MERV ADELSON in (`-1986) = 19(-)86 = (`-67) = 6x7 = (`-42) = 20+22 = `-DEATH/YEAR for AMERICAN BROADCAST JOURNALIST BARBARA JILL WALTERS!!!~'

`-DIVORCED MERV ADELSON in (`-1992) = `-BIRTH/YEAR = (`-1929) = "SWIPE ONE (`-9) to the `-LEFT"!!!~'

(`-1992) = 9(1+9+2) = 9(12) = `-WAS `-BORN in the `-MONTH of (`-9); and, `-DIED in the `-MONTH of (`-12)!!!~'

`-MARRIED to MERV ADELSON for (`-6) `-YEARS = 9(-)3 = (`-93) = `-AGE of `-DEATH for AMERICAN BROADCAST JOURNALIST BARBARA JILL WALTERS!!!~'

`-BIRTH/DAY = 9(-)25 = (`-16)!!!~'

`-DEATH/DAY = 12(-)30 = (`-18)!!!~'

(16/18) = (68x1x1) = (`-68) = RECIPROCAL = (`-86) = `-MARRIED MERV ADELSON in (`-86)!!!~'

`-BIRTH/DAY = 9+25 = (`-34) x (`-2) = (`-68) = RECIPROCAL = (`-86) = `-MARRIED MERV ADELSON in (`-86)!!!~'

`-BIRTH/DAY = 9/25 = HALF RECIPROCAL = 9/52 = 9(-)52 = (`-43) x (`-2) = (`-86) = `-MARRIED MERV ADELSON in (`-86)!!!~'

`-DEATH/DAY = 12+30 = (`-42) = 20+22 = `-DEATH/ YEAR for AMERICAN BROADCAST JOURNALIST BARBARA JILL WALTERS!!!~'

`-BIRTH/YEAR = 19+29 = (`-48) = RECIPROCAL = (`-84)!!!~'

`-DEATH/DAY # `-NUMBER = 12+30+20+22 = (`-84)!!!~'

(84 +84) = (`-168) = 16x8 = (`-128) = 1x28 = (`-28) = RECIPROCAL = (`-82)!!!~'

`-BIRTY/DAY # `-NUMBER = 9+25+19+29 = (`-82)!!!~'

`-DEATH/DAY = 12/30 = HALF RECIPROCAL = 12/03 = 12(-)3 = 9

"TAKE the `-VERY `-LAST `-PART of the `-EQUATION = (`-39) = RECIPROCAL = (`-93) = `-AGE of `-DEATH for AMERICAN BROADCAST JOURNALIST BARBARA JILL WALTERS!!!~'

`-WAS `-BORN in the `-MONTH of (`-9); and, `-DIED in the `-MONTH of (`-12) = 9/12 = FLIP 2 to 7 = 9/17 = 9(1(-)7) = (`-96) = `-DIED this `-MANY `-DAYS from `-BIRTH-to-DEATH for AMERICAN BROADCAST JOURNALIST BARBARA JILL WALTERS!!!~'

(365 (-) 96) = (`-269) = 2x69 = (`-138) = (1+8) (3) = (`-93) = `-AGE of `-DEATH for AMERICAN BROADCAST JOURNALIST BARBARA JILL WALTERS (20/20)!!!~'

`-GOD equals a `-PERFECT `-MEMORY!!!~' When `-I say, the RESURRECTED will be brought `-BACK to `-LIFE; `-I SAY, that they will be brought back to `-LIFE; with a PERFECT MEMORY of EVERY CONCEPT of THOUGHT that THEY had EVER HAD!!!~' EVERY NOTE of a `-SONG & with a `-distinct `-NUANCE~

`-PLEASE `-KEEP this in `-MIND: When the `-DEAD are `-resurrected, `-THEY will `-INCLUDE every `-VISAGE of `-LIFE; including the `-UNBORN!!!~' For `-ALL those that had an `-ABORTION; these VISAGES of `-LIFE `-too, will be `-SEEN; and, `-ENTERTAINED as `-WELL!!!~' PLEASE keep this in `-MIND!!!~' The PROPHET~

POPE BENEDICT XVI (FORMER HEAD of the CATHOLIC CHURCH) died at the `-AGE of (`-95)!!!~'

'-WAS '-BORN in the '-MONTH of ('-4); and, '-DIED in the '-MONTH of ('-12) = 4/12 = FLIP 2 to 7 = 4/17 = 4(1(-)7) = 4/6 = '-BIRTH/DAY = 4/16 = 46x1 = ('-4/6)!!!~'

'-BIRTH/YEAR = 19+27 = ('-46)!!!~'

'-BIRTH/DAY = 4/16 = HALF RECIPROCAL = 4/61 = 4+61 = ('-65) = FLIP 6 to 9 = ('-95) = '-AGE of '-DEATH for POPE BENEDICT XVI (FORMER HEAD of the CATHOLIC CHURCH)!!!~'

'-BIRTH/YEAR = 1927 = (1x9) (2(-)7) = ('-95) = '-AGE of '-DEATH for POPE BENEDICT XVI (FORMER HEAD of the CATHOLIC CHURCH)!!!~'

'-WAS '-BORN in the '-MONTH of ('-4); and, '-DIED in the '-MONTH of ('-12) = 4/12 = 4x12 = ('-48) = RECIPROCAL = ('-84) = '-BIRTH/DAY of POPE JOHN PAUL II (FORMER HEAD of the CATHOLIC CHURCH) = 5/18 = RECIPROCAL = 81/5 = 8(1(-)5) = ('-84)!!!~'

POPE JOHN PAUL II (FORMER HEAD of the CATHOLIC CHURCH) '-BIRTH/DAY = 5/18 = RECIPROCAL = 81/5 = 8(1(-)5) = ('-84) = **The '-VERY '-AGE of '-DEATH** from '-**BIRTH/DAY** for POPE JOHN PAUL II (FORMER HEAD of the CATHOLIC CHURCH)!!!~'

POPE JOHN PAUL II (FORMER HEAD of the CATHOLIC CHURCH) '-AGE of '-DEATH = ('-**84**) = RECIPROCAL = ('-48) = **4/8** = '-**DATE OF '-BURIAL** for POPE JOHN PAUL II (FORMER HEAD of the CATHOLIC CHURCH)!!!~'

POPE FRANCIS `-BIRTH/DAY # `-NUMBER = 12+17+19+36 = (`-84)!!!~'

POPE FRANCIS `-CURRENT `-AGE = (`-86) = 8x6 = (`-48) = RECIPROCAL = (`-84)!!!~'

(84 + 84) = (`-168) = 1x68 = (`-68) = RECIPROCAL = (`-86)!!!~'

POPE FRANCIS `-BIRTH/YEAR = (`-36) = 3(6's) = (`-666) = "The `-PATTERN"!!!~'

POPE BENEDICT XVI (FORMER HEAD of the CATHOLIC CHURCH) `-DIED (`-106) `-DAYS from `-BIRTH-to-DEATH = 10+6 = (`-16) = `-DAY of `-BIRTH / for POPE BENEDICT XVI (FORMER HEAD of the CATHOLIC CHURCH)!!!~'

(365 (-) 106) = (`-259) = RECIPROCAL = 95(2) = (95)(too) = `-AGE of `-DEATH (`-**95**) for POPE BENEDICT XVI (FORMER HEAD of the CATHOLIC CHURCH)!!!~'

`-DEATH/DAY = 12/31 = HALF RECIPROCAL = 12/13 = 12x13 = (`-156) = RECIPROCAL = (`-651) = 65(-)1 = (`-64)!!!~'

`-BIRTH/DAY = 4/16 = RECIPROCAL = 61/4 = 6x1/4 = (`-**64**)!!!~'

`-AGE of `-DEATH (`-95) for POPE BENEDICT XVI (FORMER HEAD of the CATHOLIC CHURCH) = 9x5 = (`-**45**) = `-BIRTH/DAY = 4/16 = 4(1(-)6) = (`-45) = 9x5 = (`-**95**) = `-AGE of `-DEATH for POPE BENEDICT XVI (FORMER HEAD of the CATHOLIC CHURCH)!!!~'

POPE JOHN PAUL II (FORMER HEAD of the CATHOLIC CHURCH) `-DIED in the `-MONTH of (`-4); and, `-WAS `-BORN in the `-MONTH of (`-5) = (`-**45**) = 9x5 = (`-**95**) = `-AGE of `-DEATH for POPE BENEDICT XVI (FORMER HEAD of the CATHOLIC CHURCH)!!!~'

POPE JOHN PAUL II (FORMER HEAD of the CATHOLIC CHURCH) `-**BIRTH/DAY** = **5/18** = 5x18 = (`-**90**) / DIVIDED by (`-2) = (`-**45**) = "SEE `-ABOVE" – **DIED** in the `-MONTH of &`-WAS `-**BORN** in the `-MONTH of!!!~'

POPE JOHN PAUL II (FORMER HEAD of the CATHOLIC CHURCH) became `-POPE in (`-**1978**) = 19(-)78 = (`-**59**) = RECIPROCAL = (`-**95**) = `-**AGE of `-DEATH** for POPE BENEDICT XVI (FORMER HEAD of the CATHOLIC CHURCH)!!!~'

POPE JOHN PAUL II (FORMER HEAD of the CATHOLIC CHURCH) `-BIRTH/DAY # `-NUMBER = 5+18+19+20 = (`-62) = "SEE `-BELOW"!!!~'

POPE JOHN PAUL II (FORMER HEAD of the CATHOLIC CHURCH) `-**PARTIAL** `-**DEATH/DAY #** `-**NUMBER** = 4+2+20 = (`-26) = RECIPROCAL = (`-62)

= `-**BIRTH/DAY** # `-NUMBER for POPE JOHN PAUL II (FORMER HEAD of the CATHOLIC CHURCH)!!!~'

POPE JOHN PAUL II (FORMER HEAD of the CATHOLIC CHURCH) `-DEATH/DAY # `-NUMBER = 4+2+20+05 = (`-31) = `-DAY of `-DEATH (`-31st) for POPE BENEDICT XVI (FORMER HEAD of the CATHOLIC CHURCH)!!!~'

POPE JOHN PAUL II (FORMER HEAD of the CATHOLIC CHURCH) `-**DEATH/DAY** = **4/2** = (`-42) = (**20+22**) = `-**DEATH/YEAR for the** `-**NEXT** `-**POPE** = POPE BENEDICT XVI (FORMER HEAD of the CATHOLIC CHURCH)!!!~'

POPE JOHN PAUL II (FORMER HEAD of the CATHOLIC CHURCH) `-DIED (`-**46**) `-DAYS from `-BIRTH-to-DEATH = POPE BENEDICT XVI (FORMER HEAD of the CATHOLIC CHURCH) `-**BIRTH/DAY** = **4**/1**6** = 46x1 = (`-**46**)!!!~'

POPE BENEDICT XVI (FORMER HEAD of the CATHOLIC CHURCH) `-**BIRTH/YEAR** = 19+27 = (`-**46**)!!!~'

POPE BENEDICT XVI (FORMER HEAD of the CATHOLIC CHURCH) `-**BIRTH/DAY** = 4/16 = 4x16 = (`-**64**) = RECIPROCAL = (`-**46**) = **"SEE `-ABOVE"!!!~'**

POPE JOHN PAUL II = **(365 (-) 46)** = (`-279) = **RECIPROCAL = (972) = 9(7(-)2)** = (`-95) = `-AGE of `-DEATH for **POPE BENEDICT XVI** (FORMER HEAD of the CATHOLIC CHURCH)!!!~'

For POPE BENEDICT XVI (FORMER HEAD of the CATHOLIC CHURCH) =

`-DEATH/DAY # `-NUMBER = 12+31+20+22 = (`-85) = RECIPROCAL = (`-58) = **POPE JOHN PAUL II** (FORMER HEAD of the CATHOLIC CHURCH) `-**BIRTH/DAY** = **5**/**18**= 5/1x8 = (`-58)!!!~'

`-PARTIAL `-DEATH/DAY # `-NUMBER = 12+31+20 = (`-63) = RECIPROCAL = (`-36) = 3(6's) = (`-**666**)!!!~'

`-BIRTH/DAY # `-NUMBER = 4+16+19+27 = (`-66) = 6x6 = (`-36) = 3(6's) = (`-**666**)!!!~'

(666 (+) 666) = (`-**13/32**) = `-**CARDINAL (KEY) #'s `-NUMBERS** for `-**R**ECIPROCAL-**S**EQUENCING-**N**UMEROLOGY-**RSN**!!!~' (**DWA**)!!!~'

The `-TALK'S / AMANDA KLOOTS' HUSBAND NICHOLAS EDUARDO ALBERTO CORDERO is in MY 9ᵗʰ BOOK – The GOD BOOK of NUMEROLOGY!!!~' I didn't PUT this in MY BOOK; but, HERE'S the SIMPLE `-EQUATION = NICK'S `-BIRTH/DAY # `-NUMBER = 9+17+19+78 = (`-123)!!!~' SIMPLY `-DIVIDE by (`-3) = (`-41)

31

= `-HIS `-VERY `-OWN `-AGE of `-DEATH!!!~' HE will be `-RESURRECTED!!!~' The PROPHET has `-SPOKEN!!!~'

AMANDA KLOOTS `-BIRTH/DAY # `-NUMBER = 3+19+19+82 = (`-123) = `-The `-VERY `-SAME # `-NUMBER as `-HER `-HUSBAND!!!~'

AMANDA KLOOTS `-PARTIAL `-BIRTH/DAY # `-NUMBER = 3+19+19 = (`-41) = `-HER `-CURRENT `-AGE; and, `-also the `-AGE of `-DEATH of `-her `-HUSBAND = (`-41)!!!~'

(41 + 41) = (`-82) = AMANDA KLOOTS `-BIRTH/YEAR = (`-82) = `-HER `-HUSBAND `-DIED (`-74) DAYS from `-BIRTH-to-DEATH = 7x4 = (`-28) = RECIPROCAL = (`-82)!!!~'

`-REVERSE `-LOOKUP on AMANDA KLOOTS' `-BIRTH/DAY # `-NUMBER = (82(-)19(-)19(-)3) = (`-41) = "SEE the `-PREVIOUS `-WRITINGS"!!!~'

AMANDA KLOOTS `-BIRTH/DAY = (3/19)!!!~' The `-PROPHET'S `-BIRTH/DAY (Dwayne W. Anderson) = (3/20)!!!~'

CHARLES FRAZIER STANLEY (AMERICAN BAPTIST PASTOR & WRITER) died at the `-AGE of (`-90)!!!~'

`-WAS `-BORN in the `-MONTH of (`-9); and, `-DIED in the `-MONTH of (`-4) = **9/4** = **RECIPROCAL** = **4/9** = `-DEATH/DAY = 4/18 = 4/1+8 = (`-**49**)!!!~'

CHARLES FRAZIER STANLEY `-WAS the `-SENIOR PASTOR at FIRST BAPTIST CHURCH in ATLANTA for (`-**49**) `-YEARS!!!~'

(`-94) (-) (`-49) = (`-45) X TIMES (`-2) = (`-90) = `-AGE of `-DEATH for CHARLES FRAZIER STANLEY (AMERICAN BAPTIST PASTOR & WRITER)!!!~'

(94) (+) (`-49) = (`-143) = 1x43 = (`-43) = 20+23 = `-DEATH/YEAR!!!~'

CHARLES FRAZIER STANLEY'S (EX-WIFE) ANNA J. STANLEY `-DEATH/DAY # `-NUMBER = 11+10+20+14 = (`-55) = `-THEY were `-MARRIED in 19(55) for (`-45) `-YEARS = (`-45) X TIMES (`-2) = (`-90) = `-AGE of `-DEATH for CHARLES FRAZIER STANLEY (AMERICAN BAPTIST PASTOR & WRITER)!!!~'

EX-WIFE ANNA J. STANLEY'S `-DEATH/YEAR = 2014 = 20+14 = (`-34) = "SEE `-BELOW"!!!~'

CHARLES FRAZIER STANLEY `-BIRTH/DAY = 9/25 = 9+25 = (`-34) = RECIPROCAL = (`-43) = (20+23) = `-HIS `-DEATH/YEAR!!!~'

`-DAY of `-BIRTH = (`-25ᵗʰ) /|\ `-DAY of `-DEATH = (`-18ᵗʰ) /|\ (25 + 18) = (`-43)-` = 20+23 = `-DEATH/YEAR = "SEE `-ABOVE `-ALSO"!!!~'

`-AGE of `-DEATH = (`-90) x (`-2) = (`-180) = 18+0 = (`-18ᵗʰ) = `-DAY of `-DEATH!!!~'

`-DAY of `-BIRTH = (`-25ᵗʰ) = 2(5's) = (`-55) = `-MARRIED in 19(55)!!!~'

CHARLES FRAZIER STANLEY (AMERICAN BAPTIST PASTOR & WRITER) `-BIRTH/DAY # `-NUMBER = 9+25+19+32 = (`-85) = RECIPROCAL = (`-58) = `-DEATH/ DAY = 4/18 = (4+1)/8 = (`-58)!!!~'

CHARLES FRAZIER STANLEY (AMERICAN BAPTIST PASTOR & WRITER) `-BIRTH/DAY # `-NUMBER = 9+25+19+32 = (`-85) = `-DEATH/DAY = 4/18 = RECIPROCAL = 81/4 = (8)/1+4 = (`-85)!!!~'

(85 (+) 58) = (`-143) = 1x43 = (`-43) = 20+23 = `-DEATH/ YEAR for CHARLES FRAZIER STANLEY!!!~'

`-BIRTH/YEAR = 1932 = 9/1(-)3(-)2 = (`-90) = `-AGE of `-DEATH for CHARLES FRAZIER STANLEY (AMERICAN BAPTIST PASTOR & WRITER)!!!~'

CHARLES FRAZIER STANLEY `-DIED (`-160) DAYS from `-BIRTH-to-DEATH = 1x60 = (`-60) = FLIP 6 to 9 = (`-90) = `-AGE of `-DEATH for CHARLES FRAZIER

STANLEY (AMERICAN BAPTIST PASTOR & WRITER)!!!~'

CHARLES FRAZIER STANLEY (AMERICAN BAPTIST PASTOR & WRITER) `-BIRTH/YEAR = (`-32) = RECIPROCAL = (`-23) = `-DEATH/YEAR!!!~'

SAN FRANCISCO 49'ers LINEBACKER DAVID WILCOX died at the AGE of (`-80)!!!~'

`-WAS `-BORN in the `-MONTH of (`-9); and, `-DIED in the `-MONTH of (`-4) = (`-94) = RECIPROCAL = (`-49) = `-HE was a (`-49)'er!!!~'

`-WAS `-BORN in the `-MONTH of (`-9); and, `-DIED in the `-MONTH of (`-4) = (`-94) = RECIPROCAL = (`-49) = DEATH/DAY = 4/19 = 4/1x9 = (`-49)!!!~'

`-DEATH/DAY = 4/19 = 4/1x9 = (`-49'ers) LINEBACKER of SAN FRANCISCO!!!~'

`-BIRTH/YEAR = (`-42) = 40(2) = 40x2 = (`-80) = `-AGE of `-DEATH for SAN FRANCISCO 49'ers LINEBACKER DAVID WILCOX = "A COMMON `-PATTERN of this CONFIGURATION"!!!~'

`-BIRTH/YEAR = 1942 = 19(-)42 = (`-23) = `-DEATH/ YEAR!!!~'

`-DEATH/DAY = 4/19 = 4+19 = (`-23) = 19(-)42 = `-BIRTH/ YEAR!!!~'

`-DEATH/DAY = 4/19 = 4+19 = (`-23) = `-DEATH/ YEAR!!!~'

`-DEATH/DAY = 4/19 = 4x19 = (`-76) = 7x6 = (`-42) = `-BIRTH/YEAR!!!~'

(23 + 23) = (`-46) = FLIP 6 to 9 = (`-49'er) = "SEE the `-PREVIOUS `-PATTERNS"!!!~'

(23 + 23) = (`-46) = RECIPROCAL = (`-64) = `-BECAME a SAN FRANCISCO (49'ER) in (`-64)!!!~'

`-BIRTH/DAY = 9/29 = 9+29 = (`-38) = RECIPROCAL = (`-83) = 19+64 = (`-83)!!!~'

`-BIRTH/DAY # `-NUMBER = 9+29+19+42 = (`-99)!!!~'

`-DEATH/DAY # `-NUMBER = 4+19+20+23 = (`-66)!!!~'

(99 (+) 66) = (`-165) = 16x5 = (`-80) = `-AGE of `-DEATH for SAN FRANCISCO 49'ers LINEBACKER DAVID WILCOX!!!~'

(`-99) = RECIPROCAL / (flip the # `-NUMBER - UPSIDE DOWN) = (`-66)

`-BIRTH/DAY = 9/29 = 9-to-9 = (9x9) = (`-81) = `-DIED in `-HIS `-YEAR of `-TURNING (`-81)!!!~'

`-BIRTH/DAY # `-NUMBER = (`-99) = 9x9 = (`-81) = `-DIED in `-HIS `-YEAR of `-TURNING (`-81)!!!~'

`-FRAGMENTED `-BIRTH/DAY # `-NUMBER = 9+2+9+1+9+4+2 = (`-36) = (9x4) = `-WAS `-BORN in the `-MONTH of (`-9); and, `-DIED in the `-MONTH of (`-4)!!!~'

`-DEATH/DAY # `-NUMBER = (`-66) = 6x6 = (`-36) = (9x4) = `-WAS `-BORN in the `-MONTH of (`-9); and, `-DIED in the `-MONTH of (`-4)!!!~'

`-DEATH/DAY # `-NUMBER = (`-66) = 6x6 = (`-36) = `-FRAGMENTED `-BIRTH/DAY # `-NUMBER = 9+2+9+1+9+4+2 = (`-36)!!!~'

`-FRAGMENTED `-DEATH/DAY # `-NUMBER = 4+1+9+2+0+2+3 = (`-21)!!!~'

`-FRAG `-BIRTH # `-NUMBER (`-36) (+) `-FRAG `-DEATH # `-NUMBER (`-21) = (`-57)!!!~'

`-PARTIAL `-BIRTH/DAY # `-NUMBER = 9+29+19 = (`-57)!!!~'

(`-57) = RECIPROCAL = (`-75)

(57 + 75) = (`-132) = 1x32 = (`-32) = RECIPROCAL = (`-23) = `-DEATH/YEAR!!!~'

DWAYNE W. ANDERSON

AUSTRALIAN COMEDIAN/ACTOR/AUTHOR JOHN BARRY HUMPHRIES died at the AGE of (`-89)!!!~'

`-WAS `-BORN in the `-MONTH of (`-2); and, `-DIED in the `-MONTH of (`-4) = (`-24) = RECIPROCAL = (`-42) = `-DEATH/DAY = (`-4/22)!!!~'

`-BIRTH/DAY # `-NUMBER = 2+17+19+34 = (`-72) = 8x9 = (`-89) = `-AGE of `-DEATH for AUSTRALIAN COMEDIAN/ACTOR/AUTHOR JOHN BARRY HUMPHRIES!!!~'

`-DEATH/DAY # `-NUMBER = 4+22+20+23 = (`-69) = 6+9 = (`-15) = 19(-)34 = `-BIRTH/YEAR!!!~'

FRAGMENTED `-BIRTH/DAY # `-NUMBER = 2+1+7+1+9+3+4 = (`-27) = 3x9 = (`-39) = FLIP 3 to 8 = (`-89) = `-AGE of `-DEATH for AUSTRALIAN COMEDIAN/ ACTOR/AUTHOR JOHN BARRY HUMPHRIES!!!~'

FRAGMENTED `-DEATH/DAY # `-NUMBER = 4+2+2+2+0+2+3 = (`-15) = 19(-)34 = `-BIRTH/YEAR!!!~'

FRAG `-BIRTHDAY # `-NUMBER (`-27) (+) PLUS (+) FRAG `-DEATHDAY # `-NUMBER (`-15) = (`-42) = RECIPROCAL = (`-24) = `-WAS `-BORN in the `-MONTH of (`-2); and, `-DIED in the `-MONTH of (`-4) = (`-24) = RECIPROCAL = (`-42) = DEATH/DAY = (`-4/22)!!!~'

`-DEATH/DAY = 4/22 = 4+22 = (`-26) = FLIP 2 to 7 = (`-76) = 7x6 = (`-42) = RECIPROCAL = (`-24) = `-WAS `-BORN

38

in the `-MONTH of (`-2); and, `-DIED in the `-MONTH of (`-4)!!!~'

`-BIRTH/YEAR = 1934 = (1+3+4) (9) = (`-89) = `-AGE of `-DEATH for AUSTRALIAN COMEDIAN/ACTOR/ AUTHOR JOHN BARRY HUMPHRIES!!!~'

`-BIRTH/YEAR = 1934 = 19+34 = (`-53) = RECIPROCAL = (`-35)!!!~'

(53 (+) 35) = (`-88) = `-DEATH/DAY = 4/22 = 4x22 = (`-88) = `-DIED the `-VERY `-NEXT `-YEAR of `-AGE at the `-AGE of (`-89)!!!~'

`-DIED (`-64) `-DAYS from `-BIRTH-to-DEATH = 2x32 = (to)x(32) = RECIPROCAL = (to)x(23) = `-DEATH/ YEAR!!!~'

`-DIED (`-64) `-DAYS from `-BIRTH-to-DEATH = (`-64) = 6x4 = (`-24) = `-WAS `-BORN in the `-MONTH of (`-2); and, `-DIED in the `-MONTH of (`-4) = (`-24)!!!~'

`-DAY of `-BIRTH = (`-17th) /|\ `-DAY of `-DEATH = (`-22nd)

(17 (+) 22) = (`-39) = FLIP 3 to 8 = (`-89) = `-AGE of `-DEATH for AUSTRALIAN COMEDIAN/ACTOR/ AUTHOR JOHN BARRY HUMPHRIES!!!~'

`-BIRTH/DAY = 2/17 = 2x17 = (`-34) = RECIPROCAL = (`-43) = 20+23 = `-DEATH/YEAR!!!~'

`-BIRTH/YEAR = (`-34) = RECIPROCAL = (`-43) = 20+23 = `-DEATH/YEAR!!!~'

LEONARD GORDON GOODMAN (ENGLISH PROFESSIONAL BALLROOM DANCER, DANCE JUDGE; and, DANCE COACH) died at the AGE of (`-78)!!!~'

WAS `-BORN in the `-MONTH of (`-4); and, `-DIED in the `-MONTH of (`-4) = (`-44) = `-BIRTH/YEAR = (`-44)!!!~'

`-BIRTH/DAY # `-NUMBER = 4+25+19+44 = (`-92)!!!~'

`-DEATH/DAY # `-NUMBER = 4+22+20+23 = (`-69)!!!~'

(92 (-) 69) = (`-23) = `-DEATH/YEAR!!!~'

(92 (-) 29) = (`-63) = 19+44 = `-BIRTH/YEAR!!!~'

(69 (+) 15) = (`-84) = 8x4 = (`-32) = RECIPROCAL = (`-23) = `-DEATH/YEAR!!!~'

`-PARTIAL `-BIRTH/DAY # `-NUMBER = 4+25+19 = (`-48) = RECIPROCAL = (`-84) = 8x4 = (`-32) = RECIPROCAL = (`-23) = `-DEATH/YEAR!!!~'

FRAGMENTED `-BIRTH/DAY # `-NUMBER = 4+2+5+1+9+4+4 = (`-29)!!!~'

FRAGMENTED `-DEATH/DAY # `-NUMBER = 4+2+2+2+0+2+3 = (`-15) = `-WAS `-MARRIED to CHERRY KINGSTON for (`-15) `-YEARS from 1972-to-1987!!!~'

FRAGMENTED `-DEATH/DAY # `-NUMBER = 4+2+2+2+0+2+3 = (`-15) = 7+8 = (`-78) = `-AGE of `-DEATH for LEONARD GORDON GOODMAN (ENGLISH PROFESSIONAL BALLROOM DANCER, DANCE JUDGE; and, DANCE COACH)!!!~'

(29 + 15) = (`-44) = `-BIRTH/YEAR!!!~'

`-DIED (`-3) DAYS from `-BIRTH/DAY-to-DEATH/DAY!!!~'

(365 (-) 3) = (`-362) = 3x62 = (`-186) = 1+6/8 = (`-78) = `-AGE of `-DEATH for LEONARD GORDON GOODMAN (ENGLISH PROFESSIONAL BALLROOM DANCER, DANCE JUDGE; and, DANCE COACH)!!!~'

(365 (-) 3) = (`-362) = 36x2 = (`-72) = FLIP 7 to 2 = (`-22) = `-DAY of `-DEATH!!!~'

`-BIRTH/YEAR = 1944 = 19(-)44 = (`-25) = `-DAY of `-BIRTH = (`-25th)!!!~'

(365 (-) 3) = (`-362) = 36x2 = (`-72) = `-MARRIED CHERRY KINGSTON in (`-72)!!!~'

`-DIVORCED CHERRY KINGSTON in (`-87) = RECIPROCAL = (`-78) = `-AGE of `-DEATH for

LEONARD GORDON GOODMAN (ENGLISH PROFESSIONAL BALLROOM DANCER, DANCE JUDGE; and, DANCE COACH)!!!~'

`-MARRIED SUE GOODMAN in (`-2012) = 20+12 = (`-32) = RECIPROCAL = (`-23) = `-DEATH/YEAR!!!~'

`-DAY of `-BIRTH = (`-25$^{th}$) /|\ `-DAY of `-DEATH = (`-22nd)

(25 (+) 22) = (`-47) = `-BIRTH/DAY = 4/2+5 = (`-47)!!!~'

`-DEATH/DAY = 4/22 = 4/2+2 = (`-44) = `-BIRTH/YEAR!!!~'

AMERICAN SINGER, ACTIVIST; and, ACTOR HARRY BELAFONTE died at the `-AGE of (`-96)!!!~'

`-AGE of `-DEATH = (`-96) = 9x6 = (`-54) = `-DEATH/DAY = 4/25 = RECIPROCAL = 52/4 = (5-to-4)!!!~'

`-WAS `-BORN in the `-MONTH of (`-3); and, `-DIED in the `-MONTH of (`-4) = (`-34) = RECIPROCAL = (`-43) = 20+23 = `-DEATH/YEAR!!!~'

`-AGE of `-DEATH = (`-96) / DIVIDED by (`-3) = (`-32) = RECIPROCAL = (`-23) = `-DEATH/YEAR!!!~'

`-BIRTH/DAY = 3/1 = FLIP 3 to 8 = 8/1 = (`-81) = 9x9 = (`-99) = FLIP 9 to 6 = (`-96) = `-AGE of `-DEATH for

AMERICAN SINGER, ACTIVIST; and, ACTOR HARRY BELAFONTE!!!~'

`-BIRTH/DAY # `-NUMBER = 3+1+19+27 = (`-50) = `-WAS `-MARRIED to JULIE ROBINSON for (`-50) `-YEARS!!!~'

`-PARTIAL `-BIRTH/DAY # `-NUMBER = 3+1+19 = (`-23) = `-DEATH/YEAR!!!~'

`-DEATH/DAY # `-NUMBER = 4+25+20+23 = (`-72) = RECIPROCAL = (`-27) = `-BIRTH/YEAR!!!~'

(50/72) = 57(two) = `-WAS `-MARRIED to `-FORMER `-WIFE JULIE ROBINSON in (`-57) & `-DIVORCED FORMER `-WIFE MARGUERITE BELAFONTE in (`-57)!!!~'

FRAGMENTED `-BIRTH/DAY # `-NUMBER = 3+1+1+9+2+7 = (`-23) = `-DEATH/YEAR!!!~'

FRAGMENTED `-DEATH/DAY # `-NUMBER = 4+2+5+2+0+2+3 = (`-18) = 2x9 = 2(9's) = (`-99) = FLIP 9 to 6 = (`-96) = `-AGE of `-DEATH for AMERICAN SINGER, ACTIVIST; and, ACTOR HARRY BELAFONTE!!!~'

FROM `-BIRTH-to-DEATH there are (`-55) `-DAYS = 2(5's) = (`-25ᵗʰ) = `-DAY of `-DEATH!!!~'

FROM `-BIRTH-to-DEATH there are (`-55) `-DAYS = 5x5 = (`-25ᵗʰ) = `-DAY of `-DEATH!!!~'

(365 (-) 55) = (`-310) = 31+0 = (`-31) = `-BIRTH/DAY = (3/1)!!!~'

`-HARRY BELAFONTE was `-MARRIED to PAMELA FRANK from 2008 to 2023 = (`-15) `-YEARS = 9+6 = (`-96) = `-AGE of `-DEATH for AMERICAN SINGER, ACTIVIST; and, ACTOR HARRY BELAFONTE!!!~'

`-MARRIED & `-DIVORCED in (`-2008) = 20+08 = (`-28) X TIMES (`-3) = (`-84) = RECIPROCAL = (`-48) X TIMES (`-2) = (`-96) = `-AGE of `-DEATH for AMERICAN SINGER, ACTIVIST; and, ACTOR HARRY BELAFONTE!!!~'

`-FORMER `-WIFE JULIE ROBINSON'S `-BIRTH/ DAY = 9/14 = 9+14 = (`-23) = `-DEATH/YEAR of `-HER `-FORMER `-HUSBAND AMERICAN SINGER, ACTIVIST; and, ACTOR HARRY BELAFONTE!!!~'

`-FORMER `-WIFE JULIE ROBINSON'S `-BIRTH/DAY = 9/14 = 94x1 = (`-94) = `-HER `-CURRENT `-AGE at the `-TIME of `-DEATH of `-HER `-FORMER `-HUSBAND AMERICAN SINGER, ACTIVIST; and, ACTOR HARRY BELAFONTE!!!~'

`-FORMER `-WIFE JULIE ROBINSON'S `-BIRTH/ YEAR = 1928 = 19+28 = (`-47) = `-DEATH/DAY of `-HER `-FORMER `-HUSBAND AMERICAN SINGER, ACTIVIST; and, ACTOR HARRY BELAFONTE = 4/25 = 4/2+5 = (`-47)!!!~'

(47 (+) 47) = (`-94) = "SEE the `-LINKAGES" = RECIPROCAL = (`-49)!!!~'

HARRY BELAFONTE `-YEARS `-ACTIVE = 19(49)-to-2023 = (`-74) `-YEARS = RECIPROCAL = (`-47)!!!~'

(CO-STAR) SIDNEY POITIER BIRTH/YEAR = 1927 = 9/(7-2-1) = (`-94) = AGE of DEATH for (CO-STAR) SIDNEY POITIER!~' DEATH/DAY # `-NUMBER for (CO-STAR) SIDNEY POITIER = 1+6+20+22 = (`-49) = RECIPROCAL = (`-94) = `-HIS `-VERY `-OWN `-AGE of `-DEATH!~' FRAGMENTED BIRTH/DAY # `-NUMBER FOR (CO-STAR) SIDNEY POITIER = 2+2+0+1+9+2+7 = (`-23) (`-JUST; `-AS `-WELL) = RECIPROCAL = (`-32) = (&) (CO-STAR) SIDNEY POITIER `-DIED (`-320) DAYS from BIRTHDAY-to-DEATH/DAY!!!~'

`-FOR: AMERICAN SINGER, ACTIVIST; and, ACTOR HARRY BELAFONTE:

`-FORMER `-WIFE MARGUERITE BELAFONTE was `-BORN in (`-23) = `-DEATH/YEAR for `-HER `-FORMER `-HUSBAND AMERICAN SINGER, ACTIVIST; and, ACTOR HARRY BELAFONTE!!!~'

HARRY BELAFONTE `-WAS `-MARRIED to `-FORMER `-WIFE MARGUERITE BELAFONTE in (`-48) X TIMES (`-2) = (`-96) = `-AGE of `-DEATH for `-HER `-FORMER `-HUSBAND AMERICAN SINGER, ACTIVIST; and, ACTOR HARRY BELAFONTE!!!~'

AMERICAN SINGER, ACTIVIST; and, ACTOR HARRY BELAFONTE `-BIRTH/YEAR = 1927 = 9/1(-)2(-)7 = (`-96) = `-AGE of `-DEATH for AMERICAN SINGER, ACTIVIST; and, ACTOR HARRY BELAFONTE!!!~'

AMERICAN SINGER, ACTIVIST; and, ACTOR HARRY BELAFONTE `-DEATH/DAY = 4/25 = HALF RECIPROCAL = 4/52 = 4(-)52 = (`-48) X TIMES (`-2) = (`-96) = `-AGE of `-DEATH for AMERICAN SINGER, ACTIVIST; and, ACTOR HARRY BELAFONTE!!!~'

AMERICAN SINGER, ACTIVIST; and, ACTOR HARRY BELAFONTE `-DEATH/DAY = 4/25 = RECIPROCAL = 52/4 = 52(-)4 = (`-48) X TIMES (`-2) = (`-96) = `-AGE of `-DEATH for AMERICAN SINGER, ACTIVIST; and, ACTOR HARRY BELAFONTE!!!~'

AMERICAN NOVELIST JUDITH KRANTZ `-**DIED** on JUNE 22nd within `-20**19**!!!~' `-SHE was `-**BORN** on *JANUARY 9th* in `-**1928**!!!~' `-SHE `-**DIED** at the `-AGE of (`-**91**)!!!~'

`-BIRTH/DAY = 1/9** = `-DEATH/YEAR = (`-19**)!!!~'

`-BIRTH/DAY** = (**1/9**) = (`-19**) = RECIPROCAL = (`-**91**) = "AGE of `-DEATH for AMERICAN NOVELIST JUDITH KRANTZ (`-**91**)"!!!~'

'-DEATH/YEAR = ('-19) = RECIPROCAL = ('-91) = "AGE of '-DEATH for AMERICAN NOVELIST JUDITH KRANTZ ('-91)"!!!~'

'-BIRTH/YEAR = 1928 = 9 (1+2+8) = ('-**911**) = 91x1 = ('-**91**) = "SEE the '-PREVIOUS '-LINKAGES"!!!~'

'-DEATH/DAY = 6/22 = 6(-)22 = ('-**16**) = FLIP 6 to 9 = ('-**19**) = "SEE the '-PREVIOUS '-LINKAGES"!!!~'

'-WAS '-**BORN** in the '-MONTH of ('-**1**); and, '-**DIED** in the '-MONTH of ('-**6**) = **1/6** = FLIP 6 to 9 = **1/9** = "SEE the '-PREVIOUS '-LINKAGES"!!!~'

OIL TYCOON T. BOONE PICKENS '-**DIED** at the '-AGE of ('-**91**) & was '-**BORN** in ('-**1928**) '-*BIRTH/YEAR* = 9(1+2+8) = ('-**911**) = 91x1 = ('-**91**) = HIS '-AGE of '-DEATH ('-**91**) & **DEATH/DAY** ('-**9/11**) from = EQUALS = '-**BIRTH/YEAR**!!!~' '-HE too; '-**DIED**, in the '-**YEAR** of ('-**19**) at the '-**AGE** *of* '-*RECIPROCAL* ('-**91**) = "SEE the '-LINKAGES"!!!~'

AMERICAN TELEVISION HOST (LEE PHILLIP BELL) '-AGE of '-DEATH = ('-**91**) (BIRTH: **JUNE 10**, **1928**) (DEATH: **FEBRUARY 25**, 2020)

`-**BIRTH/YEAR** = (**1928**) = (9) (1+2+8) = (`-**911**) = 91x1 = (`-**91**) = `-**AGE of** `-**DEATH for AMERICAN TELEVISION HOST LEE PHILLIP BELL** (`-**91**)!!!~'

`-**BIRTH/DAY** = (**6/1**0) = (6 + 10) = (`-**16**) = RECIPROCAL = (`-**61**) = FLIP (`-**6**) to (`-**9**) = (`-**91**) = "**AGE of** `-**DEATH for AMERICAN TELEVISION HOST LEE PHILLIP BELL** (`-**91**)"!!!~'

SHE DIED (`-**106**) DAYS BEFORE HER NEXT BIRTHDAY = 10 + 6 = (`-**16**) = RECIPROCAL = (`-**61**) = FLIP (`-**6**) to (`-**9**) = (`-**91**) = `-**AGE of** `-**DEATH for AMERICAN TELEVISION HOST LEE PHILLIP BELL** (`-**91**)"!!!~'

(`-**106**) = RECIPROCAL = (`-**6/01**) = HALF RECIPROCAL = (`-**6/10**) = "**BIRTHDAY for AMERICAN TELEVISION HOST LEE PHILLIP BELL**"!!!~'

(366 (-) 106) = (`-**260**) = (26 + 0) = (`-**26**) = `-**DIED in the** `-**MONTH of** (`-**2**); and, `-**WAS** `-**BORN in the** `-**MONTH of** (`-**6**) = (`-**2/6**) & `-**DIED** `-**AGAIN;** (`-**260**) **DAYS AWAY from** `-**BIRTH/DAY-to-DEATH/DAY**!!!~'

FRAGMENTED `-**BIRTH/DAY # **`-**NUMBER** = (6 + 1 + 0 + 1 + 9 + 2 + 8) = (`-**27**)!!!~'

`-FRAGMENTED `-BIRTHDAY # `-NUMBER = (`-27) = (2 + 25) = (2/25) = "DAY of `-DEATH for AMERICAN TELEVISION HOST LEE PHILLIP BELL"!!!~'

AMERICAN ENTREPRENEUR JOSEPH HARDIN COULOMBE "FOUNDER of GROCERY STORE CHAIN (TRADER JOE'S)" (`-89) (BIRTH: JUNE 3, 1930) (DEATH: FEBRUARY 28, 2020)

`-**BORN** in the `-**YEAR** of (`-30) = **MONTH; and, DAY** `-**HE** `-**DIED** = (2/28) = (2 + 28) = (`-30)!!!~'

`-**1930** = (19 + 30) = (`-49) = (4 x 9) = (`-36) = RECIPROCAL = (`-63) = `-**BIRTHDAY for AMERICAN ENTREPRENEUR JOSEPH HARDIN COULOMBE (JUNE 3ʳᵈ)!!!~'**

FOUNDED "TRADER JOE'S" in (`-1967); AND, was `-MARRIED for (`-67) YEARS to `-HIS `-WIFE ALICE COULOMBE!!!~' THEY were `-MARRIED in (`-1953)!!!~'

`-**1953** = (19 + 53) = (`-72) = (8 x 9) = (`-89) = `-**AGE of** `-**DEATH for AMERICAN ENTREPRENEUR JOSEPH HARDIN COULOMBE "FOUNDER of GROCERY STORE CHAIN (TRADER JOE'S)" (`-89)!!!~'**

HE DIED (`-96) DAYS BEFORE HIS NEXT BIRTHDAY!!!~'

(366 (-) 96) = (`-**270**) = (27 + 0) = (`-**27**) = RECIPROCAL = (`-**72**) = "SEE `-BELOW"!!!~'

HE DIED AT THE `-AGE of (`-**89**) = (8 x 9) = (`-**72**) = RECIPROCAL = (`-**27**) = `-**DIED** (`-**270**) **DAYS AWAY from `-BIRTH/DAY-to-DEATH/DAY!!!~'**

`-**DIED in the `-MONTH of (`-2); and, `-WAS `-BORN in the `-MONTH of (`-6)** = (`-**2/6**) = **RECIPROCAL = (`-6/2)!!!~'**

(62 + 26) = (`-**88**) = `-**DIED the `-NEXT `-YEAR `-AFTERWARD at the `-AGE of (`-89)!!!~'**

AMERICAN FILM ACTOR STUART MAXWELL WHITMAN `-AGE of `-DEATH = (`-**92**) (BIRTH: FEBRUARY 1, 19**2**8) (DEATH: MARCH 16, 2020)!!!~'

`-**BIRTH/YEAR** = (1928) = (9) (1+2+8) = (`-**911**) = 91+1 = (`-**92**) = `-**AGE of `-DEATH for AMERICAN FILM ACTOR STUART MAXWELL WHITMAN (`-92)!!!~'**

`-**AGE** of `-**DEATH** = (`-**92**) = (9 x 2) = (`-**18**) = `-**WHAT'S `-REMAINING** from **"SEE `-ABOVE** at (`-1**9**28)"!!!~'

`-**BIRTH/DAY** = FEBRUARY 1 = (2 x 1) = (`-**2**)!!!~'

`-**DEATH/DAY** = MARCH 16 = (3 + 16) = (`-**19**) = (1 x 9) = (`-**9**)!!!~'

(`-**29**) = RECIPROCAL = (`-**92**) = **"AGE of `-DEATH"!!!~'**

`-BIRTHDAY # `-NUMBER = (2 + 1 + 19 + 28) = **50**

`-DEATH/DAY # `-NUMBER = (3 + 16 + 20 + 20) = **59**

(59 (-) 50) = (`-**9**)**!!!~'**

(59 + 50) = (`-**109**)**!!!~'**

(109 + 9) = (`-**1/18**) – (1 x 18) – (`-**18**) = (9 x 2) = (`-**92**) = **"AGE of `-DEATH for AMERICAN FILM ACTOR STUART MAXWELL WHITMAN (`-92)!!!~'**

HE DIED (`-**44**) DAYS AFTER HIS LAST BIRTHDAY!!!~'

(366 (-) 44) = (`-**322**) = *(3(to)2) = RECIPROCAL = (2(to)3)!!!~'*

`-FRAGMENTED `-BIRTH/DAY # `-NUMBER =** FEBRUARY 1, 1928 = (2 + 1 + 1 + 9 + 2 + 8) = (`-23**) = **`-WAS `-BORN in the `-MONTH of (`-2); and, `-DIED in the `-MONTH of (`-3)!!!~'**

MUSIC ARTIST JONI SLEDGE from "SISTER SLEDGE" `-DIED on *MARCH 10[th]* within `-2017!!!~' `-SHE was `-BORN on **SEPTEMBER 13**[th] in `-19**56**!!!~' `-SHE `-DIED at the `-AGE of (`-**60**)!!!~'

MUSIC ARTIST JONI SLEDGE `-WAS `-**BORN** in the `-MONTH of (`-**9**); and, `-**DIED** in the `-MONTH of (`-**3**) = 9/3 = `-**BIRTH/DAY** = 9/13 = 9/1x3 = (`-**93**)!!!~'

`-**DEATH/DAY** = 3/10 = 3x10 = (`-**30**) X TIMES (`-2) = (`-**60**) = `-**AGE of** `-**DEATH for MUSIC ARTIST JONI SLEDGE!!!**~'

`-**BIRTH/YEAR** = (1956) = 19(-)56 = (`-**37**) = `-DEATH/ YEAR = 20+17 = (`-**37**)!!!~'

`-**DEATH/DAY** = (**3/10**) = RECIPROCAL = `-**BIRTH/ DAY** (SEPTEMBER 13th) = (**9/13**) = RECIPROCAL = (**31/9**) = (3) (1 + 9) = (**3/10**)!!!~'

`-**BIRTH/YEAR** = (`-**56**) = 5x6 = (`-**30**) = `-**DEATH/DAY** = **3/10** = 3x10 = (`-**30**)!!!~'

(30 + 30) = (`-**60**) = `-**AGE of** `-**DEATH for MUSIC ARTIST JONI SLEDGE from the MUSICAL GROUP of the "SISTER SLEDGE"!!!**~'

ENTERTAINER, LAWYER; & FORMER MAYOR of CINCINNATI JERRY SPRINGER died at the `-AGE of (`-79)!!!~'

`-AGE of `-DEATH = 79 = 7+9 = (`-16) X TIMES (`-2) = (`-32) = RECIPROCAL = (`-23) = `-DEATH/YEAR!!!~'

'-WAS '-BORN in the '-MONTH of ('-2); and, '-DIED in the '-MONTH of ('-4) = 2/4 = '-BIRTH/DAY = 2/13 = 2/1+3 = ('-24)!!!~'

'-BIRTH/YEAR = 1944 = 19+44 = ('-63) = 7x9 = ('-79) = '-AGE of '-DEATH for ENTERTAINER, LAWYER; & FORMER MAYOR of CINCINNATI JERRY SPRINGER!!!~'

'-BIRTH/DAY = 2/13 = 2x13 = ('-26) = FLIP 2 to 7; FLIP 6 to 9 = ('-79) = '-AGE of '-DEATH for ENTERTAINER, LAWYER; & FORMER MAYOR of CINCINNATI JERRY SPRINGER!!!~'

'-BIRTH/DAY = 2/13 = 23x1 = ('-23) = '-DEATH/ YEAR; '-ALSO = "SEE '-PREVIOUS '-EXAMPLES in this '-BOOK of AMERICAN COMPOSER (GERALD FRIED) & OAKLAND A'S (SALVATORE LEONARD BANDO) = '-BIRTH/DAY = 2/13 & '-DEATH/YEAR = ('-23)!!!~'

'-BIRTH/DAY = 2/13 = HALF RECIPROCAL = 2/31 = 2(-)31 = ('-29) = FLIP 2 to 7 = ('-79) = '-AGE of '-DEATH for ENTERTAINER, LAWYER; & FORMER MAYOR of CINCINNATI JERRY SPRINGER!!!~'

'-DEATH/DAY = 4/27 = 4(-)27 = ('-23) = '-DEATH/ YEAR!!!~'

'-DEATH/DAY = 4/27 = 4(-)27 = ('-23) = '-BIRTH/DAY = 2/13 = 23x1 = ('-23)!!!~'

`-BIRTH/DAY # `-NUMBER = 2+13+19+44 = (`-78) = `-DIED the `-VERY `-NEXT `-YEAR of `-AGE `-afterward = (`-79)!!!~'

`-BIRTH/DAY # `-NUMBER = 2+13+19+44 = (`-78) = `-WAS `-MAYOR from 1977-to-19(78)!!!~'

(`-1977) = 19+77 = (`-96) = 9x6 = (`-54) = 5x4 = (`-20) = `-FRAGMENTED `-DEATH/DAY # `-NUMBER!!!~'

(`-1977) = 19+77 = (`-96) = RECIPROCAL = (`-69) = `-MET `-FORMER `-WIFE MICKI VELTON in (`-69) on a `-BLIND `-DATE!!!~'

(`-1978) = 19+78 = (`-97) = RECIPROCAL = (`-79) = `-AGE of `-DEATH for ENTERTAINER, LAWYER; & FORMER MAYOR of CINCINNATI JERRY SPRINGER!!!~'

`-BIRTH/DAY # `-NUMBER = 2+13+19+44 = (`-78) = FLIP 8 to 3 = (`-73) = FROM `-BIRTH-to-DEATH there are (`-73) `-DAYS!!!~'

`-PARTIAL `-BIRTH/DAY # `-NUMBER = 2+13+19 = (`-34) = RECIPROCAL = (`-43) = 20+23 = `-DEATH/YEAR!!!~'

`-DEATH/DAY # `-NUMBER = 4+27+20+23 = (`-74) = RECIPROCAL = (`-47) = `-DEATH/DAY = 4/27 = 4-to-7!!!~'

`-DEATH/DAY = 4/27 = HALF RECIPROCAL = 4/72 = 4+72 = (`-76) = FLIP 6 to 9 = (`-79) = `-AGE of `-DEATH for ENTERTAINER, LAWYER; & FORMER MAYOR of CINCINNATI JERRY SPRINGER!!!~'

`-DEATH/DAY = 4/27 = RECIPROCAL = 72/4 = 72+4 = (`-76) = FLIP 6 to 9 = (`-79) = `-AGE of `-DEATH for ENTERTAINER, LAWYER; & FORMER MAYOR of CINCINNATI JERRY SPRINGER!!!~'

`-DEATH/DAY = 4/27 = HALF RECIPROCAL = 4/72 = 4(-)72 = (`-68) = FLIP 8 to 3 = (`-63) = 19+44 = `-BIRTH/YEAR!!!~'

`-DEATH/DAY = 4/27 = RECIPROCAL = 72/4 = 72(-)4 = (`-68) = FLIP 8 to 3 = (`-63) = 19+44 = `-BIRTH/YEAR!!!~'

FRAGMENTED `-BIRTH/DAY # `-NUMBER = 2+1+3+1+9+4+4 = (`-24) = `-WAS `-BORN in the `-MONTH of (`-2); and, `-DIED in the `-MONTH of (`-4) = (`-24)!!!~'

FRAGMENTED `-DEATH/DAY # `-NUMBER = 4+2+7+2+0+2+3 = (`-20) = 5x4 = (`-54) = 19(-)73 = `-WAS `-MARRIED to MICKI VELTON in (`-1973)!!!~'

FROM `-BIRTH-to-DEATH there are (`-73) `-DAYS = FLIP 3 to 8 = (`-78) = `-BIRTH/DAY # `-NUMBER!!!~'

FROM `-BIRTH-to-DEATH there are (`-73) `-DAYS = `-WAS `-MARRIED to MICKI VELTON in 19(73)!!!~'

(`-1973) = 19+73 = (`-92) = RECIPROCAL = (`-29) = FLIP 2 to 7 = (`-79) = `-AGE of `-DEATH for ENTERTAINER, LAWYER; & FORMER MAYOR of CINCINNATI JERRY SPRINGER!!!~'

`-DIVORCED MICKI VELTON in (`-1994) = HALF RECIPROCAL = 19/49 = 19+49 = (`-68) = FLIP 8 to 3 = (`-63) = 19+44 = `-BIRTH/YEAR!!!~'

`-DIVORCED MICKI VELTON in (`-1994) = 19+94 = (`-113) = 11x3 = (`-33) = `-BIRTH/DAY = 2/13 = HALF RECIPROCAL = 2/31 = 2+31 = (`-33)!!!~'

`-MARRIED to MICKI VELTON for (`-21) `-YEARS = 7x3 = (`-73) = FROM `-BIRTH-to-DEATH there are (`-73) `-DAYS & `-THEY were `-MARRIED in (`-73)!!!~'

ENTERTAINER, LAWYER; & FORMER MAYOR of CINCINNATI JERRY SPRINGER `-BIRTH/YEAR = 1944 = (1(-)4+4) (9) = (`-79) = `-AGE of `-DEATH for ENTERTAINER, LAWYER; & FORMER MAYOR of CINCINNATI JERRY SPRINGER!!!~'

ACTOR ADAM WEST (ANDERSON) (**BATMAN**) `-DIED on *JUNE 9th* within `-2017!!!~' `-HE was `-BORN on *SEPTEMBER 19th* in `-19**28**!!!~' `-HE `-DIED at the `-AGE of (`-**88**)!!!~'

`-**BIRTH/YEAR** = (1928) = (1(-)9) (28) = 8/28 = (8-to-8) = `-**AGE of** `-**DEATH for ACTOR ADAM WEST (ANDERSON) (BATMAN)** (`-**88**)!!!~'

`-**DIED** in the `-**MONTH** of (`-**6**); and, `-**WAS** `-**BORN** in the `-**MONTH** of (`-**9**) = (`-**69**) = `-**HIS** `-**VERY** `-**OWN** `-**DEATH/DAY** = "JUNE 9ᵗʰ")!!!~'

ACTOR MARTIN LANDAU `-DIED on *JULY 15ᵗʰ* within `-**2017**!!!~' `-HE was `-BORN on *JUNE 20ᵗʰ* in `-**1928**!!!~' `-HE `-DIED at the `-AGE of (`-**89**)!!!~'

`-**BIRTH/YEAR** = (1928) = RECIPROCAL = (8291) – (8-to-9-ONE TIME) = `-**AGE of** `-**DEATH for ACTOR MARTIN LANDAU** (`-**89**)!!!~'

ACTOR BOB CRANE from "HOGAN'S HEROES" `-DIED on **JUNE 29**ᵗʰ within `-**1978**!!!~' `-HE was `-BORN on *JULY 13ᵗʰ* in `-19**28**!!!~' `-HE `-DIED at the `-AGE of (`-**49**)!!!~'

`-**DEATH/YEAR** = (1978) = FLIP 7 to 2 = (1928) = `-**BIRTH/YEAR**!!!~'

`-**BIRTH/YEAR** = (1928) = (ONE-9-to-8) = (`-**98**) DIVIDED by (`-2) = (`-**49**) = `-**AGE of** `-**DEATH for**

ACTOR BOB CRANE from "HOGAN'S HEROES" (`-49)!!!~'

ACTOR BOB CRANE from "HOGAN'S HEROES" `-BIRTHDAY # `-NUMBER = `-EQUALS = (7 + 13 + 19 + 28) = `-67 = `-DIED in the `-MONTH of (`-6); and, `-WAS `-BORN in the `-MONTH of (`-7)!!!~'

`-BIRTH/DAY = (7/13) = FLIP 3 to 8 = (7/18) = (7-ONE-8) = `-DIED in the `-YEAR of (`-78)!!!~'

MUSICIAN ANTOINE "FAT'S" DOMINO JR. `-DIED on *OCTOBER 24th* within `-2017!!!~' `-HE was `-BORN on *FEBRUARY 26th* in `-1928!!!~' `-HE `-DIED at the `-AGE of (`-89)!!!~

`-BIRTH/YEAR = (1928) = RECIPROCAL = (8291) = (8-to-9-ONE TIME) = `-AGE of `-DEATH for MUSICIAN ANTOINE "FAT'S" DOMINO JR. (`-89)!!!~'

AMERICAN ACTOR RANCE HOWARD (FATHER of RON & CLINT HOWARD) `-DIED on *NOVEMBER 25th* within `-2017!!!~' `-HE was `-BORN on *NOVEMBER 17th* in `-1928!!!~' `-HE `-DIED at the `-AGE of (`-89)!!!~'

`-BIRTH/YEAR = (1928) = RECIPROCAL = (8291) = (8-to-9-ONE TIME) = `-AGE of `-DEATH for AMERICAN

ACTOR RANCE HOWARD (FATHER of RON & CLINT HOWARD) (`-89)!!!~'

`-**BIRTH/DAY** = (11/17) = (1 + 1) (17) = 2(0)17 = `-**DEATH/ YEAR!!!~'**

`-**DEATH/DAY** = (11/25) = 11+25 = (`-**36**) = FLIP 3 to 8; FLIP 6 to 9 = (`-**89**) = `-**AGE of `-DEATH for AMERICAN ACTOR RANCE HOWARD (FATHER of RON & CLINT HOWARD) (`-89)!!!~'**

AMERICAN SINGER VIC DAMONE `-DIED on *FEBRUARY 11^(th)* within `-**2018**!!!~' `-HE was `-BORN on *JUNE 12^(th)* in `-***1928***!!!~' `-HE `-DIED at the `-AGE of (`-**89**)!!!~'

`-**BIRTH/YEAR** = (1928) = RECIPROCAL = (8291) = (8-to-9-ONE TIME) = `-**AGE of `-DEATH for AMERICAN SINGER VIC DAMONE (`-89)!!!~'**

`-**BIRTH/DAY** = (**6/12**) = (6 x 12) = (`-**72**) = (8 x 9) = (`-**89**) = "**AGE of `-DEATH for AMERICAN SINGER VIC DAMONE (`-89)**"!!!~'

`-WAS `-**BORN** in the `-**MONTH** of (`-**6**); and, `-DIED in the `-MONTH of (`-**2**) = (6/2) = `-**BIRTH/DAY** = (6-one-2)!!!~'

AMERICAN ACTOR & COMEDIAN RICHARD (DICK) VINCENT (VAN) (PATTEN) `-DIED** at the `-AGE of (`-86**)!!!~' (**BIRTH/DAY**: DECEMBER 9th, 1928) (**DEATH/DAY**: JUNE 23rd, 2015)!!!~'

`-DIED in the `-MONTH of (`-**6**); and, `-WAS `-BORN in the `-MONTH of (`-**12**) = (**6/12**) = FLIP 2 to 7 = (6/17) = (6) (1 + 7) = (`-**68**) = RECIPROCAL = (`-**86**) = `-**AGE of `-DEATH for AMERICAN ACTOR & COMEDIAN RICHARD (DICK) VINCENT (VAN) (PATTEN) (`-86)!!!~'**

`-FRAGMENTED `-BIRTH/DAY # `-NUMBER = (1 + 2 + 9 + 1 + 9 + 2 + 8) = (`-**32**) = RECIPROCAL = (`-**23**) = `-**DAY of `-DEATH** = (`-**23**rd)!!!~'

`-FRAGMENTED `-DEATH/DAY # `-NUMBER = (6 + 2 + 3 + 2 + 0 + 1 + 5) = (`-**19**) = `-**BIRTH/DAY** = (1-to-9) = (**12/9**)!!!~'

/|\ `-BIRTH/DAY # `-NUMBER = (12 + 9 + 19 + 28) = (`-**68**) = RECIPROCAL = (`-**86**) = `-**AGE of `-DEATH for AMERICAN ACTOR & COMEDIAN RICHARD (DICK) VINCENT (VAN) (PATTEN) (`-86)!!!~'** /|\

`-DEATH/DAY # `-NUMBER = (6 + 23 + 20 + 15) = (`-**64**) DIVIDED by (`-2) = (`-**32**) = `-**FRAGMENTED `-BIRTH/ DAY # `-NUMBER = (`-32)!!!~'**

FROM `-BIRTH-to-DEATH there are (`-169) `-DAYS = 1x69 = (`-69) = 6x9 = (`-54) = `-WAS `-MARRIED to PAT VAN PATTEN in 19(54)!!!~'

`-*MARRIAGE* `-BEGAN = (19 (-) 54) = `-(`-35)-` = (20 (+) 15) = `-*MARRIAGE* `-ENDED!!!~'

`-DIED in the `-MONTH of (`-6); and, `-WAS `-BORN in the `-MONTH of (`-12) = (6/12) = (61-TOO) = `-WAS `-MARRIED to PAT VAN PATTEN for (`-61) `-YEARS!!!~'

FROM `-BIRTH-to-DEATH there are (365 (-) 169) = (`-196) `-DAYS = (1 (-) 9) (6) = (`-86) = `-AGE of `-DEATH for AMERICAN ACTOR & COMEDIAN RICHARD (DICK) VINCENT (VAN) (PATTEN) (`-86)!!!~'

`-BIRTH/YEAR = (1928) = (1 (-) 9) (2 (-) 8) = (`-86) = `-AGE of `-DEATH for AMERICAN ACTOR & COMEDIAN RICHARD (DICK) VINCENT (VAN) (PATTEN) (`-86)!!!~'

AMERICAN SINGER & ACTRESS IRENE CARA ESCALERA died at the `-AGE of (`-63)!!!~'

`-BIRTH/DAY # `-NUMBER = 3+18+19+59 = (`-99) = 9x9 = (`-81) = RECIPROCAL = (`-18) = 6x3 = (`-63) = `-AGE of `-DEATH for AMERICAN SINGER & ACTRESS IRENE CARA ESCALERA!!!~'

`-BIRTH/YEAR = (1959) = 19+59 = (`-78) = `-DEATH/DAY # `-NUMBER!!!~'

`-DEATH/DAY # `-NUMBER = 11+25+20+22 = (`-78) = `-BIRTH/DAY = 3/18 = HALF RECIPROCAL = 3/81 = 3(-)81 = (`-78)!!!~'

`-DEATH/DAY # `-NUMBER = 11+25+20+22 = (`-78) = 7x8 = (`-56) = FLIP 6 to 9 = (`-59) = `-BIRTH/YEAR!!!~'

`-DEATH/DAY#`-NUMBER= 11+25+20+22 = (`-78) = `-AGE of `-FORMER `-HUSBAND CONRAD E. PALMISANO at the `-TIME of `-HER `-DEATH - AMERICAN SINGER & ACTRESS IRENE CARA ESCALERA!!!~'

`-DEATH/DAY = 11/25 = 11+25 = (`-36) = RECIPROCAL = (`-63) = `-AGE of `-DEATH for AMERICAN SINGER & ACTRESS IRENE CARA ESCALERA!!!~'

`-DEATH/DAY = 11/25 = HALF RECIPROCAL = 11/52 = 11+52 = (`-63) = `-AGE of `-DEATH for AMERICAN SINGER & ACTRESS IRENE CARA ESCALERA!!!~'

/|\ FRAGMENTED `-BIRTH/DAY # `-NUMBER = 3+1+8+1+9+5+9 = (`-36) = RECIPROCAL = (`-63) = `-AGE of `-DEATH for AMERICAN SINGER & ACTRESS IRENE CARA ESCALERA!!!~' /|\

FRAGMENTED `-DEATH/DAY # `-NUMBER = 1+1+2+5+2+0+2+2 = (`-15) = `-BIRTH/DAY = 3(-)18 = (`-15)!!!~'

FROM `-BIRTH-to-DEATH there are (`-113) `-DAYS = 11/3 = `-DIED in the `-MONTH of (`-11); and, `-WAS `-BORN in the `-MONTH of (`-3)!!!~'

`-BIRTH/DAY = 3/18 = HALF RECIPROCAL = 3/81 = 3+81 = (`-84) DIVIDED by (`-2) = (`-42) = 20+22 = `-DEATH/YEAR!!!~'

`-MARRIED ιω CONRAD E. PALMISANO in (1986) = 19(-)86 = (`-67) = 6x7 = (`-42) = 20+22 = `-DEATH/YEAR!!!~'

`-DIVORCED CONRAD E. PALMISANO in (1991) = 19(-)91 = (`-72) = 9x8 = (`-98) = FLIP 9 to 6; FLIP 8 to 3 = (`-63) = `-AGE of `-DEATH for AMERICAN SINGER & ACTRESS IRENE CARA ESCALERA!!!~'

RUSSIAN DESIGNER VALENTIN ABRAMOVICH YUDASHKIN died at the `-AGE of (`-59)!!!~'

`-HEIGHT = 5' 6" = FLIP 6 to 9 = 5' 9" = (`-59) = `-AGE of `-DEATH for RUSSIAN DESIGNER VALENTIN ABRAMOVICH YUDASHKIN!!!~'

`-BIRTH/DAY # `-NUMBER = 10 + 14 + 19 + 63 = (`-106)!!!~'

`-DAUGHTER GALINA YUDASHKINA was `-BORN in (1990) = 19+90 = (`-109) = FLIP 9 to 6 = (`-106) = `-HER

`-FATHER'S `-BIRTH/DAY # `-NUMBER = (`-106) = RUSSIAN DESIGNER VALENTIN ABRAMOVICH YUDASHKIN!!!~'

(1990) = 19(-)90 = (`-71) = RECIPROCAL = (`-17)!!!~'

(71 (-) 17) = (`-54) = RECIPROCAL = (`-45) = 5x9 = (`-59) = `-AGE of `-DEATH of `-HER `-FATHER RUSSIAN DESIGNER VALENTIN ABRAMOVICH YUDASHKIN!!!~'

(17 (+) 71) = (`-88) = FLIP 8 to 3 = (`-33) = `-AGE of DAUGHTER GALINA YUDASHKINA at the `-TIME of `-HER `-FATHER'S `-DEATH = RUSSIAN DESIGNER VALENTIN ABRAMOVICH YUDASHKIN!!!~'

RUSSIAN DESIGNER VALENTIN ABRAMOVICH YUDASHKIN `-BIRTH/DAY # `-NUMBER = (`-106) / DIVIDED by (`-2) = (`-53) = RECIPROCAL = (`-35) = 20+15 = `-YEAR `-DAUGHTER GALINA YUDASHKINA was `-MARRIED to PETER MAKSAKOV!!!~'

RUSSIAN DESIGNER VALENTIN ABRAMOVICH YUDASHKIN `-BIRTH/DAY # `-NUMBER = (`-106) / DIVIDED by (`-2) = (`-53) = FLIP 3 to 8 = (`-58) = `-WIFE MARINA V. YUDASHKIN was `-BORN in the `-YEAR of (`-58)!!!~'

FOR = RUSSIAN DESIGNER VALENTIN ABRAMOVICH YUDASHKIN:

`-BIRTH/MONTH = OCTOBER with (`-31) `-DAYS /|\
`-DAY of `-BIRTH = 14

(31 (-) 14) = (`-17) = RECIPROCAL = (`-71)!!!~'

(17 (-) 71) = (`-54) = RECIPROCAL = (`-45) = 5x9 = (`-59) = `-AGE of `-DEATH for RUSSIAN DESIGNER VALENTIN ABRAMOVICH YUDASHKIN!!!~'

`-DEATH/DAY # `-NUMBER = 5 + 2 + 20 + 23 = (`-50) = `-DIED in the `-MONTH of (`-5); and, `-WAS `-BORN in the `-MONTH of (`-10) = 5/10 = 5x10 = (`-50)!!!~'

FRAGMENTED `-BIRTH/DAY # `-NUMBER = 1 + 0 + 1 + 4 + 1 + 9 + 6 + 3 = (`-25) = X TIMES (`-2) = (`-50) = `-DEATH/DAY # `-NUMBER!!!~'

FRAGMENTED `-DEATH/DAY # `-NUMBER = 5 + 2 + 2 + 0 + 2 + 3 = (`-14) = 5+9 = (`-59) = `-AGE of `-DEATH for RUSSIAN DESIGNER VALENTIN ABRAMOVICH YUDASHKIN!!!~'

FRAGMENTED `-DEATH/DAY # `-NUMBER = 5 + 2 + 2 + 0 + 2 + 3 = (`-14) = `-DAY of `-BIRTH = (`-14th)!!!~'

(14 (+) 14) = (`-28) = RECIPROCAL = (`-82) = 19+63 = `-BIRTH/YEAR!!!~'

FROM `-BIRTH-to-DEATH there are (`-165) `-DAYS = RECIPROCAL = (`-561) = 56x1 = (`-56) = `-WAS (5' 6") in `-HEIGHT for RUSSIAN DESIGNER VALENTIN ABRAMOVICH YUDASHKIN!!!~'

(365 (-) 165) = (`-200) = 20+0 = (`-20) = `-REVERSE `-LOOKUP with RUSSIAN DESIGNER VALENTIN ABRAMOVICH YUDASHKIN `-BIRTH/DAY # `-NUMBER (in `-REVERSE) = (63(-)19(-)14(-)10) = (`-20)!!!~'

FROM `-BIRTH-to-DEATH there are (`-165) `-DAYS = RECIPROCAL = (`-561) = 56x1 = (`-56) = FLIP 6 to 9 = (`-59) = `-AGE of `-DEATH for RUSSIAN DESIGNER VALENTIN ABRAMOVICH YUDASHKIN!!!~'

FROM `-BIRTH-to-DEATH there are (`-165) `-DAYS = 1x65 = (`-65) = `-WIFE MARINA V. YUDASHKIN was (`-65) `-years OF `-AGE at the `-TIME of `-HER `-HUSBAND'S `-DEATH = RUSSIAN DESIGNER VALENTIN ABRAMOVICH YUDASHKIN = **RECIPROCAL** = `-HER `-HUSBAND was at the `-LEVEL of (5' 6") in `-HEIGHT!!!~'

`-WIFE MARINA V. YUDASHKIN was `-BORN in the `-YEAR of (`-**58**); and, `-HER `-HUSBAND RUSSIAN DESIGNER VALENTIN ABRAMOVICH YUDASHKIN `-**DIED** the `-VERY `-NEXT `-YEAR `-**AFTERWARD** at the `-AGE of (`-**59**)!!!~'

CANADIAN SINGER-SONGWRITER-GUITARIST GORDON MEREDITH LIGHTFOOT JR. died at the `-AGE of (`-84)!!!~'

`-DIED in the `-MONTH of (`-5); and, `-WAS `-BORN in the `-MONTH of (`-11) = 5/11 = (5/1) = `-DEATH/DAY!!!~'

`-DIED in the `-MONTH of (`-5); and, `-WAS `-BORN in the `-MONTH of (`-11) = 5/11 = 51x1 = (5/1) = `-DEATH/DAY!!!~'

`-BIRTH/DAY # `-NUMBER = 11 + 17 + 19 + 38 = (`-85) = `-DIED within `-HIS (`-85th) `-YEAR of `-EXISTENCE!!!~'

`-DEATH/DAY # `-NUMBER = 5 + 1 + 20 + 23 = (`-49) = X TIMES (`-2) = (`-98) = RECIPROCAL = (`-89) = `-MARRIED FORMER `-WIFE ELIZABETH MOON in (`-89)!!!~'

`-DEATH/DAY # `-NUMBER = 5 + 1 + 20 + 23 = (`-49) = 4+9 = (`-13) = FRAGMENTED `-DEATH/DAY # `-NUMBER = RECIPROCAL = (`-31) = FRAGMENTED `-BIRTH/DAY # `-NUMBER!!!~'

`-FRAGMENTED `-BIRTH/DAY # `-NUMBER = 1 + 1 + 1 + 7 + 1 + 9 + 3 + 8 = (`-31)!!!~'

`-DIVORCED FORMER WIFE ELIZABETH MOON in (2011) = 20+11 = (`-31) = `-FRAGMENTED `-BIRTH/DAY # `-NUMBER = (`-31)!!!~'

`-FRAGMENTED `-BIRTH/DAY # `-NUMBER = (`-31) = RECIPROCAL = (`-13) = `-FRAGMENTED `-DEATH/ DAY # `-NUMBER!!!~'

`-FRAGMENTED `-DEATH/DAY # `-NUMBER = 5 + 1 + 2 + 0 + 2 + 3 = (`-13)!!!~'

`-BIRTH/MONTH = NOVEMBER with (`-30) `-DAYS /|\ `-DAY of `-BIRTH = 17

(30 (-) 17) = (`-13) = `-FRAGMENTED `-DEATH/DAY # `-NUMBER = (`-13)!!!~'

FROM `-BIRTH-to-DEATH there are (`-165) `-DAYS = 1x65 = (`-65) = CANADIAN SINGER-SONGWRITER-GUITARIST GORDON MEREDITH LIGHTFOOT JR. & BRITA INGEGERD OLAISSON'S `-DAUGHTER INGRID LIGHTFOOT was `-BORN in (`-65)!!!~'

`-DAUGHTER INGRID LIGHTFOOT was `-BORN in (`-1965) = 19+65 = (`-84) = `-AGE of `-DEATH for `-HER `-VERY `-OWN `-FATHER = CANADIAN SINGER-SONGWRITER-GUITARIST GORDON MEREDITH LIGHTFOOT JR. (`-84)!!!~'

`-BIRTH/YEAR = 1938 = RECIPROCAL = 8391 = (8) (3+9+1) = (8/13) = (8) (1+3) = (`-84) = `-AGE of `-DEATH for CANADIAN SINGER-SONGWRITER-GUITARIST GORDON MEREDITH LIGHTFOOT JR. (`-84)!!!~'

`-DEATH/YEAR = 2023 = 20+23 = (`-43) = FLIP 3 to 8 = (`-48) = RECIPROCAL = (`-84) = `-AGE of `-DEATH for CANADIAN SINGER-SONGWRITER-GUITARIST GORDON MEREDITH LIGHTFOOT JR. (`-84)!!!~'

`-MARRIED FORMER `-WIFE ELIZABETH MOON in (1989) = 19+89 = (`-108) = `-DIVIDED by (`-2) = `-(`-**54**)-` = 19(-)73 = `-year `-HE DIVORCED `-FORMER `-WIFE BRITA INGEGERD OLAISSON!!!~'

`-MARRIED FORMER `-WIFE BRITA INGEGERD OLAISSON in (1963) = 19+63 = (`-82) = RECIPROCAL = (`-28) = (11+17) = `-BIRTH/DAY of CANADIAN SINGER-SONGWRITER-GUITARIST GORDON MEREDITH LIGHTFOOT JR.!!!~'

`-MARRIED FORMER `-WIFE BRITA INGEGERD OLAISSON in (1963) = 19+63 = (`-82) / DIVIDED by (`-2) = (`-41) = RECIPROCAL = (`-14) = `-MARRIED KIM HASSE in (`-14)!!!~'

`-WAS `-MARRIED to KIM HASSE in (2014) = 20+14 = (`-34) = RECIPROCAL = (`-43) = 20+23 = `-DEATH/YEAR of `-HER `-HUSBAND CANADIAN SINGER-SONGWRITER-GUITARIST GORDON MEREDITH LIGHTFOOT JR.!!!~'

CANADIAN SINGER-SONGWRITER-GUITARIST GORDON MEREDITH LIGHTFOOT JR. & ELIZABETH MOON'S `-SON MILES LIGHTFOOT was (`-32) YEARS of `-AGE at the `-TIME of `-HIS `-FATHER'S

`-DEATH = RECIPROCAL = (`-23) = `-HIS VERY OWN `-FATHER'S `-DEATH/YEAR!!!~'

CANADIAN SINGER-SONGWRITER-GUITARIST GORDON MEREDITH LIGHTFOOT JR. `-AGE of `-DEATH = (`-**84**) = 8x4 = (`-**32**) = RECIPROCAL = (`-**23**) = `-**DEATH/YEAR!!!~'**

FRENTORISH "TORI" BOWIE (TRACK & FIELD 2017 100M WORLD CHAMPION) died at the `-AGE of (`-**32**)!!!~'

`-DIED in the `-MONTH of (`-5); and, `-WAS `-BORN in the `-MONTH of (`-8) = (`-58) = FLIP 8 to 3 = (`-5/3) = `-DEATH/DAY!!!~'

`-BIRTH/DAY = 8/27 = 8+27 = (`-35) = RECIPROCAL = (`-5/3) = `-DEATH/DAY!!!~'

`-PARTIAL `-BIRTH/DAY # `-NUMBER = 8 + 27 + 19 = (`-54) = RECIPROCAL = (`-45) = 5x9 = (`-59) = 5' 9" in `-HEIGHT for FRENTORISH "TORI" BOWIE (TRACK & FIELD 2017 100M WORLD CHAMPION)!!!~'

`-BIRTH/DAY # `-NUMBER = 8 + 27 + 19 + 90 = (`-144) = 14x4 = (`-56) = FLIP 6 to 9 = (`-59) = 5' 9" in `-HEIGHT for FRENTORISH "TORI" BOWIE (TRACK & FIELD 2017 100M WORLD CHAMPION)!!!~'

'-DEATH/DAY # '-NUMBER = 5 + 3 + 20 + 23 = ('-51)!!!~'

FRAGMENTED '-BIRTH/DAY # '-NUMBER = 8 + 2 + 7 + 1 + 9 + 9 + 0 = ('-36)!!!~'

REVERSE '-LOOKUP on '-BIRTH/DAY # '-NUMBER (in '-REVERSE) = (90(-)19(-)27(-)8) = ('-36)!!!~'

('-**SIBLING**) TAMARA BOWIE'S ` BIRTH/DAY _ 6/3 = RECIPROCAL = ('-3/6) = "SEE '-ABOVE" for REVERSE '-LOOKUP & '-FRAGMENTED '-BIRTH/DAY # '-NUMBER = ('-36) for ('-**SIBLING**) FRENTORISH "TORI" BOWIE (TRACK & FIELD 2017 100M WORLD CHAMPION)!!!~'

REVERSE '-LOOKUP on ('-**SIBLING**) TAMARA BOWIE'S '-BIRTH/DAY # '-NUMBER (in '-REVERSE) = (81(-)19(-)3(-)6) = ('-5/3) = (MAY 3rd) = '-DEATH/DAY of ('-**SIBLING**) FRENTORISH "TORI" BOWIE (TRACK & FIELD 2017 100M WORLD CHAMPION)!!!~'

FRAGMENTED '-DEATH/DAY # '-NUMBER = 5 + 3 + 2 + 0 + 2 + 3 = ('-15) = RECIPROCAL = ('-51) = '-DEATH/ DAY # '-NUMBER!!!~'

(15 + 51) = ('-66) / DIVIDED by ('-2) = ('-33) = '-DIED within '-HER ('-33rd) '-YEAR of '-EXISTENCE!!!~'

(15 (-) 51) = ('-36) = "SEE '-ABOVE & '-PREVIOUS" = '-BIRTH/DAY # '-NUMBER in '-REVERSE &

`-FRAGMENTED `-BIRTH/DAY # `-NUMBER = (`-36)!!!~'

FROM `-BIRTH-to-DEATH there are (`-116) `-DAYS = 11x6 = (`-66) / DIVIDED by (`-2) = (`-33) = `-DIED within `-HER (`-33rd) `-YEAR of `-EXISTENCE!!!~'

(365 (-) 116) = (`-249) = 24+9 = (`-33) = `-DIED within `-HER (`-33rd) `-YEAR of `-EXISTENCE!!!~'

(365 (-) 116) = (`-249) = 24(-)9 = (`-15) = `-FRAGMENTED `-DEATH/DAY # `-NUMBER = RECIPROCAL = (`-51) = `-DEATH/DAY # `-NUMBER!!!~'

`-BIRTH/DAY = 8/27 = HALF RECIPROCAL = 8/72 = 8(-)72 = (`-64) = DIVIDED by (`-2) = (`-32) = `-AGE of `-DEATH for FRENTORISH "TORI" BOWIE (TRACK & FIELD 2017 100M WORLD CHAMPION)!!!~'

`-AGE of `-DEATH (`-**32**) for FRENTORISH "TORI" BOWIE (TRACK & FIELD 2017 100M WORLD CHAMPION) = (`-**32**) = RECIPROCAL = (`-**23**) = **`-DEATH/YEAR!!!~'**

AMERICAN PROFESSIONAL BASEBALL PLAYER (**VIDA** ROCHELLE **BLUE** JR.) died at the `-AGE of (`-**73**)!!!~'

`-DIED in the `-MONTH of (`-5); and, `-WAS `-BORN in the `-MONTH of (`-7) = (`-5/7) = 5x7 = (`-**#35**) OAKLAND A's = for AMERICAN PROFESSIONAL BASEBALL PLAYER (VIDA ROCHELLE BLUE JR.)!!!~'

`-DEATH/YEAR = (`-23) = FLIP 2 to 7 = (`-73) = `-AGE of `-DEATH for AMERICAN PROFESSIONAL BASEBALL PLAYER (VIDA ROCHELLE BLUE JR.) (`-73)!!!~'

`-BIRTH/DAY # `-NUMBER = 7 + 28 + 19 + 49 = (`-103)!!!~'

`-PARTIAL `-DEATH/DAY # `-NUMBER = 6 + 20 + 23 = (`-49) = `-BIRTH/YEAR!!!~'

`-DEATH/DAY = 5/6 = 7x8 = (`-78) = FLIP 8 to 3 = (`-73) = `-AGE of `-DEATH for AMERICAN PROFESSIONAL BASEBALL PLAYER (VIDA ROCHELLE BLUE JR.) (`-73)!!!~'

`-DEATH/DAY # `-NUMBER = 5 + 6 + 20 + 23 = (`-54)!!!~'

`-PARTIAL `-BIRTH/DAY # `-NUMBER = 7 + 28 + 19 = (`-**54**) = `-DEATH/DAY # `-NUMBER = (`-**54**) = 6x9 = (`-**69**) = **"SEE `-BELOW"!!!~'**

(54 (+) 54) = (`-108) = FLIP 8 to 3 = (`-103) = `-BIRTH/DAY # `-NUMBER!!!~'

`-WAS a `-LEFT-HANDED `-PITCHER in `-MAJOR `-LEAGUE `-BASEBALL from 19(**69**) to 19(**86**) = **"SEE; ALSO, `-BELOW"!!!~'**

`-BIRTH/YEAR = 19+49 = (`-**68**) = RECIPROCAL = (`-**86**) = "SEE; ALSO, `-ABOVE"!!!~'

(69 (+) 86) = (`-155) = 1(-)55 = (`-54) = `-DEATH/DAY # `-NUMBER!!!~'

(103 (+) 54) = (`-157) = 1(-)57 = (`-5/6) = `-DEATH/DAY!!!~'

(103 (+) 54) = (`-157) = 1+57 = (`-58) = `-FRAGMENTED `-BIRTH/DAY # `-NUMBER (`-40) (+) `-FRAGMENTED `-DEATH/DAY # `-NUMBER (`-18) / `-ADDED `-UP `-TOGETHER = (`-58)!!!~'

(103 (-) 54) = (`-**49**) = `-BIRTH/YEAR for AMERICAN PROFESSIONAL BASEBALL PLAYER (VIDA ROCHELLE BLUE JR.)!!!~'

`-WAS `-MARRIED in (`-89) to PEGGY SHANNON = 8x9 = (`-72) = `-DIED the `-VERY `-NEXT `-YEAR `-AFTERWARD at the `-AGE of (`-73) for AMERICAN PROFESSIONAL BASEBALL PLAYER (VIDA ROCHELLE BLUE JR.) (`-73)!!!~'

`-BIRTH/YEAR = 19/49 = 19+49 = (`-68) = RECIPROCAL = (`-86) = FLIP 6 to 9 = (`-89) = `-MARRIED `-FORMER `-WIFE PEGGY SHANNON in (`-89)!!!~'

`-MARRIED in (**198**9) = (1(-)8) (9+9) = 7(18) = FLIP 8 to 3 = 7(13) = 73x1 = (`-73) = `-AGE of `-DEATH for AMERICAN PROFESSIONAL BASEBALL PLAYER (VIDA ROCHELLE BLUE JR.) (`-73)!!!~'

`-DIVORCED in (199**6**) = (1+6) (9+9) = 7(18) = FLIP 8 to 3 = 7(13) = 73x1 = (`-73) = `-AGE of `-DEATH for AMERICAN PROFESSIONAL BASEBALL PLAYER (VIDA ROCHELLE BLUE JR.) (`-73)!!!~'

FRAGMENTED `-BIRTH/DAY # `-NUMBER = 7 + 2 + 8 + 1 + 9 + 4 + 9 = (`-40)!!!~'

FRAGMENTED `-DEATH/DAY # `-NUMBER = 5 + 6 + 2 + 0 + 2 + 3 = (`-18)!!!~'

(40 (+) 18) = (`-**58**) = **"SEE `-<u>ABOVE</u> & `-<u>BELOW</u>"!!!~'**

FROM `-BIRTH-to-DEATH there are (`-82) `-DAYS = RECIPROCAL – (`-28) = `-DAY of `-BIRTH = (28th)!!!~'

(365 (-) 82) = (`-283) = (2+8) (3) = (10) (3) = (`-103) = `-BIRTH/DAY # `-NUMBER!!!~'

(365 (-) 82) = (`-283) = 28x3 = (`-84) = RECIPROCAL = (`-48) = X TIMES (`-2) = (`-96) = `-DIVORCED FORMER `-WIFE PEGGY SHANNON in (`-96)!!!~'

(365 (-) 82) = (`-283) = 2+83 = (`-85) = RECIPROCAL = (`-58) = `-FRAGMENTED `-BIRTH/DAY # `-NUMBER (`-40) (+) `-FRAGMENTED `-DEATH/DAY # `-NUMBER (`-18) / `-ADDED `-UP `-TOGETHER = (`-58)!!!~'

(365 (-) 82) = (`-283) = 2+83 = (`-85) = FLIP 8 to 3 = (`-35) = **"SEE `-BELOW" for `-<u>ASSIGNMENT</u> to `-<u>BIRTH/ DAY</u>!!!~'**

`-**BIRTH/DAY** = 7/28 = 7+28 = (`-**35**) = `-WAS # (`-**35**) for the OAKLAND A'S as THEIR `-PITCHER!!!~'

`-INTEGRAL`-MEMBER of the OAKLAND ATHLETICS `-DYNASTY that `-WON (`-3) CONSECUTIVE `-WORLD `-SERIES `-CHAMPIONSHIPS `-between 19(72) to 19(74) = `-WHAT'S in the `-MIDDLE = (`-73) = `-AGE of `-DEATH for AMERICAN PROFESSIONAL BASEBALL PLAYER (VIDA ROCHELLE BLUE JR.) (`-73)!!!~'

`-EARNED `-RUN `-AVERAGE = 3.27 = RECIPROCAL = 72.3 = 7(to)3 = (`-73) = `-AGE of `-DEATH for AMERICAN PROFESSIONAL BASEBALL PLAYER (VIDA ROCHELLE BLUE JR.) (`-73)!!!~'

`-BIRTH/MONTH = (`-**7**) JULY with (`-**31**) `-DAYS /|\ `-DAY of `-BIRTH = 28th

(31 (-) 28) = (`-**3**) = PLUS `-MONTH of `-BIRTH = (`-**7**) = RECIPROCAL = (`-**73**) = `-**AGE of `-DEATH for AMERICAN PROFESSIONAL BASEBALL PLAYER (VIDA ROCHELLE BLUE JR.) (`-73)!!!~'**

AMERICAN ACTRESS & BALLERINA (YVONNE JOYCE CRAIG); otherwise KNOWN, as `-***BATGIRL*** died at the `-AGE of (`-78)!!!~'

'-PARTIAL '-BIRTH/DAY # '-NUMBER = 5 + 16 + 19 = ('-40) = '-WAS '-BORN in the '-MONTH of ('-5); and, '-DIED in the '-MONTH of ('-8) = ('-5/8) = 5x8 = ('-40)!!!~'

'-BIRTH/YEAR = ('-37) = RECIPROCAL = ('-73) = FLIP 3 to 8 = ('-78) = '-AGE of '-DEATH for AMERICAN ACTRESS & BALLERINA (YVONNE JOYCE CRAIG); otherwise KNOWN, as '-BATGIRL ('-78)!!!~'

'-BIRTH/DAY = 5/16 = 56x1 = ('-56) = 7x8 = ('-78) = '-AGE of '-DEATH for AMERICAN ACTRESS & BALLERINA (YVONNE JOYCE CRAIG); otherwise KNOWN, as '-BATGIRL ('-78)!!!~'

'-BIRTH/DAY = 5/16 = (5) (1x6) = ('-56) = 7x8 = ('-78) = '-AGE of '-DEATH for AMERICAN ACTRESS & BALLERINA (YVONNE JOYCE CRAIG); otherwise KNOWN, as '-BATGIRL ('-78)!!!~'

'-BIRTH/DAY = 5/16 = HALF RECIPROCAL = 5/61 = 5(-)61 = ('-56) = 7x8 = ('-78) = '-AGE of '-DEATH for AMERICAN ACTRESS & BALLERINA (YVONNE JOYCE CRAIG); otherwise KNOWN, as '-BATGIRL ('-78)!!!~'

'-DEATH/DAY = 8/17 = 87x1 = ('-87) = RECIPROCAL = ('-78) = '-AGE of '-DEATH for AMERICAN ACTRESS & BALLERINA (YVONNE JOYCE CRAIG); otherwise KNOWN, as '-BATGIRL ('-78)!!!~'

`-DEATH/DAY = 8/17 = (8) (1x7) = (`-87) = RECIPROCAL = (`-78) = `-AGE of `-DEATH for AMERICAN ACTRESS & BALLERINA (YVONNE JOYCE CRAIG); otherwise KNOWN, as `-BATGIRL (`-78)!!!~'

`-BIRTH/DAY = 5/16 = HALF RECIPROCAL = 5/61 = 5+61 = (`-66) = 6x6 = (`-36) = RECIPROCAL = (`-63)!!!~'

`-DEATH/DAY = 8/17 = HALF RECIPROCAL = 8/71 = 8(-)71 = (`-63)!!!~'

`-BIRTH/DAY # `-NUMBER = 5 + 16 + 19 + 37 = (`-77) = `-DIED the `-VERY `-NEXT `-YEAR `-AFTERWARD at the `-AGE of (`-78) for AMERICAN ACTRESS & BALLERINA (YVONNE JOYCE CRAIG); otherwise KNOWN, as `-BATGIRL (`-78)!!!~'

`-PARTIAL `-DEATH/DAY # `-NUMBER = 8 + 17 + 20 = (`-45) = RECIPROCAL = (`-54) = `-WAS (5' 4") in `-HEIGHT!!!~'

`-DEATH/DAY # `-NUMBER = 8 + 17 + 20 + 15 = (`-60) = `-MARRIED `-FORMER `-HUSBAND JIMMY BOYD in (`-60)!!!~'

`-DEATH/DAY # `-NUMBER = 8 + 17 + 20 + 15 = (`-60) = 30x2 = (3) (0) (2) = `-FRAGMENTED `-BIRTH/DAY # `-NUMBER = (`-32)!!!~'

(77 (+) 60) = (`-137) = 1x37 = (`-37) = `-BIRTH/YEAR!!!~'

(77 (+) 60) = (`-137) = RECIPROCAL = (`-731) = FLIP 3 to 8 = (`-781) = 78x1 = (`-78) = `-AGE of `-DEATH for AMERICAN ACTRESS & BALLERINA (YVONNE JOYCE CRAIG); otherwise KNOWN, as `-BATGIRL (`-78)!!!~'

(77 (+) 60) = (`-137) = FLIP 3 to 8 = (`-187) = "SWIPE 1 to the `-RIGHT" = (`-8/17) = `-DEATH/DAY!!!~'

FRAGMENTED `-BIRTH/DAY # `-NUMBER = 5 + 1 + 6 + 1 + 9 + 3 + 7 = (`-32) = RECIPROCAL = (`-23) = FLIP 2 to 7; FLIP 3 to 8 = (`-78) = `-AGE of `-DEATH for AMERICAN ACTRESS & BALLERINA (YVONNE JOYCE CRAIG); otherwise KNOWN, as `-BATGIRL (`-78)!!!~'

FRAGMENTED `-DEATH/DAY # `-NUMBER = 8 + 1 + 7 + 2 + 0 + 1 + 5 = (`-24)!!!~'

(32 (+) 24) = (`-56) = `-BIRTH/DAY = (5/16)!!!~'

FROM `-BIRTH-to-DEATH there are (`-93) `-DAYS = 9x3 = (`-27) = (X) TIMES (`-2) = (`-54) = `-WAS (5' 4") in `-HEIGHT!!!~'

FROM `-BIRTH-to-DEATH there are (`-93) `-DAYS = FLIP 3 to 8 = (`-98) = 9x8 = (`-72) = RECIPROCAL = (`-27) = (X) TIMES (`-2) = (`-54) = `-WAS (5' 4") in `-HEIGHT!!!~'

(365 (-) 93) = (272) = 27x2 = (`-54) = `-WAS (5' 4") in `-HEIGHT!!!~'

(365 (-) 93) = (272) = **R**ECIPROCAL-**S**EQUENCING-**N**UMEROLOGY-**RSN** = "SEE the `-PREVIOUS"!!!~'

`-BIRTH/YEAR = (1937) = RECIPROCAL = (7391) = (7) (3+9+1) = (7) (13) = (7) (1x3) = (`-73) = FLIP 3 to 8 = (`-78) = `-AGE of `-DEATH for AMERICAN ACTRESS & BALLERINA (YVONNE JOYCE CRAIG); otherwise KNOWN, as `-BATGIRL (`-78)!!!~'

`-DEATH/YEAR = (`-15) = 7+8 = (`-78) = `-AGE of `-DEATH for AMERICAN ACTRESS & BALLERINA (YVONNE JOYCE CRAIG); otherwise KNOWN, as `-BATGIRL (`-78)!!!~'

`-BIRTH/DAY = 5/16 = 5+16 = (`-21) = 7x3 = (`-73) = FLIP 3 to 8 = (`-78) = `-AGE of `-DEATH for AMERICAN ACTRESS & BALLERINA (YVONNE JOYCE CRAIG); otherwise KNOWN, as `-BATGIRL (`-78)!!!~'

`-BIRTH/MONTH (`-5) MAY with (`-31) `-DAYS /|\ `-DAY of `-BIRTH = (`-16ᵗʰ)

(31 (-) 16) = (`-**15**) = `-**DEATH/YEAR** for AMERICAN ACTRESS & BALLERINA (YVONNE JOYCE CRAIG); otherwise KNOWN, as `-BATGIRL (`-78)!!!~'

(31 (-) 16) = (`-**15**) = 7+8 = (`-**78**) = `-AGE of `-DEATH for AMERICAN ACTRESS & BALLERINA (YVONNE JOYCE CRAIG); otherwise KNOWN, as `-BATGIRL (`-**78**)!!!~'

'-WAS '-MARRIED to KENNETH ALDRICH from (1988) to (2015) for = ('-**27**) '-YEARS = (X) TIMES ('-2) = ('-**54**) = '-**WAS 5' 4" in '-HEIGHT!!!~'**

'-WAS '-MARRIED to '-FORMER '-HUSBAND JIMMY BOYD from (1960) to (1962) for = ('-**2**) '-YEARS!!!~'

'-**TOTAL '-YEARS '-MARRIED** = ALDRICH (**27**) BOYD (**2**) – FROM '-**BIRTH-to-DEATH** there were ('-**272**) '-DAYS = **R**ECIPROCAL-**S**EQUENCING-**N**UMEROLOGY-**RSN** = "SEE the '-PREVIOUS '-linkages"!!!~'

'-WAS '-MARRIED to '-FORMER '-HUSBAND JIMMY BOYD in (1960) = 19+60 = ('-79) = '-DIED the '-VERY '-YEAR '-PRIOR at the '-AGE of ('-78) for AMERICAN ACTRESS & BALLERINA (YVONNE JOYCE CRAIG); otherwise KNOWN, as '-BATGIRL ('-78)!!!~'

'-DEATH/DAY = 8/17 = HALF RECIPROCAL = 8/71 = 8+71 = ('-79) = '-WAS '-MARRIED to '-FORMER '-HUSBAND JIMMY BOYD in (1960) = 19+60 = ('-79)!!!~'

'-DEATH/DAY = 8/17 = 8x17 = ('-136) = 13x6 = ('-78) = '-AGE of '-DEATH for AMERICAN ACTRESS & BALLERINA (YVONNE JOYCE CRAIG); otherwise KNOWN, as '-BATGIRL ('-78)!!!~'

'-**BROKEN** '-**DEATH/DAY** # '-**NUMBER** = 8/**17/20**/15!!!!~'

(17 (+) 20) = (`-**37**) = `-**BIRTH/YEAR!!!~**'

(8 (+) 15) = (`-**23**) = FLIP 2 to 7; FLIP 3 to 8 = (`-**78**) = `-**AGE of** `-**DEATH for AMERICAN ACTRESS & BALLERINA (YVONNE JOYCE CRAIG); otherwise KNOWN, as** `-**BATGIRL** (`-**78**)!!!~'

AMERICAN FOOTBALL PLAYER & COACH (**JOSEPH ROBERT KAPP**) died at the `-AGE of (`-**85**)!!!~'

`-WAS `-BORN in the `-MONTH of (`-3); and, `-DIED in the `-MONTH of (`-5) = (`-35) = FLIP 3 to 8 = (`-85) = `-AGE of `-DEATH for AMERICAN FOOTBALL PLAYER & COACH (JOSEPH ROBERT KAPP) (`-85)!!!~'

`-BIRTH/YEAR = 1938 = RECIPROCAL = 8391 = (8) (3(-)9(-)1) = (`-**85**) = `-AGE of `-DEATH for AMERICAN FOOTBALL PLAYER & COACH (JOSEPH ROBERT KAPP) (`-85)!!!~'

`-BIRTH/DAY # `-NUMBER = 3 + 19 + 19 + 38 = (`-79)!!!~'

`-DEATH/DAY # `-NUMBER = 5 + 8 + 20 + 23 = (`-56)!!!~'

(79 (-) 56) = (`-23) = `-DEATH/YEAR!!!~'

(79 (+) 56) = (`-135) = 1x35 = (`-35) = FLIP 3 to 8 = (`-85) = `-AGE of `-DEATH for AMERICAN FOOTBALL PLAYER & COACH (JOSEPH ROBERT KAPP) (`-85)!!!~'

(79 (+) 56) = (`-135) = 1x35 = (`-35) = `-WAS `-BORN in the `-MONTH of (`-3); and, `-DIED in the `-MONTH of (`-5) = (`-35)!!!~'

(79 (+) 56) = (`-135) = 13x5 = (`-65) = RECIPROCAL = (`-56) = `-DEATH/DAY # `-NUMBER!!!~'

`-PARTIAL `-DEATH/DAY # `-NUMBER = 5 + 8 + 20 = (`-33) = FLIP 3 to 8 = (`-38) = `-BIRTH/YEAR!!!~'

FRAGMENTED `-BIRTH/DAY # `-NUMBER = 3 + 1 + 9 + 1 + 9 + 3 + 8 = (`-34) = RECIPROCAL = (`-43) = 20+23 = `-DEATH/YEAR!!!~'

FRAGMENTED `-DEATH/DAY # `-NUMBER = 5 + 8 + 2 + 0 + 2 + 3 = (`-20) = (X) TIMES (`-2) = (`-40) = 8x5 = (`-85) = `-AGE of `-DEATH for AMERICAN FOOTBALL PLAYER & COACH (JOSEPH ROBERT KAPP) (`-85)!!!~'

(34 (+) 20) = (`-54) = 5x4 = (`-20) = `-FRAGMENTED `-DEATH/DAY # `-NUMBER!!!~'

FROM `-BIRTH-to-DEATH there are (`-50) `-DAYS!!!~'

(365 (-) 50) = (`-315) = 35x1 = (`-35) = `-WAS `-BORN in the `-MONTH of (`-3); and, `-DIED in the `-MONTH of (`-5) = (`-35) = FLIP 3 to 8 = (`-85) = `-AGE of `-DEATH for AMERICAN FOOTBALL PLAYER & COACH (JOSEPH ROBERT KAPP) (`-85)!!!~'

(365 (-) 50) = (`-315) = (3) (1x5) = (`-35) = `-WAS `-BORN in the `-MONTH of (`-3); and, `-DIED in the `-MONTH of (`-5) = (`-35) = FLIP 3 to 8 = (`-85) = `-AGE of `-DEATH for AMERICAN FOOTBALL PLAYER & COACH (JOSEPH ROBERT KAPP) (`-85)!!!~'

/|\ `-DEATH/DAY = 5/8 = RECIPROCAL = (`-85) = `-AGE of `-DEATH for AMERICAN FOOTBALL PLAYER & COACH (JOSEPH ROBERT KAPP) (`-85)!!!~' /|

/|\ `-A `-VERY `-COMMON `-PATTERN!!!~' /|

/|\ SOCCER PLAYER JACK CHARLTON `-**DIED** at the `-**AGE** of (`-**85**)!!!~'

`-**BIRTHDAY** = (**5**/**8**/19/**35**) = (**5** + **8** + 19 + **35**) = (`-**67**) = RECIPROCAL = (`-**76**) = FLIP 6 to 9 = (`-**79**)!!!~'

`-**BIRTH/DAY** = (**5/8**) = RECIPROCAL = (`-**85**) = `-**AGE of** `-**DEATH for (SOCCER PLAYER) JACK CHARLTON** (`-**85**)!!!~'

`-**AGE of** `-**DEATH for (SOCCER PLAYER) JACK CHARLTON** = (`-**85**) = RECIPROCAL = (`-**58**)- while being `-MARRIED in (`-19**58**) to PAT KEMP!!!~'

`-BIRTH/YEAR = (`-**35**) = FLIP 3 to 8 = (`-**85**) = `-`-**AGE of** `-**DEATH for (SOCCER PLAYER) JACK CHARLTON** (`-**85**)!!!~' /|\

AMERICAN SCHOOLTEACHER (**MARY KAY LETOURNEAU**) `-**DIED** at the `-**AGE** of (`-**58**)!!!~'

AMERICAN SCHOOLTEACHER (**MARY KAY LETOURNEAU**) `-**DIED** (`-**158**) DAYS AWAY from `-**HER** `-**BIRTHDAY; WHILE** `-**DYING at the** `-**AGE of** (`-**58**)!!!~'

/|\ FILM ACTOR (**RICHARD BURTON**) `-**DIED** at the `-**AGE** of (`-**58**)!!!~'

`-**AGE of** `-**DEATH** = (`-**58**) = RECIPROCAL = (`-**85**) = `-**DEATH/DAY** of (**8/5**) for FILM ACTOR (RICHARD BURTON) = (**AUGUST 5**[th])!!!~'

FILM ACTOR (**RICHARD BURTON**) `-**DEATH/DAY** = (**8/5**/19/**84**) = (**8** + **5** + 19 + **84**) = (`-**116**) = (`-**116**) / `-*DIVIDED by* (`-**2**) = (`-**58**) = `-**AGE of** `-**DEATH for FILM ACTOR (RICHARD BURTON)** (`-**58**)"!!!~'

FRAGMENTED `-**DEATH/DAY** # `-**NUMBER** = (8 + 5 + 1 + 9 + 8 + 4) = (`-**35**) = RECIPROCAL = (`-**53**) = FLIP

3 to 8 = (`-**58**) = `-**AGE of** `-**DEATH for FILM ACTOR (RICHARD BURTON)** (`-**58**)"!!!~`

FRAGMENTED `-**DEATH/DAY** # `-**NUMBER** = (8 + 5 + 1 + 9 + 8 + 4) = (`-**35**) = FLIP 3 to 8 = (`-**85**) = RECIPROCAL = (`-**58**) = `-**AGE of** `-**DEATH for FILM ACTOR (RICHARD BURTON)** (`-**58**)"!!!~` /|\

/|\ The `-PROPHET (DWAYNE W. ANDERSON'S) `-**UNCLE** (**GERALD ANDERSON**) was `-**BORN** in the `-MONTH of (`-**8**); and, `-**DIED** in the `-MONTH of (`-**5**) = (`-**85**)!!!~`

`-UNCLE GERALD ANDERSON'S `-**BIRTH/MONTH** = (0**8**)!!!~`

`-UNCLE GERALD ANDERSON'S `-**BIRTH/YEAR** = (**5**0)!!!~`

!!!-`(0**8**)(**5**0)`-!!!

`-UNCLE GERALD ANDERSON `-**DIED** (`-**85**) **DAYS** `-**AWAY** from `-**BIRTH-to-DEATH**!!!~`

(`-**85**) = RECIPROCAL = (`-**58**)

`-UNCLE GERALD ANDERSON `-**DIED** on (`-**5/8**) = (**MAY 8**th) = ___RECIPROCAL___ = (`-**85**)!!!~` /|\

AMERICAN ACTRESS JACKLYN ZEMAN died at the `-AGE of (`-**70**)!!!~'

AMERICAN ACTRESS JACKLYN ZEMAN `-AGE of `-DEATH = (`-**70**) / `-DIVIDED by (`-2) = (`-**35**) = `-WAS `-BORN in the `-MONTH of (`-**3**); and, `-DIED in the `-MONTH of (`-**5**) = (`-**35**)!!!~'

`-WAS `-BORN in the `-MONTH of (`-**3**); and, `-DIED in the `-MONTH of (`-**5**) = (`-**35**) = RECIPROCAL = (`-**53**) = `-**BIRTH/YEAR!!!~'**

ACTRESS JACKLYN ZEMAN was a `-**PLAYBOY** `-**BUNNY at the** `-**PLAYBOY** `-**CLUB** in (1972) = 19(-)72 = (`-**53**) = `-**HER** `-**VERY** `-**OWN** `-**BIRTH/YEAR!!!~'**

`-WAS `-BORN in the `-MONTH of (`-3); and, `-DIED in the `-MONTH of (`-5) = (`-35) = **(X) TIMES (`-2) =** (`-70) = `-AGE of `-DEATH for AMERICAN ACTRESS JACKLYN ZEMAN (`-70)!!!~'

`-BIRTH/DAY # `-NUMBER = 3 + 6 + 19 + 53 = (`-81) = `-DIVORCED FORMER HUSBAND (MURRAY the K) in (`-81)!!!~'

`-FORMER `-HUSBAND MURRAY KAUFMAN (MURRAY the K) died in (`-1982) = 19(-)82 = (`-63) = RECIPROCAL = (`-36) = `-BIRTH/DAY = 3/6 = for `-FORMER `-WIFE / AMERICAN ACTRESS JACKLYN ZEMAN!!!~'

`-FORMER `-HUSBAND MURRAY KAUFMAN (MURRAY the K) `-PARTIAL `-BIRTH/DAY # `-NUMBER = 2 + 14 + 19 = (`-35) = "SEE the `-LINKAGES for `-FORMER `-WIFE / AMERICAN ACTRESS JACKLYN ZEMAN!!!~'

`-FORMER `-HUSBAND MURRAY KAUFMAN (MURRAY the K) `-BIRTH/DAY # `-NUMBER = 2 + 14 + 19 + 22 = (`-57) = 5x7 = (`-35) = "SEE the `-LINKAGES for `-FORMER `-WIFE / AMERICAN ACTRESS JACKLYN ZEMAN!!!~'

(35 + 35) = (`-70) = `-AGE of `-DEATH for `-FORMER `-WIFE / AMERICAN ACTRESS JACKLYN ZEMAN (`-70)!!!~'

`-FORMER `-HUSBAND MURRAY KAUFMAN (MURRAY the K) `-DEATH/DAY = 2/21 = 2+21 = (`-23) = `-DEATH/YEAR for `-FORMER `-WIFE / AMERICAN ACTRESS JACKLYN ZEMAN!!!~'

`-FORMER `-HUSBAND MURRAY KAUFMAN (MURRAY the K) `-DIED (`-7) `-DAYS after `-HIS `-LAST `-BIRTH/DAY = "JUST `-ADD a `-ZERO" = (`-70) = `-AGE of `-DEATH for `-FORMER `-WIFE / AMERICAN ACTRESS JACKLYN ZEMAN (`-70)!!!~'

`-MARRIED `-FORMER `-HUSBAND (GLENN GORDEN) in (1988) = 19(-)88 = (`-69) = `-DIED the `-VERY `-NEXT `-YEAR `-AFTERWARD at the `-AGE of (`-70) for AMERICAN ACTRESS JACKLYN ZEMAN (`-70)!!!~'

`-DIVORCED `-FORMER `-HUSBAND (GLENN GORDEN) in (`-07) = RECIPROCAL = (`-70) = `-AGE of `-DEATH for `-FORMER `-WIFE / AMERICAN ACTRESS JACKLYN ZEMAN (`-70)!!!~'

`-PARTIAL `-DEATH/DAY # `-NUMBER = 5 + 10 + 20 = (`-35) = `-WAS `-BORN in the `-MONTH of (`-3); and, `-DIED in the `-MONTH of (`-5) = (`-35) = "SEE the `-PREVIOUS `-LINKAGES"!!!~'

`-DEATH/DAY # `-NUMBER = 5 + 10 + 20 + 23 = (`-**58**) = FLIP 8 to 3 = (`-**53**) = `-**BIRTH/YEAR** = RECIPROCAL = (`-**35**) = `-WAS `-**BORN** in the `-**MONTH** of (`-3); and, `-**DIED** in the `-**MONTH** of (`-5) = (`-**35**)!!!~'

`-DEATH/DAY # `-NUMBER = 5 + 10 + 20 + 23 = (`-58) = RECIPROCAL = (`-85) = `-MARRIED `-FORMER `-HUSBAND (STEVE GRIBBIN) in (`-85)!!!~'

`-DEATH/DAY # `-NUMBER = 5 + 10 + 20 + 23 = (`-58) = RECIPROCAL = (`-85) = `-MARRIED `-FORMER `-HUSBAND (STEVE GRIBBIN) in (`-1985) = 19(-)85 = (`-66) = 6x6 = (`-3/6) = `-BIRTH/DAY for `-FORMER `-WIFE / AMERICAN ACTRESS JACKLYN ZEMAN!!!~'

`-**BIRTH/DAY** # `-**NUMBER** = (81 (-) 58) = `-**DEATH/ DAY** # `-**NUMBER** = (`-**23**) = `-**DEATH/YEAR**!!!~'

FRAGMENTED `-BIRTH/DAY # `-NUMBER = 3 + 6 + 1 + 9 + 5 + 3 = (`-27) = RECIPROCAL = (`-72) = 19+53 = **`-BIRTH/YEAR!!!~'**

FRAGMENTED `-DEATH/DAY # `-NUMBER = 5 + 1 + 0 + 2 + 0 + 2 + 3 = (`-13) = FLIP 3 to 8 = (`-18) = RECIPROCAL = (`-81) = `-BIRTH/DAY # `-NUMBER = (`-81)!!!~'

(27 (+) 13) = (`-**40**) = 5x8 = (`-58) = `-DEATH/DAY # `-NUMBER!!!~'

`-FORMER `-HUSBAND MURRAY KAUFMAN (MURRAY the K) `-DEATH/DAY # `-NUMBER (in `-REVERSE) = (82(-)19(-)21(-)2) = (`-**40**)!!!~'

(27 (X) 13) = (`-351) = 35x1 = (`-**35**) = `-WAS `-BORN in the `-MONTH of (`-**3**); and, `-DIED in the `-MONTH of (`-**5**) = (`-**35**) = RECIPROCAL = (`-**53**) = **`-BIRTH/YEAR!!!~'**

FROM `-BIRTH-to-DEATH there are (`-**65**) `-DAYS = `-DAY of `-BIRTH (`-**6**ᵗʰ) /|\ `-DEATH/MONTH = (`-**5**)!!!~'

(365 (-) 65) = (`-**300**) = 30+0 = (`-**30**) = **3**x**10** = `-BIRTH/MONTH (`-**3**) /|\ `-DAY of `-DEATH = (`-**10**ᵗʰ)!!!~'

`-DEATH/DAY** = 5/10 **/|\** `-BIRTH/DAY** = 3/6

(510 (-) 36) = (`-**474**) = **R**ECIPROCAL-**S**EQUENCING-**N**UMEROLOGY-**RSN** = 4(-)74 = (`-**70**) = **`-AGE of**

`-DEATH for AMERICAN ACTRESS JACKLYN ZEMAN (`-70)!!!~'

`-**BIRTH/YEAR** = 19(-)53 = (`-**34**) = RECIPROCAL = (`-**43**) = 20+23 = `-**DEATH/YEAR!!!~'**

AMERICAN UNIVERSITY PROFESSOR, ACTOR; &, AUTHOR (CLARENCE ALFRED GILYARD JR.) died at the `-AGE of (`-**66**) = 6x6 = (`-**36**) = "SEE `-**below**"!!!~'

`-BIRTH/DAY = 12/24 = 12+24 = (`-**36**) = 3(6's) = (`-**666**) = `-AGE of `-DEATH for AMERICAN UNIVERSITY PROFESSOR, ACTOR; &, AUTHOR (CLARENCE ALFRED GILYARD JR.) (`-**66**)!!!~'

`-DEATH/DAY = 11/28 = 11+28 = (`-**39**) = 3(9's) = (`-**999**) = RECIPROCAL = (`-**666**) = `-AGE of `-DEATH for AMERICAN UNIVERSITY PROFESSOR, ACTOR; &, AUTHOR (CLARENCE ALFRED GILYARD JR.) (`-**66**)!!!~'

`-PARTIAL `-BIRTH/DAY # `-NUMBER = 12 + 24 + 19 = (`-55) = `-BIRTH/YEAR = (`-55)!!!~'

`-BIRTH/DAY # `-NUMBER = 12 + 24 + 19 + 55 = (`-**110**) = `-DIVIDED by (`-3) = (`-**36.666**) = "SEE `-**ABOVE** & `-**BELOW**"!!!~'

`-DEATH/DAY # `-NUMBER = 11 + 28 + 20 + 22 = (`-**81**) = 9x9 = (`-**99**) = FLIP 9 to 6 = (`-**66**) = `-AGE of `-DEATH for AMERICAN UNIVERSITY PROFESSOR, ACTOR; &, AUTHOR (CLARENCE ALFRED GILYARD JR.) (`-**66**)!!!~'

(110 (-) 81) = (`-**29**) = 2(9's) = (`-**99**) = FLIP 9 to 6 = (`-**66**) = `-AGE of `-DEATH for AMERICAN UNIVERSITY PROFESSOR, ACTOR; &, AUTHOR (CLARENCE ALFRED GILYARD JR.) (`-**66**)!!!~'

FRAGMENTED `-BIRTH/DAY # `-NUMBER = 1 + 2 + 2 + 4 + 1 + 9 + 5 + 5 = (`-**29**) = 2(9's) = (`-**99**) = FLIP 9 to 6 = (`-**66**) = `-AGE of `-DEATH for AMERICAN UNIVERSITY PROFESSOR, ACTOR; &, AUTHOR (CLARENCE ALFRED GILYARD JR.) (`-**66**)!!!~'

FRAGMENTED `-DEATH/DAY # `-NUMBER = 1 + 1 + 2 + 8 + 2 + 0 + 2 + 2 = (`-**18**) = 2x9 = (`-**29**) = 2(9's) = (`-**99**) = FLIP 9 to 6 = (`-**66**) = `-AGE of `-DEATH for AMERICAN UNIVERSITY PROFESSOR, ACTOR; &, AUTHOR (CLARENCE ALFRED GILYARD JR.) (`-**66**)!!!~'

FROM `-BIRTH-to-DEATH there are (`-**26**) `-DAYS = 2(**6's**) = (`-**66**) = `-AGE of `-DEATH for AMERICAN UNIVERSITY PROFESSOR, ACTOR; &, AUTHOR (CLARENCE ALFRED GILYARD JR.) (`-**66**)!!!~'

`-BIRTH/YEAR = (1955) = (9) (1+5+5) = (9) (11) = 9x11 = (`-**99**) = FLIP 9 to 6 = (`-**66**) = `-AGE of `-DEATH for AMERICAN UNIVERSITY PROFESSOR, ACTOR;

&, AUTHOR (CLARENCE ALFRED GILYARD JR.) (`-**66**)!!!~'

`-WAS `-MARRIED to ELENA GILYARD from 2001 to 2022 = (`-**21**) `-years = (X) TIMES (`-3) = (`-**63**) = RECIPROCAL = (`-**36**) = 3(6's) = (`-**666**) = `-AGE of `-DEATH for AMERICAN UNIVERSITY PROFESSOR, ACTOR; &, AUTHOR (CLARENCE ALFRED GILYARD JR.) (`-**66**)!!!~'

`-WAS `-MARRIED to ELENA GILYARD from 2001 to 2022 = (`-**21**) `-years = (X) TIMES (`-3) = (`-**63**) = RECIPROCAL = (`-**36**) = **6**x**6** = (`-**66**) = `-AGE of `-DEATH for AMERICAN UNIVERSITY PROFESSOR, ACTOR; &, AUTHOR (CLARENCE ALFRED GILYARD JR.) (`-**66**)!!!~'

AMERICAN MUSICIAN & SINGER-SONGWRITER (**DAVID** VAN CORTLANDT **CROSBY**) died at the `-AGE of (`-**81**)!!!~'

`-WAS `-BORN in the `-MONTH of (`-**8**); and, `-DIED in the `-MONTH of (`-**1**) = (`-**81**) = `-AGE of `-DEATH for AMERICAN MUSICIAN & SINGER-SONGWRITER (DAVID VAN CORTLANDT CROSBY) (`-**81**)!!!~'

`-**DEATH/DAY** = 1/18 = RECIPROCAL = 81/1 = 81x1 = (`-**81**) = `-WAS `-BORN in the `-MONTH of (`-8); and, `-DIED in the `-MONTH of (`-1) = (`-**81**) = ALSO; `-AGE of `-DEATH for AMERICAN MUSICIAN & SINGER-SONGWRITER (DAVID VAN CORTLANDT CROSBY) (`-81)!!!~'

`-DAY of `-DEATH = (`-18th) = RECIPROCAL = (`-81) = `-WAS `-BORN in the `-MONTH of (`-8); and, `-DIED in the `-MONTH of (`-1) = (`-81) = ALSO; `-AGE of `-DEATH for AMERICAN MUSICIAN & SINGER-SONGWRITER (DAVID VAN CORTLANDT CROSBY) (`-81)!!!~'

`-BIRTH/DAY # `-NUMBER = 8 + 14 + 19 + 41 = (`-**82**) = `-DIED within `-HIS (`-**82**nd) `-YEAR of `-EXISTENCE!!!~'

`-PARTIAL `-BIRTH/DAY # `-NUMBER = 8 + 14 + 19 = (`-41) = `-BIRTH/YEAR = (`-41)!!!~'

`-DEATH/DAY = 1/18 = HALF RECIPROCAL = 1/81 = 1+81 = (`-82) = `-BIRTH/DAY # `-NUMBER!!!~'

`-BIRTH/DAY # `-NUMBER = 8 + 14 + 19 + 41 = (`-82) = RECIPROCAL = (`-28) = "JUST `-INSERT a `-ZERO" = (`-208) = `-DIED this `-MANY `-DAYS from `-BIRTH-to-DEATH / for AMERICAN MUSICIAN & SINGER-SONGWRITER (DAVID VAN CORTLANDT CROSBY)!!!~'

`-DEATH/DAY # `-NUMBER = 1 + 18 + 20 + 23 = (`-62) = DIVIDED by (`-2) = (`-31) = FLIP 3 to 8 = (`-81) = `-WAS `-BORN in the `-MONTH of (`-8); and, `-DIED in the `-MONTH of (`-1) = (`-81) = ALSO; `-AGE of `-DEATH for

AMERICAN MUSICIAN & SINGER-SONGWRITER (DAVID VAN CORTLANDT CROSBY) ('-81)!!!~'

FRAGMENTED '-BIRTH/DAY # '-NUMBER = 8 + 1 + 4 + 1 + 9 + 4 + 1 = ('-28) = "JUST '-INSERT a '-ZERO" = ('-208) = '-DIED this '-MANY '-DAYS from '-BIRTH-to-DEATH / for AMERICAN MUSICIAN & SINGER-SONGWRITER (DAVID VAN CORTLANDT CROSBY)!!!~'

FRAGMENTED '-BIRTH/DAY # '-NUMBER = 8 + 1 + 4 + 1 + 9 + 4 + 1 = ('-28) = RECIPROCAL = ('-82) = '-BIRTH/DAY # '-NUMBER!!!~'

FRAGMENTED '-DEATH/DAY # '-NUMBER = 1 + 1 + 8 + 2 + 0 + 2 + 3 = ('-17) = (X) TIMES ('-2) = ('-34) = RECIPROCAL = ('-43) = 20+23 = '-DEATH/YEAR!!!~'

'-BIRTH/MONTH ('-8) AUGUST with ('-31) DAYS /|\ '-DAY of '-BIRTH = ('-14th)

(31 (-) 14) = ('-17) = '-FRAGMENTED '-DEATH/DAY # '-NUMBER = ('-17)!!!~'

FROM '-BIRTH-to-DEATH there are ('-**208**) '-DAYS = 20+8 = ('-28) = '-FRAGMENTED '-BIRTH/DAY # '-NUMBER = RECIPROCAL = ('-82) = '-BIRTH/DAY # '-NUMBER!!!~'

(365 (-) 208) = ('-**157**) = 15+7 = ('-22) = 8+14 = '-**BIRTH/ DAY**!!!~'

`-MARRIED to JAN DANCE from (1987) to (2023) = `-EQUALS = (`-36) `-YEARS = 3x6 = (`-18) = RECIPROCAL = (`-81) = WAS `-BORN in the `-MONTH of (`-8); and, `-DIED in the `-MONTH of (`-1) = (`-81) = ALSO; `-AGE of `-DEATH for AMERICAN MUSICIAN & SINGER-SONGWRITER (DAVID VAN CORTLANDT CROSBY) (`-81)!!!~'

`-FROM `-ANOTHER `-MOTHER** / DAVID VAN CORTLANDT CROSBY'S `-SON** (**JAMES RAYMOND**) was `-BORN in (**1962**) = 19+62 = (`-**81**) = `-**FATHER** / WAS `-BORN in the `-MONTH of (`-**8**); and, `-DIED in the `-MONTH of (`-**1**) = (`-**81**) = ALSO; `-AGE of `-DEATH for `-**FATHER** / AMERICAN MUSICIAN & SINGER-SONGWRITER (DAVID VAN CORTLANDT CROSBY) (`-**81**)!!!~'

`-FROM `-ANOTHER `-MOTHER** / DAVID VAN CORTLANDT CROSBY'S `-SON** (**JAMES RAYMOND**) was `-BORN in (**1962**) = 19(-)62 = (`-**43**) = 20+23 = `-**DEATH/YEAR** for `-**FATHER** / AMERICAN MUSICIAN & SINGER-SONGWRITER (DAVID VAN CORTLANDT CROSBY)!!!~'

AMERICAN MUSICIAN & SINGER-SONGWRITER (DAVID VAN CORTLANDT CROSBY) `-DAY of `-DEATH (`-**18**[th]) (+) `-DAY of `-BIRTH (`-**14**) = (`-**32**) = RECIPROCAL = (`-**23**) = `-**DEATH/YEAR for**

AMERICAN MUSICIAN & SINGER-SONGWRITER (DAVID VAN CORTLANDT CROSBY)!!!~'

DOYLE F. BRUNSON "The GODFATHER of POKER" died at the `-AGE of (`-89)!!!~'

`-WAS `-BORN in the `-MONTH (`-8); and, `-DIED in the `-MONTH of (`-5) = (`-85) = FLIP 8 to 3 = (`-35) = (X) TIMES (`-2) = (`-70) = `-BIRTH/DAY # `-NUMBER (`-70)!!!~'

`-SON / TODD ALAN BRUNSON `-BIRTH/DAY # `-NUMBER (in `-REVERSE) = (69(-)19(-)7(-)8) = (`-35) = (X) TIMES (`-2) = (`-70) = `-BIRTH/DAY # `-NUMBER (`-70) of `-HIS `-FATHER / DOYLE F. BRUNSON "The GODFATHER of POKER"!!!~'

`-SON / TODD ALAN BRUNSON `-PARTIAL `-BIRTH/DAY # `-NUMBER (in `-REVERSE) = (69(-)19(-)7) = (`-**43**) = 20+23 = `-DEATH/YEAR of `-HIS `-FATHER / DOYLE F. BRUNSON "The GODFATHER of POKER"!!!~'

(`-**43**) = RECIPROCAL = (`-**34**)!!!~'

`-SON / TODD ALAN BRUNSON `-PARTIAL `-BIRTH/DAY # `-NUMBER = 8 + 7 + 19 = (`-**34**) = (X) times (`-2) = (`-68) = RECIPROCAL = (`-86) = FLIP 6 to 9 = (`-89) = `-AGE of `-DEATH for `-FATHER / DOYLE F. BRUNSON "The GODFATHER of POKER" (`-89)!!!~'

`-BIRTH/DAY = 8/10 = 8+10 = (`-18) = 3x6 = (`-36) = FLIP 3 to 8; FLIP 6 to 9 = (`-89) = `-AGE of `-DEATH for DOYLE F. BRUNSON "The GODFATHER of POKER" (`-89)!!!~'

`-BIRTH/DAY # `-NUMBER = 8 + 10 + 19 + 33 = (`-70) = "SEE `-PREVIOUS"!!!~'

`-DEATH/DAY = 5/14 = 5x14 = (`-70) = `-BIRTH/DAY # `-NUMBER!!!~'

`-DEATH/DAY = 5/14 = HALF RECIPROCAL = 5/41 = 5(-)41 = (`-36) = FLIP 3 to 8; FLIP 6 to 9 = (`-89) = `-AGE of `-DEATH for DOYLE F. BRUNSON "The GODFATHER of POKER" (`-89)!!!~'

`-DEATH/DAY # `-NUMBER = 5 + 14 + 20 + 23 = (`-62) = `-MARRIED LOUISE BRUNSON in 19(62)!!!~'

(70 (+) 62) = (`-132) = FLIP 3 to 8; FLIP 2 to 7 = (`-**187**) = (1(-)87) = (`-86) = FLIP 6 to 9 = (`-89) = `-AGE of `-DEATH for DOYLE F. BRUNSON "The GODFATHER of POKER" (`-89)!!!~'

(70 (+) 62) = (`-132) = FLIP 3 to 8; FLIP 2 to 7 = (`-**187**) = 1+87 = (`-88) = `-DIED this `-MANY `-DAYS from `-BIRTH-to-DEATH for DOYLE F. BRUNSON "The GODFATHER of POKER"!!!~'

`-SON / TODD ALAN BRUNSON `-BIRTH/DAY = (`-**8/7**)!!!~'

`-SON / TODD ALAN BRUNSON `-BIRTH/YEAR = (1969) = 19+69 = (`-**88**) = `-HIS `-FATHER / DOYLE F. BRUNSON "The GODFATHER of POKER" / `-DIED this `-MANY `-DAYS from `-BIRTH-to-DEATH = (`-**88**)!!!~'

`-SON / TODD ALAN BRUNSON `-BIRTH/YEAR = (`-69) = 6x9 = (`-54) = RECIPROCAL = (`-45) = (X) TIMES (`-2) = (`-90) = `-HIS `-FATHER `-DIED the `-VERY `-YEAR `-PRIOR at the `-AGE of (`-89) for DOYLE F. BRUNSON "The GODFATHER of POKER"!!!~'

`-SON / TODD ALAN BRUNSON `-BIRTH/YEAR = (`-69) = 6x9 = (`-**54**) = `-FATHER / DOYLE F. BRUNSON'S "The GODFATHER of POKER" / `-DEATH/DAY = (`-**5**/1**4**)!!!~

`-PARTIAL `-DEATH/DAY # `-NUMBER = 5 + 14 + 20 = (`-39) = FLIP 3 to 8 = (`-89) = `-AGE of `-DEATH for DOYLE F. BRUNSON "The GODFATHER of POKER" (`-89)!!!~'

FRAGMENTED `-BIRTH/DAY # `-NUMBER = 8 + 1 + 0 + 1 + 9 + 3 + 3 = (`-25)!!!~'

FRAGMENTED `-DEATH/DAY # `-NUMBER = 5 + 1 + 4 + 2 + 0 + 2 + 3 = (`-17) = 8+9 = (`-89) = `-AGE of `-DEATH for DOYLE F. BRUNSON "The GODFATHER of POKER" (`-89)!!!~'

`-DAY of `-DEATH = (`-14th) = RECIPROCAL = (`-**41**)!!!~'

(25 (+) 17) = ('-**42**)!!!~'

'-DEATH/YEAR = 20+23 = ('-**43**)!!!~'

(41,42,43) = **"LINEAR '-PROGRESSION"!!!~'**

(41 (+) 42 (+) 43) = ('-126) = RECIPROCAL = ('-621) = 62x1 = ('-62) = '-MARRIED LOUISE BRUNSON in 19(62) = & = '-DEATH/DAY # '-NUMBER = ('-62)!!!~'

(41 (+) 42 (+) 43) = ('-126) = 12x6 = ('-72) = 8x9 = ('-89) = '-AGE of '-DEATH for DOYLE F. BRUNSON "The GODFATHER of POKER" ('-89)!!!~'

'-BIRTH/YEAR = ('-33) = FLIP 3 to 8 = ('-88) = FROM '-BIRTH-to-DEATH there are ('-88) '-DAYS!!!~'

FROM '-BIRTH-to-DEATH there are ('-88) '-DAYS = '-DIED the '-VERY '-NEXT '-YEAR '-AFTERWARD at the '-AGE of ('-89)!!!~'

'-DEATH/MONTH was ('-5) MAY with ('-31) '-DAYS /|\ '-DAY of '-DEATH = ('-14th)

(31 (-) 14) = ('-17) = 8+9 = ('-89) = '-AGE of '-DEATH for DOYLE F. BRUNSON "The GODFATHER of POKER" ('-89)!!!~'

'-BIRTH/YEAR = (1933) = (1(-)9) (3+3) = ('-86) = FLIP 6 to 9 = ('-89) = '-AGE of '-DEATH for DOYLE F. BRUNSON "The GODFATHER of POKER" ('-89)!!!~'

`-DEATH/YEAR = (2023) = 20+23 = (`-43) = (X) TIMES (`-2) = (`-86) = FLIP 6 to 9 = (`-89) = `-AGE of `-DEATH for DOYLE F. BRUNSON "The GODFATHER of POKER" (`-89)!!!~'

`-MARRIED LOUISE BRUNSON in (**1962**) = (1(-)9) (6+2) = (`-**88**) = `-DIED this `-MANY `-DAYS from `-BIRTH-to-DEATH for DOYLE F. BRUNSON "The GODFATHER of POKER"!!!~'

`-MARRIED LOUISE BRUNSON in (**1962**) = 19(-)62 = (`-43) = 20+23 = `-DEATH/YEAR for DOYLE F. BRUNSON "The GODFATHER of POKER"!!!~'

`-MARRIED LOUISE BRUNSON in (**1962**) = RECIPROCAL = (**2691**) = (2+6) (9x1) = (`-**89**) = `-AGE of `-DEATH for DOYLE F. BRUNSON "The GODFATHER of POKER" (`-**89**)!!!~'

SCOTTISH ACTOR (SIR SEAN CONNERY) died at the `-AGE of (`-**90**)!!!~'

`-WAS `-BORN in the `-MONTH of (`-8); and, `-DIED in the `-MONTH of (`-10) = (8/10) = (8+1) (0) = (`-90) = `-AGE of `-DEATH for SCOTTISH ACTOR (SIR SEAN CONNERY) (`-90)!!!~'

`-DEATH/DAY = 10/31 = 10x31 = (`-310) = FLIP 3 to 8 = (`-8/10) = `-WAS `-BORN in the `-MONTH of (`-8); and, `-DIED in the `-MONTH of (`-10) = (8/10)!!!~'

`-BIRTH/DAY = 8/25 = HALF RECIPROCAL = 8/52 = 8+52 = (`-60) = FLIP 6 to 9 = (`-90) = `-AGE of `-DEATH for SCOTTISH ACTOR (SIR SEAN CONNERY) (`-90)!!!~'

SCOTTISH ACTOR (SIR SEAN CONNERY) had a `-HEIGHT of (6' 2") = `-WAS `-MARRIED to DIANE CILENTO in (`-62)!!!~'

`-DIVORCED DIANE CILENTO in (1973) = 19+73 = (`-92) = FLIP 9 to 6 = (`-62) = (6' 2") = `-HEIGHT of SCOTTISH ACTOR (SIR SEAN CONNERY)!!!~'

`-WAS `-MARRIED to MICHELINE ROQUEBRUNE from (1975) to (2020) = (1975 (-) 2020) = (`-45) = (X) TIMES (`-2) = (`-90) = `-AGE of `-DEATH for SCOTTISH ACTOR (SIR SEAN CONNERY) (`-90)!!!~'

`-BIRTH/YEAR = (1930) = 19(-)30 = (`-11) = `-WAS `-MARRIED to DIANE CILENTO for (`-11) `-years = `-ALSO; `-DAY of `-BIRTH, for `-THEIR `-SON (JASON JOSEPH CONNERY)!!!~'

`-BIRTH/YEAR = (1930) = 19(+)30 = (`-49) = RECIPROCAL = (`-94) = `-SON'S (JASON JOSEPH CONNERY) `-BIRTH/DAY # `-NUMBER = (1 + 11 + 19 + 63) = (`-94)!!!~'

`-STOPPED `-STARRING as "JAMES BOND" in (1983) = 19(-)83 = (`-64) = FLIP 6 to 9 = (`-94)!!!~'

`-SON'S (JASON JOSEPH CONNERY) `-PARTIAL `-BIRTH/DAY # `-NUMBER = (1 + 11 + 19) = (`-31) = `-FATHER'S / SCOTTISH ACTOR (SIR SEAN CONNERY) = `-DAY of `-DEATH = (`-31st)!!!~

`-SON'S (JASON JOSEPH CONNERY) `-BIRTH/YEAR = 19+63 = (`-82) = "SEE `-below"!!!~'

SCOTTISH ACTOR (SIR SEAN CONNERY) `-BIRTH/ DAY # `-NUMBER = (8 + 25 + 19 + 30) = (`-82)!!!~'

SCOTTISH ACTOR (SIR SEAN CONNERY) `-DEATH/ DAY # `-NUMBER = (10 + 31 + 20 + 20) = (`-81)!!!~'

(82 (+) 81) = (`-163) = 1x63 = (`-**63**) = `-SON'S `-BIRTH/ YEAR & `-GRANDSON'S `-BIRTH/DAY = (**6/3**)!!!~'

SCOTTISH ACTOR (SIR SEAN CONNERY) `-DEATH/ DAY = 10/31 = 10(-)31 = (`-**21**) = `-STARRED as BRITISH SECRET AGENT "JAMES BOND" for (`-**21**) `-years FROM (19**62**) to (19**83**)!!!~'

(21 (+) 21) = (`-**42**) = `-**BIRTH/DAY** of `-**FORMER `-WIFE (DIANE CILENTO)** = (**4/2**) = (**APRIL 2nd**)!!!~'

SCOTTISH ACTOR (SIR SEAN CONNERY) `-DEATH/ DAY = 10/31 = HALF RECIPROCAL = 10/13 = (10 + 13) = (`-**23**) = `-PLUS the `-REST of `-HIS `-DEATH/DAY #

`-NUMBER = (23 + 20 + 20) = (`-**63**) = `-SON'S (JASON JOSEPH CONNERY) `-**BIRTH/YEAR** = 19(**63**)!!!~'

SCOTTISH ACTOR (SIR SEAN CONNERY) `-GRANDCHILD/`-GRANDSON (**DASHIELL CONNERY**) `-**BIRTH/DAY** = (**6/3**)!!!~'

SCOTTISH ACTOR (SIR SEAN CONNERY) `-GRANDCHILD/`-GRANDSON (**DASHIELL CONNERY**) `-BIRTH/DAY # `-NUMBER = (6 + 3 + 19 + 97) = (`-**125**) = 12x5 = (`-**60**) = FLIP 6 to 9 = (`-**90**) = `-AGE of `-DEATH for (GRANDFATHER) / SCOTTISH ACTOR (SIR SEAN CONNERY) (`-**90**)!!!~'

SCOTTISH ACTOR (SIR SEAN CONNERY) `-GRANDCHILD/`-GRANDSON (**DASHIELL CONNERY**) `-BIRTH/YEAR = (**1997**) = 19(-)97 = (`-**78**) = FLIP 8 to 3 = (`-**73**) = `-year `-HIS GRANDPARENTS / SCOTTISH ACTOR (SIR SEAN CONNERY) & `-WIFE DIANE CILENTO (`-**DIVORCED**)!!!~'

SCOTTISH ACTOR (SIR SEAN CONNERY) `-GRANDCHILD/`-GRANDSON (**DASHIELL CONNERY**) `-BIRTH/YEAR = (**1997**) = 19(-)97 = (`-**78**) = `-**GRANDMOTHER (DIANE CILENTO)** `-DIED (`-**178**) DAYS from `-***BIRTH-to-DEATH***!!!~'

(365 (-) 178) = (`-**187**)!!!~'

SCOTTISH ACTOR (SIR SEAN CONNERY) `-**FORMER** `-**WIFE (DIANE CILENTO)** `-**BIRTH/YEAR** = (`-**32**) =

RECIPROCAL = (`-**23**) = FLIP 2 to 7; FLIP 3 to 8 = (`-**78**) = **"see `-BEFORE"!!!~'**

`-*SCOTTISH ACTOR (SIR SEAN CONNERY)* =

`-BIRTH/MONTH** (**8**) **AUGUST** /|\ **`-DAY of `-BIRTH** = (`-25**th) /|\ (8) (2+5) = (`-**87**)!!!~'

`-BIRTH/MONTH** (**8**) **AUGUST** with (`-3**1) DAYS /|\ **`-DAY of `-BIRTH = (`-25**th)

(31 (-) 25) = (`-**6**) = FLIP 6 to 9 = (`-**9**) = "JUST `-ADD a `-ZERO" = (`-**90**) = `-AGE of `-DEATH for SCOTTISH ACTOR (SIR SEAN CONNERY) (`-**90**)!!!~'

`-*COUNTING `-DAYS until `-DEATH/DAY* =

SEPTEMBER with (`-30) `-days = (**6** + **30**) = (`-**36**) = RECIPROCAL = (`-**63**) = "SON'S `-BIRTH/YEAR 19(**63**) & GRANDSON'S `-BIRTH/DAY" = (**6/3**)!!!~'

OCTOBER with (`-31) `-days = `-death/day = (`-31st) = (**36** + **31**) = (`-**67**) = **`-days FROM `-BIRTH-to-DEATH!!!~'**

SCOTTISH ACTOR (SIR SEAN CONNERY) **`-DIED** (`-**67**) **`-DAYS** from **`-BIRTH-to-DEATH** = (6x7) = (`-**42**) = **`-BIRTH/DAY** of **`-FORMER `-WIFE (DIANE CILENTO)** = (**4/2**) = (**APRIL 2**nd)!!!~'

`-FORMER `-WIFE (DIANE CILENTO) `-DEATH/ DAY** = **10/6** = 10x6 = (`-60**) = FLIP 6 to 9 = (`-**90**) = `-AGE of `-DEATH for `-former `-husband / SCOTTISH ACTOR (SIR SEAN CONNERY) (`-**90**)!!!~'

`-GRANDSON,     `-GRANDFATHER;   AND, `-GREAT-GRANDFATHER!!!~'

BENJAMIN KEOUGH (LISA MARIE PRESLEY'S SON) `-**DIED** at the `-**AGE** of (`-**27**) = 2(7's) = (`-**77**) = `-YEAR `-HIS `-GRANDFATHER ELVIS AARON PRESLEY `-**DIED**!!!~'

ELVIS AARON PRESLEY'S FORMER WIFE (PRISCILLA ANN PRESLEY) was (`-**77**) `-YEARS of `-AGE at the `-TIME of `-HER `-DAUGHTER'S `-DEATH (LISA MARIE PRESLEY) / BENJAMIN KEOUGH'S `-MOTHER!!!~'

GREAT-GRANDMOTHER GLADYS LOVE PRESLEY `-**DEATH/YEAR** = 1958 = 19 + 58 = (`-**77**) = `-AGE of `-DAUGHTER-IN-LAW (PRISCILLA ANN PRESLEY) at the `-**TIME** of `-HER `-GRANDDAUGHTER'S `-DEATH (LISA MARIE PRESLEY)!!!~'

GREAT-GRANDFATHER VERNON PRESLEY `-**DIED** (`-**77**) DAYS `-AWAY from `-BIRTH/DAY-to-DEATH/DAY!!!~'

`-**EQUATION** = (77 x TIMES (`-2)) = (`-**154**) = "**SEE** the `-**LINKAGES**"!!!~'

BENJAMIN KEOUGH (LISA MARIE PRESLEY'S SON) `-**BIRTHDAY** # `-NUMBER = (10/21/19/92) = (10 + 21 + 19 + 92) = (`-**142**) = 1x42 = (`-**42**) = `-AGE of `-DEATH of `-**GRANDFATHER ELVIS AARON PRESLEY!!!**~'

BENJAMIN KEOUGH (LISA MARIE PRESLEY'S SON) `-**BIRTH/YEAR** = (`-**92**) = DIVIDED by (`-2) = (`-**46**) = `-AGE of `-DEATH of `-GREAT-GRANDMOTHER GLADYS LOVE PRESLEY!!!~'

`-MOTHER (LISA MARIE PRESLEY) `-BIRTH/DAY # `-NUMBER in `-REVERSE = (68 (-) 19 (-) 1 (-) 2) = (`-**46**) = `-AGE of `-DEATH of `-HER `-GRANDMOTHER GLADYS LOVE PRESLEY!!!~'

BENJAMIN KEOUGH (LISA MARIE PRESLEY'S SON) `-**DEATH/DAY** # `-NUMBER = (7/12/20/20) = (7 + 12 + 20 + 20) = (`-**59**) = 5x9 = (`-**45**) = "**SEE the `-FOLLOWING `-BELOW**"!!!~'

ELVIS AARON PRESLEY `-BIRTH/YEAR** = (`-1935**) = (19 + 35) = (`-**54**) = RECIPROCAL = (`-**45**) = "'-ELVIS AARON PRESLEY DIED (`-145) *DAYS AWAY* from `-HIS `-BIRTH/DAY**"!!!~'

ELVIS AARON PRESLEY'S FORMER WIFE (PRISCILLA ANN PRESLEY) was `-BORN in (`-45), HER `-BIRTH/DAY = (5/24) = (5-to-4), SHE'S 5' 4" in `-HEIGHT, `-HER CURRENT `-AGE at the `-TIME of `-HER `-DAUGHTER'S `-DEATH = (`-77); `-EQUATION (77 x TIMES (2)) = (`-154)!!!~'

(`-LISA MARIE PRESLEY); BENJAMIN KEOUGH'S MOTHER, `-<u>DIED</u> at the `-AGE of (`-<u>54</u>)!!!~'

GREAT-GRANDMOTHER GLADYS LOVE PRESLEY `-<u>DIED</u> (`-<u>2(54)</u>) = (too(54)) = DAYS from `-BIRTH/DAY-to-DEATH/DAY!!!~'

`-<u>DEATH/DAY</u> for BENJAMIN KEOUGH = (<u>7</u>/1<u>2</u>) = RECIPROCAL = (2<u>1</u>/<u>7</u>) = (2x1/7) = (`-<u>27</u>) = "AGE of `-DEATH for BENJAMIN KEOUGH (LISA MARIE PRESLEY'S SON)"!!!~'

`-GREAT-GRANDFATHER VERNON PRESLEY `-BIRTH/DAY # `-NUMBER = (4 + 10 + 19 + 16) = (`-<u>49</u>) = 4x9 = (`-36) = RECIPROCAL = (`-63) = `-HIS `-VERY `-OWN `-AGE of `-DEATH!!!~'

ELVIS AARON PRESLEY'S FRAGMENTED BIRTHDAY # `-NUMBER = JANUARY 8, 1935 = (1 + 8 + 1 + 9 + 3 + 5) = (`-<u>27</u>) = GRANDSON BENJAMIN KEOUGH'S `-AGE of `-DEATH = `-<u>EQUATION</u> = (27 x TIMES (`-2)) = (`-<u>54</u>) = `-<u>SEE</u> the `-<u>LINKAGES</u>!!!~'

`-GRANDSON BENJAMIN KEOUGH'S `-BIRTH/DAY # `-NUMBER = `-GRANDFATHER ELVIS AARON PRESLEY'S `-AGE of `-DEATH!!!~'

`-GRANDFATHER ELVIS AARON PRESLEY'S `-FRAGMENTED `-BIRTH/DAY # `-NUMBER = `-GRANDSON BENJAMIN KEOUGH'S `-AGE of `-DEATH!!!~'

GRANDSON BENJAMIN KEOUGH `-**DIED** at the `-**AGE** of (`-**27**) x TIMES (`-**2**) = (`-**54**)**!!!~'**

BENJAMIN KEOUGH (LISA MARIE PRESLEY'S SON) `-**DIED** (`-**101**) DAYS AWAY from `-**HIS** `-**BIRTHDAY!!!~'**

(365 (-) 101) = (`-**264**) = (**to64**) = RECIPROCAL = (`-**46**) = `-**AGE** of `-**DEATH** of **GREAT-GRANDMOTHER GLADYS LOVE PRESLEY!!!~'**

GRANDMOTHER (PRISCILLA ANN PRESLEY) `-**BIRTH/YEAR** = 1945 = (19 + 45) = (`-**64**)**!!!~'**

ELVIS AARON PRESLEY'S `-**BIRTHDAY #** `-**NUMBER** = (1 + 8 + 19 + 35) = (`-**63**) = `-**AGE** of `-**DEATH** of `-**HIS** `-**VERY** `-**OWN** `-**FATHER VERNON PRESLEY!!!~'**

ELVIS AARON PRESLEY'S `-**BIRTHDAY #** `-**NUMBER** = (1 + 8 + 19 + 35) = (`-**63**) = FLIP *the* 6 to 9 = (`-**93**) / DIVIDED by (`-2) = (`-**46.5**) = `-**AGE** of `-**DEATH** of `-**HIS** `-**VERY** `-**OWN** `-**MOTHER GLADYS LOVE PRESLEY;** `-**too!!!~'**

`-**AGES** of `-**DEATH, for** `-**BOTH** of `-**HIS** `-**PARENTS;** from `-**ONE, and the SAME;** `-**BIRTH/DAY #** `-**NUMBER** = (`-63) = from **ELVIS AARON PRESLEY!!!~'**

BOOK - "GOD = THE GOD MATRIX!!!~'"

109

`-RECIPROCAL-SEQUENCING-NUMEROLOGY-RSN (=) "the MASTER `-KEY"!!!~'

When WE look to HOW much GOD has REVEALED HIMSELF to US; We only WONDER on HOW FAR and to WHAT LEVELS HE has REVEALED HIMSELF ULTIMATELY to ALL/ of HIS other CREATIONS throughout the ENTIRE UNENDING UNIVERSE!!!~' Are THEY still in some SORT of DINOSAUR AGES; or, OF SIMILAR & VARIED `-MEANS in THEIR UNDERSTANDING of `-HIM; and, HIS `-GLORIOUS `-POWER? This, is the QUESTION!!!~

`-CLEARLY, from WHAT MYSELF; "THE PROPHET" (DWAYNE W. ANDERSON), has PROVIDED in MY (`-13) BOOKS, the `-RESURRECTION is "NO PROBLEM"!!!~' AGAIN, whether IT IS the "BIG BANG THEORY"; the "EDGE of SPACE"; or, what was BEFORE GOD and BEFORE that; and, BEFORE that; it NEVER ENDS!!!~'

"I" SEE the RESURRECTION of the DINOSAURS on the PLANET MERCURY!!!~' "I" SEE the RESURRECTION of HUMANS, here on the PLANET EARTH!!!~' "I" SEE a TERRAFORMING on the PLANET MARS and HUMANS TRAVELING (to & fro) BETWEEN the PLANET EARTH & the PLANET MARS!!!~' The PROPHET has SPOKEN!'

DISCOVERED & ORIGINATED by: AUTHOR – DWAYNE W. ANDERSON!!!~'

RELIGIOUS BROADCASTER & SOUTHERN BAPTIST MINISTER (MARION GORDON "PAT" ROBERTSON) died at the `-AGE of (`-93)!!!~'

`-WAS `-BORN in the `-MONTH of (`-3); and, `-DIED in the `-MONTH of (`-6) = (`-3/6) = RECIPROCAL = (`-6/3) = FLIP 6 to 9 = (`-93) = `-AGE of `-DEATH for RELIGIOUS BROADCASTER & SOUTHERN BAPTIST MINISTER (MARION GORDON "PAT" ROBERTSON) (`-93)!!!~'

`-BIRTH/DAY = 3/22 = 3(x)22 = (`-66) = 6(x)6 = (`-36) = `-WAS `-BORN in the `-MONTH of (`-3); and, `-DIED in the `-MONTH of (`-6)!!!~'

`-BIRTH/DAY = 3/22 = 3(x)22 = (`-66) = 6(x)6 = (`-36) = RECIPROCAL = (`-63) = FLIP 6 to 9 = (`-93) = `-AGE of `-DEATH for RELIGIOUS BROADCASTER & SOUTHERN BAPTIST MINISTER (MARION GORDON "PAT" ROBERTSON) (`-93)!!!~'

`-BIRTH/YEAR = (1930) = (1(x)93(+)0) = (`-93) = `-AGE of `-DEATH for RELIGIOUS BROADCASTER & SOUTHERN BAPTIST MINISTER (MARION GORDON "PAT" ROBERTSON) (`-93)!!!~'

`-BIRTH/YEAR = (1930) = 19(+)30 = (`-49) = 4(x)9 = (`-36) = `-WAS `-BORN in the `-MONTH of (`-3); and, `-DIED in the `-MONTH of (`-6) = (`-3/6) = RECIPROCAL = (`-6/3) = FLIP 6 to 9 = (`-93) = `-AGE of `-DEATH for RELIGIOUS BROADCASTER & SOUTHERN BAPTIST MINISTER (MARION GORDON "PAT" ROBERTSON) (`-93)!!!~'

`-DEATH/DAY = 6/8 = FLIP 6 to 9; FLIP 8 to 3 = (`-93) = `-AGE of `-DEATH for RELIGIOUS BROADCASTER & SOUTHERN BAPTIST MINISTER (MARION GORDON "PAT" ROBERTSON) (`-93)!!!~'

`-WAS `-MARRIED to ADELIA ELMER ROBERTSON from (1954) to (2022) for (`-**68**) `-YEARS = `-**DEATH/DAY** = (`-**6/8**) = "**JUNE 8ᵗʰ**")!!!~'

`-WIFE / ADELIA ELMER ROBERTSON was `-BORN in the `-MONTH of (`-12); and, `-DIED in the `-MONTH of (`-4) = (`-12/4) = 12(x)4 = (`-48) = 6(x)8 = (`-**68**) = `-WAS `-MARRIED for (`-**68**) `-YEARS = & = `-DAY of `-DEATH (`-**6/8**) of `-HER `-HUSBAND / RELIGIOUS BROADCASTER & SOUTHERN BAPTIST MINISTER (MARION GORDON "PAT" ROBERTSON)!!!~'

ADELIA ELMER ROBERTSON `-BIRTH/DAY = 12/3 = 12(x)3 = (`-36) = `-HUSBAND / "PAT" ROBERTSON `-was `-BORN in the `-MONTH of (`-3); and, `-DIED in the `-MONTH of (`-6) = (`-3/6) = RECIPROCAL = (`-6/3) = FLIP 6 to 9 = (`-93) = `-AGE of `-DEATH for `-HUSBAND / RELIGIOUS BROADCASTER & SOUTHERN BAPTIST MINISTER (MARION GORDON "PAT" ROBERTSON) (`-93)!!!~'

ADELIA ELMER ROBERTSON `-DEATH/DAY = 4/19 = 4(+)19 = (`-23) = `-DEATH/YEAR of `-HUSBAND / "PAT" ROBERTSON!!!~'

`-BIRTH/YEAR for "PAT" ROBERTSON = (1930) = 19(+)30 = (`-49) = `-WIFE (ADELIA ELMER ROBERTSON'S) `-DEATH/DAY = (4/19)!!!~'

`-BIRTH/DAY # `-NUMBER = 3 + 22 + 19 + 30 = (`-74)

FRAGMENTED `-BIRTH/DAY # `-NUMBER = 3 + 2 + 2 + 1 + 9 + 3 + 0 = (`-20)

(74 (+) 20) = (`-**94**) = RECIPROCAL = (`-**49**) = "**SEE** the `-**PREVIOUS** `-**LINKAGES** `-**ABOVE**"!!!~'

`-DEATH/DAY # `-NUMBER = 6 + 8 + 20 + 23 = (`-57)

FRAGMENTED `-DEATH/DAY # `-NUMBER = 6 + 8 + 2 + 0 + 2 + 3 = (`-21)

(57 (+) 21) = (`-**78**) = "SEE `-RIGHT `-BELOW"!!!~'

FROM `-BIRTH-to-DEATH there are (`-**78**) `-DAYS = RECIPROCAL = (`-**87**)!!!~'

`-SON / GORDON P. ROBERTSON'S `-BIRTH/DAY # `-NUMBER = 6 + 4 + 19 + 58 = (`-**87**) = "REVIEW the `-LINKAGES (**ABOVE** & **BELOW**)" = 8(x)7 = (`-**56**) = RECIPROCAL = (`-65) = `-AGE of `-SON / GORDON P. ROBERTSON at the `-TIME of `-HIS `-FATHER'S `-DEATH / RELIGIOUS BROADCASTER & SOUTHERN BAPTIST MINISTER (MARION GORDON "PAT" ROBERTSON)!!!~'

(365 (-) 78) = (`-287) = 2(x)87 = (`-174) = 1(x)74 = (`-74) = `-BIRTH/DAY # `-NUMBER!!!~'

(365 (-) 78) = (`-287) = 2(x)87 = (`-174) = 17(x)4 = (`-68) = `-DEATH/DAY = 6/8 = "JUNE 8th")

`-SON / GORDON P. ROBERTSON was `-BORN in (1958) = 19(-)58 = (`-39) = RECIPROCAL = (`-93) = `-AGE of `-DEATH for `-HIS `-FATHER / RELIGIOUS BROADCASTER & SOUTHERN BAPTIST MINISTER (MARION GORDON "PAT" ROBERTSON) (`-93)!!!~'

`-GOD; `-DO `-YOU `-NEED `-MORE???

LYRICIST CYNTHIA WEIL died at the `-AGE of (`-82) = 8x2 = (`-16) = RECIPROCAL = (`-61) = `-WAS `-BORN in the `-MONTH of (`-10); and, `-DIED in the `-MONTH of (`-6) = (10/6) = 10+6 = (`-16) = RECIPROCAL = (`-61) = `-WAS `-MARRIED in (`-61) to BARRY MANN; and, `-WAS `-MARRIED to BARRY MANN for (`-61) `-YEARS!!!~' `-DEATH/DAY for LYRICIST CYNTHIA WEIL = (`-6/1)!!!~' `-BIRTH/DAY = 10/18 = 10+18 = (`-28) = RECIPROCAL = (`-82) = `-AGE of `-DEATH for LYRICIST CYNTHIA WEIL!!!~' `-BIRTH/DAY # `-NUMBER = 10+18+19+40 = (`-87) = FLIP 7 to 2 = (`-82) = `-AGE of `-DEATH for LYRICIST CYNTHIA WEIL!!!~' "ALL of `-YOU are `-LIKE `-THIS"!!!~' `-READ `-IT in `-MY (`-13) `-BOOKS by `-ME = AUTHOR/PROPHET = DWAYNE W. ANDERSON!!!~' `-BIRTH/DAY = 10/18

= RECIPROCAL = 81/01 = (81(+)01) = (`-82) = `-AGE of `-DEATH for LYRICIST CYNTHIA WEIL = `-HER `-DEATH was `-TOLD at `-HER `-BIRTH; just LIKE, `-EVERYONE `-ELSE-'!!!~'

PS: `-DEATH/MONTH = JUNE with (`-30) `-DAYS /|\ `-DAY of `-DEATH = 1ˢᵗ

(30 (-) 1) = (`-29) = 2/9 = `-HUSBAND BARRY MANN'S `-BIRTH/DAY = 2/9 = FEBRUARY 9ᵗʰ!!!~'

LYRICIST CYNTHIA WEIL `-BIRTH/YEAR = 1940 = (1(-)9) (4(+)0) = (`-84) = `-AGE of `-HUSBAND BARRY MANN at the `-TIME of `-HER (HIS `-WIFE'S) `-DEATH!!!~' "ALL of `-YOU are `-LIKE `-THIS"!!!~' `-READ `-IT in `-MY (`-13) `-BOOKS by `-ME = AUTHOR/PROPHET = DWAYNE W. ANDERSON!!!~'

LYRICIST CYNTHIA WEIL `-DIED (`-139) `-DAYS from `-BIRTH-to-DEATH = 1/39 = 1x39 = (`-39) = `-BIRTH/YEAR of `-HUSBAND BARRY MANN!!!~'

`-BIRTH/YEAR of `-HUSBAND BARRY MANN = 19/39 = 19+39 = (`-58) = `-AGE of their `-DAUGHTER (JENN MANN) at the `-TIME of `-HER `-MOTHER'S `-DEATH!!!~'

`-DAUGHTER (JENN MANN) was `-BORN in (`-1965) = 19+65 = (`-84) = `-AGE of `-FATHER at the `-TIME of `-HER `-MOTHER'S `-DEATH!!!~'

(365 days-in-the-year (-) 139) = (`-226) = 22/6 = 22+6 = (`-28) = RECIPROCAL = (`-82) = `-AGE of `-DEATH for LYRICIST CYNTHIA WEIL = "READ `-between The `-LINES"!!!~'

BASEBALL'S (SF GIANTS) MANAGER ROGER CRAIG died at the `-AGE of (`-93)!!!~'

`-BIRTH/YEAR = 1930 = (1(x)93(+)0) = (`-93) = `-AGE of `-DEATH for BASEBALL'S (SF GIANTS) MANAGER ROGER CRAIG (`-93)!!!~'

`-BIRTH/DAY # `-NUMBER = 2 + 17 + 19 + 30 = (`-68) = FLIP 6 to 9; FLIP 8 to 3 = (`-93) = `-AGE of `-DEATH for BASEBALL'S (SF GIANTS) MANAGER ROGER CRAIG (`-93)!!!~'

`-DEATH/DAY # `-NUMBER = 6 + 4 + 20 + 23 = (`-53)!!!~'

FRAGMENTED `-BIRTH/DAY # `-NUMBER = 2 + 1 + 7 + 1 + 9 + 3 + 0 = (`-23) = `-DEATH/YEAR = (`-23)!!!~'

(23 (+) 23) = (`-46) = RECIPROCAL = (`-6/4) = `-DEATH/ DAY!!!~'

FRAGMENTED `-DEATH/DAY # `-NUMBER = 6 + 4 + 2 + 0 + 2 + 3 = (`-17) = `-DAY of `-BIRTH (`-17th)!!!~'

FRAGMENTED `-DEATH/DAY # `-NUMBER = (`-17) (X) (`-4) = (`-68) = `-BIRTH/DAY # `-NUMBER!!!~'

`-DEATH/DAY # `-NUMBER (`-53) (-) = `-MINUS = (-) = `-FRAGMENTED `-DEATH/DAY # `-NUMBER (`-17) = (`-36) = RECIPROCAL = (`-63) = FLIP 6 to 9 = (`-93) = `-AGE of `-DEATH for BASEBALL'S (SF GIANTS) MANAGER ROGER CRAIG (`-93)!!!~'

FROM `-BIRTH-to-DEATH there are (`-107) `-DAYS = 10+7 = (`-17) = FRAGMENTED `-DEATH/DAY # `-NUMBER = & = `-DAY of `-BIRTH (`-17th)!!!~'

(365 (-) 107) = (`-258) = 25(-)8 = (`-17) = FRAGMENTED `-DEATH/DAY # `-NUMBER = & = `-DAY of `-BIRTH (`-17th)!!!~'

`-BIRTH/YEAR = (1930) = 19(+)30 = (`-49) = 4(x)9 = (`-36) = RECIPROCAL = (`-63) = FLIP 6 to 9 = (`-93) = `-AGE of `-DEATH for BASEBALL'S (SF GIANTS) MANAGER ROGER CRAIG (`-93)!!!~'

`-DEATH/MONTH = (`-6) JUNE with (`-30) `-DAYS /|\ `-DAY of `-DEATH (`-4th)

(30 (-) 4) = (`-26) = `-WAS `-BORN in the `-MONTH of (`-2); and, `-DIED in the `-MONTH of (`-6) = (2/6) = FLIP 2 to 7; FLIP 6 to 9 = (7/9) = 7(x)9 = (`-63) = FLIP 6 to 9 = (`-93) = `-AGE of `-DEATH for BASEBALL'S (SF GIANTS) MANAGER ROGER CRAIG (`-93)!!!~'

'-DEATH/YEAR = 20/23 = 20(+)23 = ('-43) (X) ('-2) = ('-86) = RECIPROCAL = ('-68) = '-BIRTH/DAY # '-NUMBER!!!~'

ASTRUD GILBERTO (ASTRUD EVANGELINA WEINERT) "THE GIRL from IPANEMA" SINGER died at the '-AGE of ('-83)!!!~'

'-BIRTH/DAY = 3/29 = 3(+)29 = ('-32) = RECIPROCAL = ('-23) = '-DEATH/YEAR!!!~'

'-BIRTH/DAY # '-NUMBER = 3 + 29 + 19 + 40 = ('-91) x ('-2) = ('-182) = 1(+)82 = ('-83) = '-AGE of '-DEATH for ASTRUD GILBERTO (ASTRUD EVANGELINA WEINERT) "THE GIRL from IPANEMA" SINGER ('-83)!!!~'

'-BIRTH/DAY = 3/29 = HALF RECIPROCAL = 3/92 = 3(+)92 = ('-95) = 9(x)5 = ('-45) = RECIPROCAL = ('-54) = '-DEATH/DAY # '-NUMBER!!!~'

'-BIRTH/DAY # '-NUMBER = ('-91) / '-DIVIDED by ('-2) = ('-45.5) = HALF RECIPROCAL = ('-54.5) = "SEE '-BELOW"!!!~'

'-DEATH/DAY # '-NUMBER = 6 + 5 + 20 + 23 = ('-54)

(91 (+) 54) = ('-145) = 1(x)45 = ('-45) = 5x9 = ('-59) = "SEE '-BELOW"!!!~'

FRAGMENTED `-BIRTH/DAY # `-NUMBER = 3 + 2 + 9 + 1 + 9 + 4 + 0 = (`-28) = RECIPROCAL = (`-82) = `-DIED the `-VERY `-NEXT `-YEAR `-AFTERWARD at the `-AGE of (`-83)!!!~'

FRAGMENTED `-BIRTH/DAY # `-NUMBER = (`-**28**) x (`-2) = (`-**56**) = RECIPROCAL = (`-**65**) = `-**DEATH/DAY** = (**6/5**)!!!~'

FRAGMENTED `-DEATH/DAY # `-NUMBER = 6 + 5 + 2 + 0 + 2 + 3 = (`-18) = 6(x)3 = (`-63) = `-AGE of `-SON / JOAO MARCELO GIBERTO / at the `-TIME of `-HER (`-HIS `-MOTHER'S) `-DEATH!!!~'

FRAGMENTED `-DEATH/DAY # `-NUMBER = (`-18) = 6(x)3 = `-DIED in the `-MONTH of (`-6); and, `-WAS `-BORN in the `-MONTH of (`-3)!!!~'

(28 (+) 18) = (`-46) = 23(x)2 = `-DEATH/YEAR (`-**23**) = & = **R**eciprocal-**S**equencing-**N**umerology-**RSN** (`-**232**)!!!~'

`-BIRTH/DAY = 3/29 = HALF RECIPROCAL = 3/92 = 3(-)92 = (`-89) = RECIPROCAL = (`-98) = FLIP 9 to 6 = (`-68) = "SEE `-BELOW"!!!~'

FROM `-BIRTH-to-DEATH there are (`-68) `-DAYS = FLIP 8 to 3 = (`-63) = "SEE the `-LINKAGES / `-ABOVE"!!!~'

(`-68) = 6(+)8 = (`-14) = 5(+)9 = (`-59)!!!~'

`-BIRTH/YEAR = (1940) = 19(+)40 = (`-59) = `-MARRIED JOAO GILBERTO in (`-59)!!!~'

(59 (+) 59) = (`-**118**) = `-FORMER `-HUSBAND'S `-**BIRTH/DEATH** `-**DAY** # `-**NUMBERS** `-**ADDED** `-**UP** `-**TOGETHER** & `-**PRODUCT of** `-**DEATH** = "SEE `-BELOW"!!!~'

`-MARRIED = (`-1959) = 19(+)59 = (`-78) = 7(x)8 = (`-56) = RECIPROCAL = (`-65) = `-HER / `-DEATH/DAY = (6/5)!!!~'

`-FORMER `-HUSBAND / JOAO GILBERTO / `-BIRTH/ DAY # `-NUMBER = 6 + 10 +19 + 31 = (`-66) = 6(x)6 = (`-36) = RECIPROCAL = (`-63) = "SEE `-PREVIOUS `-LINKAGES"!!!~'

`-FORMER `-HUSBAND / JOAO GILBERTO / `-DEATH/DAY # `-NUMBER = 7 + 6 + 20 + 19 = (`-52)!!!~'

(66 (-) 52) = (`-14) = 6(+)8 = 5(+)9 (!!!~')

(66 (+) 52) = (`-**118**) = **"SEE `-PREVIOUS `-LINKAGES"** = 11(x)8 = (`-**88**) = `-AGE of `-DEATH of `-FORMER `-HUSBAND / JOAO GILBERTO!!!~'

`-DIVORCED JOAO GILBERTO in (1964) = 19(+)64 = (`-83) = `-AGE of `-DEATH for ASTRUD GILBERTO (ASTRUD EVANGELINA WEINERT) "THE GIRL from IPANEMA" SINGER (`-83)!!!~'

`-SON / JOAO MARCELO GIBERTO `-BIRTH/YEAR = (1960) = 19(+)60 = (`-79) = 7(x)9 = (`-63) = `-HIS `-AGE at the `-TIME of `-HIS `-MOTHER'S `-DEATH / ASTRUD GILBERTO (ASTRUD EVANGELINA WEINERT) "THE GIRL from IPANEMA" SINGER!!!~'

`-FORMER `-HUSBAND / JOAO GILBERTO / was `-BORN in the `-MONTH of (`-6); and, `-DIED in the `-MONTH of (`-7) = (`-6/7) = RECIPROCAL = (`-7/6) = `-HIS `-VERY `-OWN `-DEATH/DAY = (JULY 6th)!!!~'

`-FORMER `-HUSBAND / JOAO GILBERTO / `-DIED at the `-AGE of (`-88) = FLIP 8 to 3 = (`-83) = `-AGE of `-DEATH of `-HIS `-FORMER `-WIFE / ASTRUD GILBERTO (ASTRUD EVANGELINA WEINERT) "THE GIRL from IPANEMA" SINGER (`-83)!!!~'

The ADDAMS FAMILY CAROLYN SUE JONES (HER FIRST MARRIAGE to AARON SPELLING was in 53) SHE died AT AGE 53! SHE DIVORCED AARON SPELLING in 1964 = 19+64 = 83 and SHE died in the YEAR of 83! Within MY NEW BOOK: "DO YOU BELIEVE in GOD??? IS DESTINY REAL???" AUTHOR: DWAYNE W. ANDERSON!!!~

AMERICAN-BORN SWISS SINGER (TINA TURNER) "The QUEEN of ROCK 'n' ROLL"; **ALSO**, died at the `-AGE; of (`-**83**)!!!~'

'-BIRTH/DAY # '-NUMBER = 11 + 26 + 19 + 39 = ('-**95**) = "SEE '-BELOW for '-LINKAGES"!!!~'

'-PARTIAL '-BIRTH/DAY # '-NUMBER = 11 + 26 + 19 = ('-56) = '-DEATH/DAY = 5/24 = 5/2(+)4 = ('-5/6)!!!~'

'-DEATH/DAY # '-NUMBER = 5 + 24 + 20 + 23 = ('-**72**) = "SEE '-BELOW for '-LINKAGES"!!!~'

(95 (-) 72) = ('-**23**) = '-**DEATH/YEAR** = ('-**23**)!!!~'

(95 (+) 72) = ('-**167**) = 1(x)67 = ('-**67**) = '-AGE of '-HUSBAND / ERWIN BACH at the '-TIME of '-HIS '-WIFE'S '-DEATH = RECIPROCAL = ('-**76**) = '-AGE of '-DEATH of '-HER '-FORMER '-HUSBAND / IKE TURNER!!!~'

FRAGMENTED '-BIRTH/DAY # '-NUMBER = 1 + 1 + 2 + 6 + 1 + 9 + 3 + 9 = ('-**32**) = RECIPROCAL = ('-**23**) = '-**DEATH/YEAR**!!!~'

'-WAS '-BORN in the '-MONTH of ('-11); and, '-DIED in the '-MONTH of ('-5) = (11/5) = 11(x)5 = ('-55) = ('-23) (+) ('-**32**)!!!~'

FRAGMENTED '-DEATH/DAY # '-NUMBER = 5 + 2 + 4 + 2 + 0 + 2 + 3 = ('-**18**) (x) ('-4) = ('-**72**) = '-DEATH/DAY # '-NUMBER!!!~'

'-DEATH/DAY # '-NUMBER ('-72) (-) = MINUS = (-) FRAGMENTED '-DEATH/DAY # '-NUMBER ('-18) =

(`-**54**) = RECIPROCAL = (`-**45**) = 9(x)5 = (`-**95**) = `-**BIRTH/ DAY # `-NUMBER!!!~**'

FROM `-BIRTH-to-DEATH there are (`-186) `-DAYS = 18(+)6 = (`-24) = `-DAY of `-DEATH = (`-24th)!!!~'

(365 (-) 186) = (`-179) = 17(+)9 = (`-26) = `-DAY of `-BIRTH = (`-26th)!!!~'

FROM `-BIRTH-to-DEATH there are (`-186) `-DAYS = RECIPROCAL = (`-681) = 68(-)1 = (`-67) = "`-SEE `-BELOW & `-ABOVE for `-LINKAGES"!!!~'

`-MARRIED IKE TURNER in (`-62) = FLIP 2 to 7 = (`-67) = `-AGE of `-CURRENT `-HUSBAND ERWIN BACH at the `-TIME of `-HIS `-WIFE'S `-DEATH = RECIPROCAL = (`-76) = `-AGE of `-DEATH (In FACT) of `-HER `-FORMER `-HUSBAND / IKE TURNER!!!~'

`-MARRIED IKE TURNER from (1962) = 19(-)62 = (`-43) = 20(+)23 = `-DEATH/YEAR for AMERICAN-BORN SWISS SINGER (TINA TURNER) "The QUEEN of ROCK 'n' ROLL"!!!~'

`-MARRIED IKE TURNER from (1962) to (1978) for (`-16) `-YEARS!!!~'

`-MARRIED ERWIN BACH from (2013) to (2023) for (`-10) = `-YEARS!!!~'

`-TOTAL `-YEARS `-MARRIED = (16 (+) 10) = (`-26) = RECIPROCAL = (`-62) = `-WAS `-FIRST `-MARRIED to IKE TURNER in (`-62)!!!~'

`-MARRIED ERWIN BACH in (2013) = 20(+)13 = (`-33) = FLIP 3 to 8 = (`-83) = `-AGE of `-DEATH for AMERICAN-BORN SWISS SINGER (TINA TURNER) "The QUEEN of ROCK 'n' ROLL" (`-83)!!!~'

`-BIRTH/DAY = 11/26 = 11(+)26 = (`-37)!!!~'

`-DEATH/DAY = 5/24 = HALF RECIPROCAL = 5/42 = 5(-)42 = (`-37)!!!~'

`-BIRTH/YEAR = (1939) = 19(+)39 = (`-58) = `-DEATH/DAY = 5/24 = 5/2(x)4 = (`-58)!!!~'

`-BIRTH/YEAR = (1939) = 1(-)9 / 3(-)9 = (8/6) = `-DAYS from `-BIRTH-to-DEATH = (`-186)!!!~'

`-BIRTH/YEAR = (1939) = 1(-)9 / 3(+)9 = 8/12 = 8/1(+)2 = (`-83) = `-AGE of `-DEATH for AMERICAN-BORN SWISS SINGER (TINA TURNER) "The QUEEN of ROCK 'n' ROLL" (`-83)!!!~'

`-**BIRTH/YEAR** = (1939) = 1(-)9 / 3(-)9 = (**8/6**) = `-DIVIDED by (`-2) = (`-**43**) = 20(+)23 = `-**DEATH/YEAR**!!!~'

`-ACTRESS (DONNA DOUGLAS) from the "BEVERLY HILLBILLIES" had a `-BIRTH/DAY of (9/26) = 9(to)6 = RECIPROCAL = 6(to)9 = `-ACTRESS (NANCY JANE KULP) died at the `-AGE of (`-69)!!!~'

`-ACTRESS (NANCY JANE KULP) from the "BEVERLY HILLBILLIES" had a `-BIRTH/DAY of / 8(to)8 = (8/28) = `-ACTRESS (DONNA DOUGLAS) died at the `-AGE of (`-82) = RECIPROCAL = (`-28)!!!~'

`-ACTRESS (IRENE RYAN) from the "BEVERLY HILLBILLIES" had a `-BIRTH/DAY of (10/17) = RECIPROCAL = (71/01) = 71(-)01 = (`-70) = `-AGE of `-DEATH for `-ACTRESS (IRENE RYAN) from the "BEVERLY HILLBILLIES"!!!~'

The `-PROPHET (Dwayne W. Anderson's) `-BIRTH/YEAR (ENCAPSULATES) the `-DEATH of `-HIS `-MOTHER & `-GRANDMOTHER!!!~'

`-BIRTH/YEAR = (1970) = 19(+)70 = (`-**89**) = `-AGE of `-DEATH of `-MOTHER'S `-MOTHER!!!~'

(`-**89**) = RECIPROCAL = (`-**98**) = FLIP 9 to 6; FLIP 8 to 3 = (`-**63**) = `-AGE of `-DEATH of `-MOTHER!!!~'

The `-PROPHET'S `-BROTHER (Shannon L. Anderson's) `-BIRTH/YEAR (ENCAPSULATES) the `-DEATH of `-HIS `-MOTHER & `-GRANDFATHER!!!~'

`-BIRTH/YEAR = (1967) = 19(+)67 = (`-**86**) = `-AGE of `-DEATH of `-MOTHER'S `-FATHER!!!~'

(`-**86**) = RECIPROCAL = (`-**68**) = FLIP 8 to 3 = (`-**63**) = `-AGE of `-DEATH of `-MOTHER!!!~'

The `-PROPHET (Dwayne W. Anderson's) `-MATERNAL `-GRANDPARENTS `-AGES of `-DEATH = (`-**89**) = FLIP 9 to 6 = (`-**86**) = **"WOVEN in `-TIME"**!!!~'

DAREDEVIL (ROBERT EDWARD KNIEVEL II) died on (1+13+20+23) = (`-**57**) = `-HIS VERY OWN `-**BIRTH/DAY** = (`-**5/7**) = (**MAY 7**[th])!!!~'

`-**FATHER** `-**DAREDEVIL** (ROBERT CRAIG KNIEVEL) `-**BIRTH/YEAR** = (1938) = 19(+)38 = (`-**57**)!!!~'

#**35**/PRESIDENT JOHN FITZGERALD KENNEDY had `-HIS `-AGE of `-DEATH; and, `-HIS `-BROTHER / ROBERT FRANCIS KENNEDY'S `-AGE of `-DEATH

(`-**EMBEDDED**) in `-HIS (JFK'S) `-**VERY** `-**OWN** `-**BIRTH/DAY #** `-**NUMBER** = 5/**29**/19/**17**!!!-'

(29 (+) 17) = (`-**46**) = **JFK'S** `-**AGE** of `-**DEATH**!!!-'

(5 (+) 19) = (`-**24**) = RECIPROCAL = (`-**42**) = **RFK'S** `-**AGE** of `-**DEATH**!!!-'

`-**GOD;** `-**DO** `-**YOU** `-**NEED** `-**MORE???**

"The `-**PROPHET**"!!!-'

AUTHOR: DWAYNE W. ANDERSON!!!-'

AMERICAN FOOTBALL FULLBACK, CIVIL RIGHTS ACTIVIST; &, ACTOR (JAMES NATHANIEL BROWN "JIM BROWN") was `-MARRIED to MONIQUE BROWN in (1997) = 19(-)97 = (`-78) = RECIPROCAL = (`-87) = `-AGE of `-DEATH of `-HER `-HUSBAND!!!~' JAMES NATHANIEL BROWN was ALSO `-MARRIED to SUE BROWN in (1959) = 19(+)59 = (`-78) = RECIPROCAL = (`-87) = `-AGE of `-DEATH of HER `-FORMER `-HUSBAND (JIM BROWN)!!!~' YOU'RE `-ALL like `-THIS!!!~' AUTHOR: DWAYNE W. ANDERSON – The `-PROPHET!!!~'

AMERICAN ACTOR (JAMES MAITLAND "JIMMY" STEWART) died at the `-AGE of (`-89) = (8x9) = (`-7/2) = His `-DEATH/DAY!!!~'

`-HIS / `-BIRTH/YEAR = (1908) = RECIPROCAL = 8091 = (8+0) (9x1) = (`-89) = `-AGE of `-DEATH for AMERICAN ACTOR (JAMES MAITLAND "JIMMY" STEWART)!!!~'

`-HIS `-WIFE / GLORIA HATRICK MCLEAN / `-BIRTH/YEAR = (1918) = RECIPROCAL = 8191 = (8x1) (9x1) = (`-89) = `-AGE of `-DEATH of `-HER `-VERY `-OWN `-HUSBAND / AMERICAN ACTOR (JAMES MAITLAND "JIMMY" STEWART)!!!~'

`-MARRIED in (`-49) = RECIPROCAL = (`-94) = `-MARRIAGE `-ENDED in (`-94) by `-WIFE'S / GLORIA

HATRICK MCLEAN'S `-DEATH!!!~' `-MARRIAGES tell THE `-DEATH!!!~'

(94 (-) 49) = (`-45)

AMERICAN ACTOR (JAMES MAITLAND "JIMMY" STEWART) `-DEATH/DAY # `-NUMBER in (`-REVERSE) = (97 (-) 19 (-) 2 (-) 7 = (`-69) = 6 x 9 = (`-54) = RECIPROCAL = (`-45) = `-WAS `-MARRIED for (`-45) `-YEARS!!!~'

AMERICAN ACTOR (JAMES MAITLAND "JIMMY" STEWART) was `-BORN in the `-MONTH of (`-5); and, `-DIED in the `-MONTH of (`-7) = (`-57) = RECIPROCAL = (`-75) = `-AGE of `-DEATH of `-HIS `-VERY `-OWN `-WIFE / GLORIA HATRICK MCLEAN!!!~'

`-WIFE / GLORIA HATRICK MCLEAN `-DEATH/DAY # `-NUMBER in (`-REVERSE) = (94 (-) 19 (-) 16 (-) 2) = (`-57) = `-HUSBAND / AMERICAN ACTOR (JAMES MAITLAND "JIMMY" STEWART) was `-BORN in the `-MONTH of (`-5); and, `-DIED in the `-MONTH of (`-7) = (`-57) = RECIPROCAL = (`-75) = `-HER `-VERY `-OWN `-AGE of `-DEATH!!!~'

`-WIFE / GLORIA HATRICK MCLEAN `-DEATH/ YEAR = (1994) = 19(-)94 = (`-75) = `-HER `-VERY `-OWN `-AGE of `-DEATH!!!~'

`-WIFE / GLORIA HATRICK MCLEAN `-DIED (`-343) `- DAYS from `-BIRTH-to-DEATH!!!~'

AMERICAN ACTOR (JAMES MAITLAND "JIMMY" STEWART) `-DIED (`-43) `-DAYS from `-BIRTH-to-DEATH!!!~'

AMERICAN ACTOR (JAMES MAITLAND "JIMMY" STEWART) `-BIRTH/DAY (5/20) (+) `-DEATH/DAY (7/2) = (5 (+) 20 (+) 7 (+) 2) = (`-34) = RECIPROCAL = (`-43) = AMERICAN ACTOR (JAMES MAITLAND "JIMMY" STEWART) `-DIED (`-43) `-DAYS from `-BIRTH-to-DEATH!!!~'

AMERICAN ACTOR (JAMES MAITLAND "JIMMY" STEWART) `-BIRTH/DAY (5/20) = 5 (+) 20 = (`-25) = FLIP the 2 OVER to a 7 = (`-75) = `-AGE of `-DEATH of `-WIFE / GLORIA HATRICK MCLEAN!!!~'

AMERICAN ACTOR (JAMES MAITLAND "JIMMY" STEWART) `-BIRTH/DAY # `-NUMBER = 5 (+) 20 (+) 19 (+) 08 = (`-52) = FLIP the 2 OVER to a 7 = (`-57) = Was `-BORN in the `-MONTH of (`-5); and, `-DIED in the `-MONTH of (`-7) = (`-57) = RECIPROCAL = (`-75) = `-AGE of `-DEATH of `-HIS `-VERY `-OWN `-WIFE / GLORIA HATRICK MCLEAN!!!~'

AMERICAN ACTOR (JAMES MAITLAND "JIMMY" STEWART) `-DEATH/DAY # `-NUMBER = 7 (+) 2 (+) 19 (+) 97 = (`-125) = RECIPROCAL = (`-521) = 52 x 1 = (`-52) = FLIP the 2 OVER to a 7 = (`-57) = Was `-BORN in the `-MONTH of (`-5); and, `-DIED in the `-MONTH of (`-7) = (`-57) = RECIPROCAL = (`-75) = `-AGE of `-DEATH of `-HIS `-VERY `-OWN `-WIFE / GLORIA HATRICK MCLEAN!!!~'

`-WIFE / GLORIA HATRICK MCLEAN `-DEATH/ DAY = 2/16 = 2 x 16 = (`-32) = SHE; `-WAS `-BORN in the `-MONTH of (`-3); and, `-DIED in the `-MONTH of (`-2)!!!~'

`-WIFE / GLORIA HATRICK MCLEAN's `-DEATH/ DAY # `-NUMBER = 2 (+) 16 (+) 19 (+) 94 = (`-131) = 13 x 1 = (`-13) = `-BIRTH/DAY = 3/10 = 3 (+) 10 = (`-13)!!!~'

(`-13) `-BOOKS, JUST like `-THIS; of `-EVERY `-CELEBRITY; and, of `-EVERY `-PRESIDENT!!!~'

`-DISCOVERED & `-ORIGINATED by; The `-PROPHET – AUTHOR: DWAYNE W. ANDERSON!!!~'

I was looking up WILT CHAMBERLAIN; and, came across NATHANIEL THURMOND in MY BOOK: "DO YOU BELIEVE in GOD??? IS DESTINY REAL???" I did not CATCH it at the TIME but NATE was MARRIED in (1993) = 19(-)93 = (`-74) = "This, in fact; was HIS `-AGE of `-DEATH", just like - ALL the REST of `-YOU!!!~'

WILT CHAMBERLAIN (GOLDEN STATE WARRIOR); just as WELL as NATE (GOLDEN STATE WARRIOR) had a `-BIRTH/YEAR of (`-36) = RECIPROCAL = (`-63) = `-HIS `-VERY `-OWN `-AGE of `-DEATH (WILT)!!!~'

This was just like BOB SAGET who was `-BORN in (`-56) = RECIPROCAL = (`-65) = `-HIS `-VERY `-OWN `-AGE of `-DEATH!!!~' There are A LOT of CELEBRITIES; just like THIS!!!~'

`-AMERICAN ACTOR ROGER EARL MOSLEY "MAGNUM P.I." (HELICOPTER PILOT) was `-BORN in (`-38) = RECIPROCAL = (`-83) = `-HIS `-VERY `-OWN `-AGE of `-DEATH; just as WELL!!!~'

`-HIS (MOSLEY'S) `-BIRTH/DAY # `-NUMBER = 12 (+) 18 (+) 19 (+) 38 = (`-87) = "HE had this BIRTH/DAY # `-NUMBER; `-his ENTIRE `-LIFE = (`-8/7) = `-HIS `-VERY `-OWN / `-DAY of `-DEATH-`!!!~'

AMERICAN ACTOR (JAMES MAITLAND "JIMMY" STEWART) died at the `-AGE of (`-89) = (8x9) = (`-7/2) = His `-DEATH/DAY!!!~'

`-MARRIED in (1949) = 19(+)49 = (`-68) = RECIPROCAL = (`-86) = FLIP the 6 OVER to a 9 = (`-89) = `-AGE of `-DEATH for AMERICAN ACTOR (JAMES MAITLAND "JIMMY" STEWART)!!!~'

`-MARRIED in (`-49) = RECIPROCAL = (`-94) = `-MARRIAGE `-ENDED in (`-94) by `-WIFE'S / GLORIA HATRICK MCLEAN'S `-DEATH!!!~' `-MARRIAGES / tell THE `-DEATH!!!~'

'-MARRIAGE '-ENDED in (1994) = 19(-)94 = ('-75) = '-AGE of '-DEATH for WIFE / GLORIA HATRICK MCLEAN!!!~'

FIRST LADY MARY TODD LINCOLN'S '-BIRTH/DAY # '-NUMBER = 12/13/18/18 = (12x13) = 156 = 1x56 = ('-56) = '-AGE of '-DEATH for #16/PRESIDENT ABRAHAM LINCOLN!!!~'

(18(+)18) = ('-36) = RECIPROCAL = ('-63) = '-AGE of '-DEATH for '-FIRST LADY MARY TODD LINCOLN / ALL of THIS from '-HER '-BIRTH/DAY # '-NUMBER!!!~' The SAME for '-QUEEN ELIZABETH (II) of the '-UNITED '-KINGDOM!!!~'

FIRST LADY JACQUELINE KENNEDY ONASSIS died on 5/19 which was (70) days away from '-her BIRTH to DEATH!!!~' CALENDAR YEAR = 365 − 70 = (295)!!!~' JOHN F. KENNEDY was BORN on (5/29) = SWIPE the ('-5) TWO '-PLACES to the RIGHT = 295!!!~' JFK'S birthday # = 5 + 29 + 19 + 17 = (70)!!!~' HUSBAND & WIFE were (LINKED TOGETHER) in BIRTH & DEATH!!!~'

#35/PRESIDENT JOHN F. KENNEDY & FIRST LADY JACQUELINE LEE KENNEDY / '-YEAR of '-MARRIAGE (JOHN & JACQUELINE KENNEDY) = (19 − 53) = 34 = '-AGE of HIS WIFE JACQUELINE KENNEDY ONASSIS at the TIME of '-HER HUSBAND'S JOHN F. KENNEDY'S '-ASSASSINATION!!!~'

JACQUELINE WAS `-MARRIED to ARISTOTLE ONASSIS from 1968 to 1975 = 7 YEARS!!!~' WAS `-MARRIED in (19/68) = (19 – 68) = 49 = RECIPROCAL = 94 = `-HER `-VERY `-OWN `-YEAR of `-DEATH = (`-94)!!!~'

JACQUELINE'S MARRIAGE `-ENDED in (19/75) to ARISTOTLE = (19 + 75) = (`-94) = `-HER `-VERY `-OWN `-DEATH/ YEAR!!!~' (`-49) = RECIPROCAL = (`-94)!!!~' DO `-YOU BELIEVE in `-GOD??? `IS, `-DESTINY `REAL??? MARRIAGE `-ENDED in (19/75) = (19 + 75) = 94 = "FLIP EVERY (`-9) OVER to a (`-6)" = 64 = AGE of DEATH for FORMER FIRST LADY JACQUELINE LEE "JACKIE" KENNEDY ONASSIS!!!~'

ABE VIGODA (The GODFATHER) was `-MARRIED in (1968) = 19(-)68 = (`-49) = RECIPROCAL = (`-94) = `-HIS `-VERY `-OWN `-AGE of `-DEATH from `-HIS `-VERY `-OWN `-MARRIAGE `-DATE!!!~'

ABE VIGODA'S `-BIRTH/YEAR = (1921) = (9) (1+2+1) = (`-94) = `-HIS `-VERY `-OWN `-AGE of `-DEATH / from `-HIS `-VERY `-OWN `-BIRTH/YEAR!!!~'

FROM `-MY `-BOOK `-ENTITLED: "The REAL PROPHET of DOOM (KISMET) – INTRODUCTION – PENDULUM FLOW – (II)"!!!~'

For the `-RESURRECTION, it will be `-LIKENED to the `-TRANSPORTER `-ROOMS -of `-STAR `-TREK!!!~' The `-DEAD `-BODIES will be `-REASSEMBLED; back into their `-YOUTHFUL `-VIGORS!!!~' A `-LITERAL `-TRANSPORTER `-ROOM will NOT be BUILT; but, `-GOD; will USE the `-PROCESS!!!~' PROPHET!!!~'

"A CHILLING PARADOX" – I seem to REALLY LIKE the "FILM" – "The ARRIVAL" with CHARLIE SHEEN!!!~' The GLOBAL WARMING depicted in the "FILM" seems to RESEMBLE the "GLOBAL WARMING" of "TODAY"!!!~' "The ARRIVAL" is FITTING; for the "PROPHET'S" ARRIVAL!!!~' R- YOU looking for ALIENS???

BRITISH ACTRESS JANE BIRKIN died on (7)/1(6) at the AGE of 76!!!~' HER BIRTH/YEAR was 46 & SHE was MARRIED in 19(-)65 = 46!!!~' HER BIRTH/DAY = 12/14 = 12x14 = 168 = 1x68 = 68 & was `-DIVORCED in (`-68)!!!~' DEATH/DAY of PRESIDENT GEORGE WASHINGTON = 12/14!!!~' DEATH/DAY of FIRST LADY MARY TODD LINCOLN = 7/16!!!~'

FOUNDING MEMBER of the EAGLES / RANDALL HERMAN MEISNER'S BIRTHDAY # = 3+8+19+46 = 76!~' RANDALL'S DEATHDAY # = (7+26)+20+23 =

76!~' 76&76&DIED on 7-to-6!~' FRAG DEATHDAY # 7+2+6+2+0+2+3 = 22 = FLIP 2 to 7 = 77 = MARRIED in 19(-)96 = 77 & LEFT the EAGLES in 77 = & = HIS VERY OWN AGE of DEATH!!!~

SHEILA Y. OLIVER - LIEUTENANT GOVERNOR of NEW JERSEY birthyear = 19+52 = 71 = AGE of DEATH!~' BIRTHMONTH JULY with 31 DAYS – MINUS – BIRTHDAY 14th = 17 = RECIPROCAL = 71 = AGE of DEATH!~ BIRTHDAY # NUMBER = 92 = RECIP = 29 = USE this FACTOR to CALCULATE her EXACT time OF DEATH!~'

SHEILA Y. OLIVER - LIEUTENANT GOVERNOR of NEW JERSEY birthday # = 7+14+19+52 = 92!~' REMOVE AGE of DEATH from BIRTHDAY # NUMBER (71) 4+1+9+5+2 = PARTIAL FRAGMENTED BIRTHDAY # NUMBER = 21 = (92(-)21 = 71 = HER very OWN AGE of DEATH from HER `-BIRTHDAY # `-NUMBERS!!!~' The PROPHET!

SHEILA Y. OLIVER - LIEUTENANT GOVERNOR of NEW JERSEY deathday # number = 8/1/20/23 = FLIP 8 to 3 = 31+20+23 = 74 = BIRTH/DAY = 7/14 = 74x1 = 74!!!~' FRAGMENTED birthday # number = 7+1+4+1+9+5+2 = 29 = 29(x)3 = 87 = RECIPROCAL = 78 = BORN in the MONTH of 7 & DIED in the MONTH of 8!!!~'

SHEILA Y. OLIVER - LIEUTENANT GOVERNOR of NEW JERSEY REVERSE birthday # = 52(-)19(-)14(-)7 = 12 = RECIPROCAL = 21 = FLIP 2 OVER to a 7 = 71 = `-her VERY OWN `-AGE of `-DEATH!!!~' FRAGMENTED BIRTH/DAY = 7+1+4 = 12 = RECIPROCAL = 21 = FLIP 2 OVER to a 7 = 71 = `-her VERY OWN `-AGE of `-DEATH!!!~'

SHEILA Y. OLIVER - LIEUTENANT GOVERNOR of NEW JERSEY fragmented birthyear = 1+9+5+2 = 17 = RECIPROCAL = 71 = `-HER VERY `-OWN `-AGE of `-DEATH!!!~' From BIRTH-to-DEATH there are 18 DAYS = RECIPROCAL = 8/1 = `-her `-DAY of `-DEATH for SHEILA Y. OLIVER - LIEUTENANT GOVERNOR of NEW JERSEY!!!~'

FINNISH-CANADIAN PHILOSOPHER MARI RUTI had a BIRTHDAY of 3(x)31 = 93 = FLIP 9 OVER to a 6; FLIP 3 OVER to an 8 = 6/8 = `-HER very OWN death/DAY!~' BIRTH/YEAR = 19(-)64 = 45 = 5(X)9 = AGE of DEATH!~' AMERICAN LABOR LEADER CESAR CHAVEZ birth/ day 3(X)31 = 93 = death/YEAR!!!~' PROPHET!!!~'

GEORGE HERMAN "BABE" RUTH died at the AGE of 53 and YOU can CALCULATE it FROM his BIRTHday # = 2/6/18/95!~' WHAT'S in the MIDDLE

6/18 = RECIPROCAL = 8/16 = HIS DEATH/DAY!~' HE ACTUALLY DIED on 8/16!!!~'

From `-HIS / BIRTH/DAY NUMBER # = 6/18 = 61(-)8 = (`-53) = `-AGE of `-DEATH from BIRTH/DAY for GEORGE HERMAN "BABE" RUTH!!!~'

AMERICAN MUSIC ARTIST / ANASTACIA LYN NEWKIRK was BORN in 68 and HER FATHER BOB NEWKIRK died at the AGE of 68 one day short of turning 69!!!~'

AMERICAN ACTRESS ("GILLIGAN'S ISLAND/ CHARACTER-MARY ANN SUMMERS") DAWN WELLS `-BIRTHDAY = *10/18* (`-*TOO*) = 10+18 = (`-28) = RECIPROCAL= (`-82) = DAWN WELL'S AGE of DEATH!!!~' `-DEATH/DAY # `-NUMBER = `-*EQUALS* = 12+30+20+20 = (`-82) = DAWN WELL'S `-AGE of `-DEATH!!!~' BIRTHYEAR = 1938 = (1-9 / 3+8) = 8/11 = 8(1+1) = (`-82) = `-AGE of `-DEATH!!!~ `-BIRTH/ DAY = 10/18 = *RECIPROCAL* = 81/01 = (81(+)01) = (`-82) = `-AGE of `-DEATH for AMERICAN ACTRESS ("GILLIGAN'S ISLAND/CHARACTER-MARY ANN SUMMERS") DAWN WELLS!!!~'

ALEX TREBEK (CANADIAN/AMERICAN - GAME SHOW HOST - JEOPARDY) (BIRTH) = 7/22/1940; and, DEATH/DAY # `-NUMBER = 11+8+20+20 = (`-59)!!!~' BIRTHYEAR = 19+40 = (`-59)!!!~' (59(+)59) = (118) =

DEATHDAY = (**11/8**) = 11x8 = (`-**88**)!!!~' BIRTH/DAY # `-NUMBER = 7+22+19+40 = (`-**88**)!!!~' `-**YEAR of** `-**BIRTH** (`-**40**) + (**20**(+)**20**) = `-**DEATH** `-**YEAR** = (`-**80**) = `-**AGE** **of** `-**DEATH for (CANADIAN/AMERICAN - GAME SHOW HOST - JEOPARDY) ALEX TREBEK!!!~'**

AMERICAN ACTRESS MARY TYLER MOORE BIRTHDAY (**12/29**)!!!~' HALF RECIPROCAL = **12/92**!!!~' (92 (-) 12) = (`-**80**) = `-**AGE of DEATH from** (`-*__BIRTHDAY__*) for AMERICAN ACTRESS MARY TYLER MOORE!!!~' AMERICAN POLITICIAN (MARCH FONG EU) BIRTHDAY (**3/29**)!!!~' HALF RECIPROCAL = **3/92**!!!~' (3 (+) 92) = (`-**95**) = `-**AGE of DEATH from** (`-*__BIRTHDAY__*) for AMERICAN POLITICIAN (MARCH FONG EU)!!!~' REREAD the BOOKS!!!~' CONVERT 3's TO 8's & 8's to 3's!!!~

AMERICAN FILM DIRECTOR WILLIAM DAVID FRIEDKIN (MOVIES-EXORCIST/The FRENCH CONNECTION) birth/day = 8/29 = 8/2(-)9 = 87 = HIS VERY OWN AGE of DEATH from BIRTHDAY = & = HIS VERY OWN DAY of DEATH from BIRTHDAY = 8/7!~' WILLIAM FRIEDKIN was MARRIED to KELLY LANGE in 87 & died at 87 on 8/7!!!~'

FIRST LADY GRACE GOODHUE COOLIDGE died at the AGE of 78 on the DAY of 7/8!~' REVERSE LOOK on HER birth/day # = 79(-)18(-)3(-)1 = 57 = HER VERY OWN DEATHYEAR!~' HER DEATHDAY # = 7+8+19+57 = 91 = RECIPROCAL = 19 = SUBTRACT from HER BIRTHYEAR 1879 = 87 = RECIPROCAL = 78 = SEE the LINKS!!!~'

DJ CASPER (WILLIE PERRY, JR.) – The CHA CHA SLIDE – died at the AGE of 58!~' HE was BORN in the MONTH of 5 and DIED in the MONTH of 8 = 58!~' DEATHDAY NUMBER # = 8+7+20+23 = 58!~' IF I showed YOU this and OTHER PATTERNS over 100 TIMES; WHAT? would YOU THINK??? The PROPHET – DWAYNE W. ANDERSON!!!~'

IRISH SINGER/SONGWRITER (SINEAD O'CONNOR) DIED at the AGE of ('-**56**) = '-SHE '-WAS '-MARRIED to JOHN REYNOLDS in the '-YEAR of ('-**87**) = 8(x)7 = ('-**56**) = '-**AGE of** '-**DEATH** for IRISH SINGER/SONGWRITER (SINEAD O'CONNOR) from '-**HER** '-**MARRIAGE** '-**YEAR of** '-**DATE!!!~'**

'-**HER** '-**DEATH/DAY** = (7/26) = 7(-)2/6 = ('-**56**) = '-**AGE of** '-**DEATH** for IRISH SINGER/SONGWRITER (SINEAD O'CONNOR) from '-**HER** '-**DEATH/DAY!!!~'**

'-**HER** '-**BIRTH/MONTH** was '-DECEMBER with 31 '-DAYS /|\ '-DAY of '-BIRTH = the ('-8th)!!!~'

31 (-) 8 = (`-**23**) = `-**SHE** `-*died* (`-**230**) **DAYS** from `-**BIRTH-to-DEATH** = **&** = `-**SHE** died in the `-**CALENDAR** `-**YEAR** of (`-**23**)!!!~'

`-**HER** `-**BIRTH/YEAR** = (**1966**) = 1(+)9(+)6/6 = 16/6 = 1(-)6/6 = (`-**56**) = `-**AGE of** `-**DEATH for IRISH SINGER/ SONGWRITER (SINEAD O'CONNOR) from** `-**HER** `-**BIRTH/YEAR**!!!~'

`-**HER** `-**BIRTH/DAY** = 12/8 = 1(x)28 = (`-**28**) x (`-2) = (`-**56**) = `-**AGE of** `-**DEATH for IRISH SINGER/ SONGWRITER (SINEAD O'CONNOR) from** `-**HER** `-**BIRTH/DAY**!!!~'

`-**HER FRAGMENTED** `-**BIRTH/DAY #** `-**NUMBER** = 12/8/19/66 = 1+2+8+1+9+6+6 = (`-**33**) = 7(+)26 = `-**DEATH/ DAY for IRISH SINGER/SONGWRITER (SINEAD O'CONNOR) from** `-**HER** `-**BIRTH/DAY**!!!~'

AMERICAN ACTOR & COMEDIAN - PAUL REUBENS (PEE WEE HERMAN) died at the `-AGE of (`-**70**)!!!~'

`-**HIS** `-**BIRTH/DAY #** `-**NUMBER** = 8 (+) 27 (+) 19 (+) 52 = (`-**106**) = 1(+)6/0 = (`-**70**) = `-**AGE of** `-**DEATH from** `-**HIS** `-**BIRTH/DAY #** `-**NUMBER**!!!~'

`-**HIS** `-**BIRTH/DAY #** `-**NUMBER** = 8 (+) 27 (+) 19 (+) 52 = (`-**106**) / `-**DIVIDED** by (`-2) = (`-**53**) = RECIPROCAL

= (`-**35**) x (`-2) = (`-**70**) = `-AGE of `-DEATH from `-HIS `-BIRTH/DAY # `-NUMBER!!!~'

`-HIS `-**BIRTH/DAY** = 8/27 = 8(to)7 = `-WAS `-BORN in the `-MONTH of (`-**8**); and, `-DIED in the `-MONTH of (`-**7**)!!!~'

`-DIED (`-**28**) DAYS from `-BIRTH-to-DEATH = FLIP 2 to 7 = (`-**78**) = RECIPROCAL = (`-**87**) = `-WAS `-BORN in the `-MONTH of (`-**8**); and, `-DIED in the `-MONTH of (`-**7**)!!!~'

`-HIS `-**BIRTH/YEAR** = (**1952**) = 19(+)52 = (`-**71**) = `-DIED the `-VERY `-YEAR `-PRIOR at the `-AGE of (`-**70**)!!!~'

`-HIS `-**BIRTH/DAY** = (8/27) = HALF RECIPROCAL = 8/72 = 8(+)72 = (`-**80**) = `-HIS `-DEATH/DAY # `-NUMBER!!!~'

`-HIS `-**DEATH/DAY # `-NUMBER** = 7 (+) 30 (+) 20 (+) 23 = (`-**80**) = "SEE `-DIRECTLY `-ABOVE for the `-**LINKS**-'!!!~'

(80 (+) 80) = (`-**160**) = 1(+)6/0 = (`-**70**) = `-AGE of `-DEATH for PAUL REUBENS (PEE WEE HERMAN)!!!~'

`-HIS `-**BIRTH/DAY** = (8/27) = 8(+)27 = (`-**35**) x (`-2) = (`-**70**) = `-AGE of `-DEATH from `-HIS `-BIRTH/DAY for AMERICAN ACTOR & COMEDIAN - PAUL REUBENS (PEE WEE HERMAN)!!!~'

`-HIS FRAGMENTED `-BIRTH/DAY # `-NUMBER = (8/27/19/52) = 8+2+7+1+9+5+2 = (`-**34**) = RECIPROCAL = (`-**43**) = 20(+)23 = `-DEATH/YEAR for AMERICAN ACTOR & COMEDIAN - PAUL REUBENS (PEE WEE HERMAN)!!!~'

CANADIAN MUSICIAN (JAIME ROYAL "ROBBIE" ROBERTSON) was `-**BORN** in the `-**YEAR** of (`-**43**) = 20(+)23 = `-HIS `-VERY `-OWN / `-**DEATH/YEAR!!!~'**

GUITARIST & SONGWRITER for "The **BAND**" until (`-**78**) = `-WAS `-**BORN** in the `-MONTH of (`-**7**); and, `-**DIED** in the `-MONTH of (`-**8**)!!!~'

ANTHONY DOMINICK BENEDETTO (TONY BENNETT) died at the AGE of (`-96) = 9x6 = (`-54) = RECIPROCAL = (`-45) = 19(+)26 = `-BIRTH/YEAR!!!~' `-BIRTH/DAY = 8/3 = 8(X)3 = (`-24) (X) (`-4) = (`-96) = `-AGE of `-DEATH from `-BIRTH/DAY!!!~' `-BIRTH/YEAR = (1926) = 19(-)26 = (`-7) = 2+0+2+3 = `-DEATH/YEAR!!!~' Was `-BORN in the `-MONTH of (`-8); and, `-DIED in the `-MONTH of (`-7) = (8/7) = 8(x)7 = (`-56) = 8(+)3(+)19(+)26 = (`-56) = `-BIRTH/DAY # `-NUMBER for ANTHONY DOMINICK BENEDETTO (`-KNOWN PROFESSIONALLY as `-TONY `-BENNETT)!!!~' DIED (`-352) DAYS from BIRTH-to-DEATH = 3(x)52 = (`-156) = 1(x)56 = (`-56) = `-BIRTH/DAY # `-NUMBER!!!~'

FRAGMENTED `-BIRTH/DAY # `-NUMBER = 8+3+1+9+2+6 = (`-29) x (`-3) = (`-87) = Was `-BORN in the `-MONTH of (`-8); and, `-DIED in the `-MONTH of (`-7) = (8/7) / for ANTHONY DOMINICK BENEDETTO (`-KNOWN PROFESSIONALLY as `-TONY `-BENNETT)!!!~' `-WAS `-DIVORCED from SANDRA GRANT BENNETT in (`-**83**) = `-HIS `-VERY `-OWN `-BIRTH/DAY (`-**8/3**) = & = `-SHE was (`-**83**) YEARS of AGE at the `-TIME of `-HIS (TONY BENNETT'S) (HER `-FORMER `-HUSBAND'S) `-DEATH!!!~'

AMERICAN SPORTSCASTER DICK ENBERG DIED at the AGE of (`-82) & was `-MARRIED to BARBARA HEDBRING from (1983 to 2017); and, MARRIED to JERI TAYLOR from (1963 to 1973)!!!~'

(1983) = 1+9+8+3 = (`-21)

(2017) = 20+17 = 37 = 3(x)7 = (`=21)

(1963) = 19(+)63 = (`-82) = `-ACTUAL `-AGE Of DEATH for `-husband & AMERICAN SPORTSCASTER DICK ENBERG!!!~' This is a RESOUNDING `-PATTERN!!!~' GO BACK & RE-READ; the `-BOOKS, `-to CONFIRM!!!~'

`-DIVORCED in (`-73) from JERI TAYLOR = 7(x)3 = (`-21) = 3(x)7 = (`-37) = 20(+)17 = `-MARRIAGE `-ENDED with BARBARA HEDBRING!!!~'

BILLIONAIRE OWNER ALEX SPANOS of the SAN DIEGO CHARGERS/ LA CHARGERS `-DIED on OCTOBER 9th within `-2018!!!~' `-HE was `-BORN on SEPTEMBER 28th in `-1923!!!~'

`-BIRTH/DAY = 9/28 = 9/2(+)8 = 9/10 = RECIPROCAL = 10/9 = `-DEATH/DAY!!!~'

`-DIED in the `-MONTH of (`-10); and, was `-BORN in the `-MONTH of (`-9) = (10/9) = `-DEATH/DAY!!!~'

This is a RESOUNDING `-PATTERN!!!~' GO BACK & RE-READ; the `-BOOKS, `-to CONFIRM!!!~'

LEGENDARY JOURNALIST COKIE ROBERTS died at the AGE of (`-75) (BIRTH: DECEMBER 27, 1943) (DEATH: SEPTEMBER 17, 2019)!!!~'

BIRTHDAY # `-NUMBER** = (12 + 27 + 19 + 43) = (`-101**)

SHE DIED (`-**101**) `-DAYS from `-**BIRTH-to-DEATH!!!~'**

SHE `-DIED in `-HER (`-76th) YEAR of EXISTENCE!!!~'

AMERICAN JOURNALIST & HUSBAND / STEVEN V. ROBERTS / was (`-76) YEARS of AGE FOR WHEN HIS `-WIFE COKIE had `-DIED!!!~'

HUSBAND STEVEN V. ROBERTS WAS BORN **FEBRUARY 11, 1943** = (2 + 11 + 19 + 43) = (`-**75**) = AGE of `-DEATH of `-HIS `-WIFE / LEGENDARY JOURNALIST COKIE ROBERTS!!!~'

LEGENDARY JOURNALIST COKIE ROBERTS `-**BIRTH/DAY** = 12/27 = RECIPROCAL = 72/21 = (**72**)+2+1 = (`-**75**) = `-**HER** `-**VERY** `-**OWN** / `-**AGE** of `-**DEATH** for **LEGENDARY JOURNALIST COKIE ROBERTS from** `-**HER** `-**VERY** `-**OWN** `-**BIRTH/DAY!!!**~'

This is a RESOUNDING `-PATTERN!!!~' GO BACK & RE-READ; the `-BOOKS, `-to CONFIRM!!!~'

AMERICAN ACTOR (JANSEN RAYNE PANETTIERE) died at the `-AGE of (`-**28**)!!!~'

`-**BIRTH/DAY** # `-**NUMBER** = 9+25+19+94 = (`-**147**)!!!~'

`-DAYS from `-BIRTH-to-DEATH = (`-**147**) `-DAYS!!!~'

CALENDAR `-YEAR (`-365) (-) (`-147) = (`-218) = 28x1 = (`-**28**) = `-**AGE of `-DEATH!!!**~'

`-**REVERSE** `-**LOOK** on `-BIRTH/DAY # `-NUMBER = 94(-)19(-)25(-)9 = (`-**41**) x (`-2) = (`-**82**) = RECIPROCAL

= (`-28) = `-AGE of `-DEATH for AMERICAN ACTOR JANSEN RAYNE PANETTIERE!!!~'

AMERICAN PROFESSIONAL BASEBALL PLAYER (**JEREMY DEAN GIAMBI**) died at the AGE of (`-**47**)!!!~'

`-**BIRTH/YEAR** = (`-**74**) = RECIPROCAL = (`-**47**) = `-AGE of `-DEATH for AMERICAN PROFESSIONAL BASEBALL PLAYER **JEREMY DEAN GIAMBI!!!~'**

`-**BIRTHDAY #** `-**NUMBER** = 9/30/19/74 = 9 + 30 + 19 + 74 = (`-**132**)!!!~'

From `-HIS / BIRTH-TO-DEATH there were (`-**132**) DAYS = `-HIS `-VERY `-OWN / BIRTH/DAY # `-NUMBER = (`-**132**)!!!~'

This is a RESOUNDING `-PATTERN!!!~' GO BACK & RE-READ; the `-BOOKS, `-to CONFIRM!!!~'

AMERICAN MUSICIAN & a FOUNDING MEMBER of the ROCK BAND the `-EAGLES (**GLENN LEWIS FREY**) was `-BORN in (`-**1948**) = 19(+)48 = (`-**67**) = `-HIS `-VERY `-OWN / `-AGE of `-DEATH for (**GLENN LEWIS FREY**)!!!~'

Terence Dale "Buffin" Griffin (DRUMMER & a FOUNDING MEMBER of the 1970'S ROCK BAND "MOTT the HOOPLE") was `-BORN in (`-**1948**) = 19(+)48 = (`-**67**) = `-*HIS* `-*VERY* `-*OWN* / `-*AGE of* `-*DEATH* for (**Terence Dale "Buffin" Griffin**)!!!~'

20ᵗʰ U.S. PRESIDENT / JAMES A. GARFIELD was `-BORN in (`-**1831**) = 18(+)31 = (`-**49**) = `-*HIS* `-*VERY* `-*OWN* / `-*AGE of* `-*DEATH* for the (**20ᵗʰ U.S. PRESIDENT / JAMES A. GARFIELD**)!!!~'

FIRST LADY LUCRETIA GARFIELD `-**BIRTH/DAY** = **4/19** = 49(x)1 = (`-**49**) = `-**AGE of** `-**DEATH / of** `-**HER** `-**HUSBAND / 20ᵗʰ U.S. PRESIDENT JAMES A. GARFIELD**!!!~'

`-THEY were `-**MARRIED** in (`-**58**) = RECIPROCAL = (`-**85**) = `-**her VERY** `-**OWN** / `-**AGE of** `-**DEATH / for FIRST LADY LUCRETIA GARFIELD**!!!~'

`-HUSBAND & `-WIFE / `-**AGES of** `-**DEATH** = (`-49) (+) (`-85) = (`-**134**) = "SWIPE the (`-**3**) to the `-LEFT" = (`-**3/14**) = `-**DEATH/DAY of & FOR / FIRST LADY LUCRETIA GARFIELD**!!!~'

`-SHE `-died IN the `-MONTH of (`-**3**); and, WAS `-born IN the `-MONTH of (`-**4**)!!!~'

29th `-PRESIDENT / WARREN G. HARDING was `-BORN in the `-MONTH of (`-**11**); and, `-DIED in the `-MONTH of (`-**8**)!!!~' (`-273) = 27(x)3 = (`-81) = 8/11 = RECIP = 11/8!!!~'

FIRST LADY FLORENCE HARDING was `-BORN in the `-MONTH of (`-**8**); and, `-DIED in the `-MONTH of (`-**11**)!!!~' (`-273) = 27(x)3 = (`-81) = 8/11!!!~'

FIRST LADY FLORENCE HARDING `-BIRTH/YEAR = (**1860**) = 18(-)60 = (`-**42**) = RECIPROCAL = (`-**24**) = **`-HER `-VERY `-OWN / `-DEATH/YEAR!!!~'**

FIRST LADY FLORENCE HARDING `-**BIRTH/DAY** = **8/15** = 8(+)15 = (`-**23**) x (`-2) = (`-**46**) = RECIPROCAL = (`-**64**) = **`-AGE of `-DEATH for FIRST LADY FLORENCE HARDING!!!~'**

FIRST LADY FLORENCE HARDING `-**DEATH/DAY** = **11/21** = 11(+)21 = (`-**32**) x (`-2) = (`-**64**) = **`-AGE of `-DEATH for FIRST LADY FLORENCE HARDING!!!~'**

`-HUSBAND & `-WIFE / `-**AGES of `-DEATH** = (`-57) (+) (`-64) = (`-**121**) = `-DEATH/DAY of FIRST LADY FLORENCE HARDING = (11/21) = (1x1)/21 = (`-**121**)!!!~'

`-HUSBAND & `-WIFE / `-**AGES of `-DEATH** = (`-57) (+) (`-64) = (`-**121**) = `-BIRTH/DAY of / 29th `-PRESIDENT WARREN G. HARDING = (11/2) = "SWIPE the (`-**2**) to the `-LEFT" = (`-**121**)!!!~'

29th `-PRESIDENT / WARREN G. HARDING `-**BIRTH/ DAY** = (**11/2**)!!!~'

FIRST LADY FLORENCE HARDING `-**DEATH/DAY** = (**11/21**) = (11/2)(x)1 = (11/2)!!!~'

29th `-PRESIDENT WARREN G. HARDING `-DIED within `-HIS (`-**57**th) `-YEAR of EXISTENCE with (`-**273**) `-DAYS from `-BIRTH-to-DEATH!!!~' (365 (-) 273) = (`-**92**) = RECIPROCAL = (`-**29**) = For the (`-**29**th) `-PRESIDENT!!!~'

(`-**273**) = 2(+)73 = (`-**75**) = RECIPROCAL = (`-**57**) = `-HIS `-VERY `-OWN / `-AGE of `-DEATH / for the 29th `-PRESIDENT WARREN G. HARDING!!!~'

(`-**273**) = 2(x)73 = (`-**146**) = RECIPROCAL = (`-**641**) = 64(x)1 = (`-**64**) = `-**AGE of `-DEATH / of `-HIS `-WIFE /- FIRST LADY FLORENCE HARDING!!!~'**

This is a RESOUNDING `-PATTERN!!!~' GO BACK & RE-READ; the `-BOOKS, `-to CONFIRM!!!~'

`-GOD; `-DO `-YOU `-NEED `-MORE???

"The `-PROPHET"!!!~'

AUTHOR: DWAYNE W. ANDERSON!!!~'

The `-MARK of `-DESTINY; and, that `-DESTINY has been `-PROVEN!!!-'

ALMOST `-ALL of `-YOU are LIKE `-THIS!!!-' `-THIS is FOR (A) `-LITTLE RICHARD `-SPECIAL!!!-'

"LITTLE RICHARD" was `-MARRIED in (`-59); and, this `-EQUALED `-HIS `-VERY `-OWN `-DAY of `-DEATH= (5/9)!!!-'

`-MARRIAGE was in (`-1959) = 19(+)59 = (`-78) = RECIPROCAL = (`-87) = `-HIS `-VERY `-OWN `-AGE of `-DEATH = (`-87)!!!-'

"LITTLE RICHARD" was `-BORN in the `-MONTH of (`-12); and, `-DIED in the `-MONTH of (`-5) = (12/5) = `-HIS `-VERY `-OWN `-BIRTH/DAY!!!-'

`-BATMAN'S ADAM WEST was `-MARRIED to `-BILLIE LOU `-YEAGER in (`-1950) = 19(+)50 = (`-69) = `-EQUALS = `-HIS `-VERY `-OWN `-DAY of `-DEATH = (`-6/9)!!!-'

`-ADAM `-WEST was `-BORN in the `-MONTH of (`-9); and, `-DIED in the `-MONTH of (`-6) = (`-96) = RECIPROCAL = (`-6/9) = `-HIS `-VERY `-OWN `-DAY of `-DEATH!!!-'

`-ADAM `-WEST was `-BORN in the `-CALENDAR `-YEAR of (`-28) = 2(8's) = (`-88) = `-HIS `-VERY `-OWN `-AGE of `-DEATH for `-MR. `-ADAM `-WEST!!!-'

`-SUPERMAN'S GEORGE REEVES was `-MARRIED to `-ELLANORA `-NEEDLES in (`-1940) = 19(+)40 = (`-59) = `-HIS `-VERY `-OWN `-YEAR of `-DEATH = (`-59)!!!~'

`-SUPERMAN'S GEORGE REEVES `-BIRTH/DAY # `-NUMBER = 1(+)5(+)19(+)14 = (`-39) = X (`-TIMES) (`-2) = (`-78) = {19(+)59} = `-HIS `-VERY `-OWN `-DEATH/ YEAR = {(19/59)} = from `-HIS `-VERY `-OWN `-BIRTH/ DAY # `-NUMBER!!!~'

`-SUPERMAN'S GEORGE REEVES `-DIVORCED `-ELLANORA `-NEEDLES in (`-1950) = (1x9) (5+0) = (`-95) = `-RECIPROCAL = (`-59) = `-HIS `-VERY `-OWN `-YEAR of `-DEATH = (`-59); and, for `-WHEN `-HIS `-MARRIAGE to `-ELLANORA NEEDLES `-BEGAN = 19(+)40 = (`-59)!!!~'

(`-59) = 5(X)9 = (`-45) = `-AGE of `-DEATH for `-SUPERMAN'S GEORGE REEVES!!!~'

`-JAMES "JIMMY" WILLIAM BUFFETT (AMERICAN SINGER-SONGWRITER) was `-DIVORCED from MARGIE WASHIECHEK in (1972) = 19(+)72 = (`-91) = `-HIS `-VERY `-OWN `-DAY of `-DEATH = (9/1)!!!~'

`-JAMES "JIMMY" WILLIAM BUFFETT (AMERICAN SINGER-SONGWRITER) `-DEATH/DAY # `-NUMBER = 9(+)1(+)20(+)23 = (`-53) = 19(-)72 = (`-53)!!!~

`-WILLIAM BLAINE RICHARDSON (III) (30th GOVERNOR of NEW MEXICO) was `-MARRIED to

153

BARBARA RICHARDSON in (1972) = 19(+)72 = (`-91) = `-HIS `-VERY `-OWN `-DAY of `-DEATH = (9/1)!!!~'

`-WILLIAM BLAINE RICHARDSON (III) (30<sup>th</sup> GOVERNOR of NEW MEXICO) `-DEATH/DAY # `-NUMBER = 9(+)1(+)20(+)23 = (`-53) = 19(-)72 = (`-53)!!!~'

`-ALFRED HITCHCOCK (FILM DIRECTOR) `-BIRTH/ DAY = (8/13) = RECIPROCAL = (31/8) = 31(+)8 = (`-39) = `-WIFE ALMA LUCY REVILLE `-DIED (`-39) DAYS from `-BIRTH-to-DEATH; and, (RECIPROCAL) = (`-93) = `-DAUGHTER PAT HITCHCOCK `-died at the `-AGE of (`-93) on (8/9) = FLIP 8 to 3 = (3/9) = RECIPROCAL = (`-93)!!!~'

`-ALFRED HITCHCOCK (FILM DIRECTOR) `-BIRTH/ DAY = (8/13) = (8+1) (3) = (`-93) = `-AGE of `-DEATH of `-DAUGHTER / PAT HITCHCOCK!!!~'

`-ALFRED HITCHCOCK `-MARRIED WIFE ALMA LUCY REVILLE in (1926) = 19(+)26 = (`-45) = (RECIPROCAL) = (`-54) = `-MARRIAGE of (`-54) `-YEARS `-ENDED by the `-DEATH of `-ALFRED `-HITCHCOCK in 19(80) = `-ALFRED'S `-AGE of `-DEATH = (`-80)!!!~' (19(+)80) = (`-99) = (45(+)54) = (`-99) = The `-YEAR (`-BOTH) were `-BORN!!!~'

`-DAUGHTER PAT HITCHCOCK was `-BORN in (`-28); and, `-HER `-MOTHER ALMA LUCY REVILLE `-died IN the `-YEAR of = (`-RECIPROCAL) = (`-82)!!!~'

'-MOTHER ALMA LUCY REVILLE was '-BORN in the '-MONTH of ('-8); and, '-DIED in the '-MONTH of ('-7) = (8/7) = FLIP 7 to 2 = (8/2) = '-AGE of '-DEATH; and, '-YEAR of '-DEATH; for '-MOTHER ALMA LUCY REVILLE = ('-82)!!!~'

'-DAUGHTER PAT HITCHCOCK was '-BORN in the '-MONTH of ('-7); and, '-DIED in the '-MONTH of ('-8) = ('-RECIPROCAL) = of '-HER '-VERY '-OWN '-MOTHER!!!~'

'-MOTHER ALMA LUCY REVILLE '-BIRTH/DAY = 8/14 = RECIPROCAL = (41/8) = 41(+)8 = ('-49) = 7(X)7 = '-BIRTH/DAY of '-DAUGHTER PAT HITCHCOCK = (7/7) = '-MOTHER ALMA LUCY REVILLE '-died the '-VERY '-DAY '-PRIOR on (7/6) of '-HER '-DAUGHTER PAT HITCHCOCK'S '-BIRTH/DAY (7/7) on (7/6) = FLIP 7 to 2 = (2/6) = '-YEAR '-MARRIAGE '-BEGAN with '-ALFRED = (1926)!!!~'

'-DAUGHTER PAT HITCHCOCK '-BIRTH/ YEAR = 1928 = RECIPROCAL = 8291 = '-DEATH/ DAY # '-NUMBER = 8/9/20/21 = '-MATCH the '-# '-NUMBERS!!!~'

'-DAUGHTER PAT HITCHCOCK '-MARRIED JOSEPH E. O'CONNELL JR. on THE '-DAY of = 1(+)17(+)19(+)52 = ('-89) = '-HER '-VERY '-OWN '-DAY of '-DEATH for '-DAUGHTER PAT HITCHCOCK!!!~'

'-MARRIAGE '-YEAR for '-PAT HITCHCOCK & JOSEPH O'CONNELL JR. = (1952) = 19(-)52 = ('-33) = '-DAUGHTER PAT HITCHCOCK '-died ('-33) days FROM '-BIRTH-to-DEATH!!!~'

'-MOTHER ALMA LUCY REVILLE '-BIRTH/DAY = (8/14) = (8) (1+4) = ('-85) = RECIPROCAL = ('-58) = '-DAUGHTER PAT HITCHCOCK'S '-DEATH/DAY # '-NUMBER = 8(+)9(+)20(+)21 = ('-58) = RECIPROCAL = ('-85) = '-MOTHER ALMA LUCY REVILLE'S '-BIRTH/DAY!!!~'

'-AMERICAN '-SINGER STEVEN SCOTT HARWELL (SMASH MOUTH) was '-BORN in the '-MONTH of ('-1); and, '-DIED in the '-MONTH of ('-9) = (1/9) = '-HIS '-VERY '-OWN '-BIRTH/DAY!!!~'

'-AMERICAN '-SINGER STEVEN SCOTT HARWELL (SMASH MOUTH) '-DEATH/DAY (LABOR DAY) # '-NUMBER = 9(+)4(+)20(+)23 = ('-56) = '-HIS '-VERY '-OWN '-AGE of '-DEATH for '-AMERICAN '-SINGER/ SONGWRITER STEVEN SCOTT HARWELL of (SMASH MOUTH)!!!~'

'-AMERICAN '-SINGER STEVEN SCOTT HARWELL (SMASH MOUTH) '-BIRTH/YEAR = (1967) = 19(+)67 = ('-86) / '-DIVIDED by ('-2) = ('-43) = 20(+)23 = '-HIS '-VERY '-OWN '-DEATH/YEAR!!!~'

'-WAS in THE '-MUSIC '-GROUP (SMASH MOUTH) SINCE 19(94) = ('-94) = '-HIS '-VERY '-OWN '-DEATH/ DAY = (9/4)!!!~'

'-AMERICAN '-SINGER STEVEN SCOTT HARWELL (SMASH MOUTH) '-died ('-238) '-DAYS from '-BIRTH-to-DEATH = 2(X)38 = ('-76) = RECIPROCAL = ('-67) = '-HIS '-VERY '-OWN '-BIRTH/YEAR!!!~'

'-AMERICAN '-SINGER STEVEN SCOTT HARWELL (SMASH MOUTH) '-BIRTH/DAY # '-NUMBER in '-REVERSE = 67(-)19(-)9(-)1 = ('-38) X ('-2) = ('-76) = RECIPROCAL = ('-67)!!!~'

'-The '-ONLY '-CHILD (PRESLEY SCOTT HARWELL) of '-AMERICAN '-SINGER STEVEN SCOTT HARWELL (SMASH MOUTH)'s / '-BIRTH/DAY # '-NUMBER = 1(+)6(+)20(+)01 = ('-28) X ('-2) = ('-56) = '-AGE of '-DEATH of '-FATHER / '-AMERICAN '-SINGER STEVEN SCOTT HARWELL of (SMASH MOUTH)!!!~'

READ; to '-SEE -HUNDREDS of '-THESE ('-**EQUATIONS**), in '-**MY** ('-**13**) '-**BOOKS**; by **AUTHOR: DWAYNE W. ANDERSON – The '-PROPHET!!!~'**

STEPHEN HILLENBURG, ANTHONY MICHAEL BOURDAIN, ARLEEN FRANCES SORKIN; and, FERNANDO BOTERO ANGULO!!!~'

STEPHEN HILLENBURG "SPONGEBOB/ SQUAREPANTS" CREATOR had a `-BIRTH/DAY # `-NUMBER = 8(+)21(+)19(+)61 = (`-109) = 10(+)9 = (`-19) x (`-3) = (`-57) = `-EQUALS = `-HIS `-VERY `-OWN `-AGE of `-DEATH from `-HIS `-VERY `-OWN `-BIRTH/DAY # `-NUMBER!!!~'

STEPHEN HILLENBURG "SPONGEBOB/ SQUAREPANTS" CREATOR had a `-DEATH/DAY # `-NUMBER = 11(+)26(+)20(+)18 = (`-75) = RECIPROCAL = (`-57) = `-EQUALS = `-HIS `-VERY `-OWN `-AGE of `-DEATH from `-HIS `-VERY `-OWN `-DEATH/DAY # `-NUMBER!!!~'

STEPHEN HILLENBURG "SPONGEBOB/ SQUAREPANTS" CREATOR had a `-PARTIAL `-DEATH/DAY # `-NUMBER = 11(+)26(+)20 = (`-57) = `-EQUALS = `-HIS `-VERY `-OWN `-AGE of `-DEATH from `-HIS `-VERY `-OWN `-PARTIAL `-DEATH/DAY # `-NUMBER!!!~'

ARLEEN FRANCES SORKIN (AMERICAN ACTRESS & SCREENWRITER) was `-MARRIED to CHRISTOPHER LLOYD in (1995) = 19(-)95 = (`-76) = RECIPROCAL = (`-67) = `-ACTUAL `-AGE of `-DEATH for ARLEEN FRANCES SORKIN (AMERICAN ACTRESS & SCREENWRITER) from `-HER `-VERY `-OWN `-ACTUAL `-DATE of `-MARRIAGE!!!~' I'VE done `-THIS for over (`-100) times WITH the `-ASSIGNED `-MARRIAGE `-DATES!!!~'

HUSBAND CHRISTOPHER LLOYD'S (AMERICAN TELEVISION PRODUCER & SCREENWRITER) `-BIRTH/DAY = 6/18 = (6) (1-8) = (`-67) = `-ACTUAL `-AGE of `-DEATH for `-HIS `-WIFE / ARLEEN FRANCES SORKIN (AMERICAN ACTRESS & SCREENWRITER)!!!~'

FERNANDO BOTERO ANGULO (COLUMBIAN FIGURATIVE ARTIST and SCULPTOR) died (`-149) DAYS from `-BIRTH-to-DEATH = (`-149) = "SWIPE the (`-1) to the `-RIGHT `-MIDDLE = (`-4/19) = `-HIS `-VERY `-OWN `-ACTUAL `-BIRTH/DAY = "HE WAS `-BORN in the `-MONTH of (`-4); and, `-DIED in the `-MONTH of (`-9) = (`-19) = RECIPROCAL = (`-91) = `-EQUALED = `-HIS `-VERY `-OWN `-AGE of `-DEATH for FERNANDO BOTERO ANGULO (COLUMBIAN FIGURATIVE ARTIST and SCULPTOR) from `-HIS `-VERY `-OWN `-BIRTH/DAY & The TIME from `-BIRTH-to-DEATH!!!~'

ANTHONY MICHAEL BOURDAIN (AMERICAN CELEBRITY CHEF, AUTHOR; and, TRAVEL DOCUMENTARIAN) `-had a `-BIRTH/DAY # `-NUMBER = 6(+)25(+)19(+)56 = (`-106) = 10(+)6 = (`-16) = RECIPROCAL = (`-61) = `-EQUALED = `-HIS `-VERY `-OWN `-AGE of `-DEATH from `-HIS `-VERY `-OWN `-BIRTH/DAY # `-NUMBER!!!~'

ANTHONY MICHAEL BOURDAIN (AMERICAN CELEBRITY CHEF, AUTHOR; and, TRAVEL

DOCUMENTARIAN) `-had a `-BIRTH/DAY # `-NUMBER = 6(+)25(+)19(+)56 = (`-106) = RECIPROCAL = (`-601) = 60(+)1 = (`-61) = `-EQUALED = `-HIS `-VERY `-OWN `-AGE of `-DEATH from `-HIS `-VERY `-OWN `-BIRTH/DAY # `-NUMBER!!!~'

ANTHONY MICHAEL BOURDAIN (AMERICAN CELEBRITY CHEF, AUTHOR; and, TRAVEL DOCUMENTARIAN) `-had a `-BIRTH/DAY of (6/25) = 6(-)25 = (`-19) = FLIP the (`-9) OVER to a (`-6) = (`-16) = RECIPROCAL = (`-61) = `-EQUALED = `-HIS `-VERY `-OWN `-AGE of `-DEATH from `-HIS `-VERY `-OWN `-BIRTH/DAY!!!~'

ANTHONY MICHAEL BOURDAIN (AMERICAN CELEBRITY CHEF, AUTHOR; and, TRAVEL DOCUMENTARIAN) `-had a `-BIRTH/DAY of (6/25) = HALF/RECIPROCAL = (6/52) = 6(-)52 = (`-46) = RECIPROCAL = (6' 4") in `-HEIGHT from `-HIS `-VERY `-OWN `-BIRTH/DAY for ANTHONY MICHAEL BOURDAIN (AMERICAN CELEBRITY CHEF, AUTHOR; and, TRAVEL DOCUMENTARIAN)!!!~'

ANTHONY MICHAEL BOURDAIN (AMERICAN CELEBRITY CHEF, AUTHOR; and, TRAVEL DOCUMENTARIAN) `-had a `-DEATH/DAY # `-NUMBER of = 6(+)8(+)20(+)18 = (`-52) = `-MARRIED in (1985) = 19(+)85 = (`-104) / DIVIDED by (`-2) = (`-52)!!!~'

ANTHONY MICHAEL BOURDAIN (AMERICAN CELEBRITY CHEF, AUTHOR; and, TRAVEL

DOCUMENTARIAN) `-was `-MARRIED in (1985) to NANCY PUTKOSKI = 19(-)85 = (`-66) = `-ANTHONY; `-WAS `-born IN THE `-month OF (`-6); and, `-DIED in the `-MONTH of (`-6)!!!~'

ANTHONY MICHAEL BOURDAIN (AMERICAN CELEBRITY CHEF, AUTHOR; and, TRAVEL DOCUMENTARIAN) `-was `-DIVORCED in (2005) FROM NANCY PUTKOSKI = 20(+)05 = (`-25) = RECIPROCAL = (`-52) = `-EQUALED = `-HIS / ANTHONY MICHAEL BOURDAIN'S (AMERICAN CELEBRITY CHEF, AUTHOR; and, TRAVEL DOCUMENTARIAN) `-DEATH/DAY # `-NUMBER of = 6(+)8(+)20(+)18 = (`-52)!!!~'

ANTHONY MICHAEL BOURDAIN (AMERICAN CELEBRITY CHEF, AUTHOR; and, TRAVEL DOCUMENTARIAN) `-BIRTH/YEAR = (1956) = (1+9+5) (6) = (15) (6) = (1+5) (6) = (`-66) = `-ANTHONY; `-WAS `-born IN THE `-month OF (`-6); and, `-DIED in the `-MONTH of (`-6)!!!~'

ANTHONY MICHAEL BOURDAIN (AMERICAN CELEBRITY CHEF, AUTHOR; and, TRAVEL DOCUMENTARIAN) had `-DIED (`-348) DAYS from `-BIRTH-to-DEATH = 34(X)2 = (`-6/8) = `-HIS `-VERY `-OWN `-ACTUAL `-DAY of `-DEATH = 6(x)8 = (`-48) = "ALL-in-ONE-#-NUMBER"!!!~'

ANTHONY MICHAEL BOURDAIN (AMERICAN CELEBRITY CHEF, AUTHOR; and, TRAVEL

DOCUMENTARIAN) `-was `-DIVORCED in (2016) FROM OTTAVIA BUSIA = `-DIVORCED in the `-YEAR of (`-16) = RECIPROCAL = (`-61) = `-AGE of `-DEATH / from `-HIS `-VERY `-OWN `-DIVORCED `-DATE / just `-LIKE the `-HUNDREDS of `-OTHERS that are JUST the `-SAME!!!~'

`-WAS `-MARRIED to OTTAVIA BUSIA for (`-9) `-years; AND, `-WAS `-MARRIED to NANCY PUTKOSKI for (`-20) `-YEARS = (9+20) = (`-29) = X TIMES (`-2) = (`-58) = RECIPROCAL = (`-85) = `-YEAR `-FIRST `-MARRIED / to NANCY PUTKOSKI!!!~'

ANTHONY MICHAEL BOURDAIN (AMERICAN CELEBRITY CHEF, AUTHOR; and, TRAVEL DOCUMENTARIAN) had a `-FRAGMENTED `-BIRTH/DAY # `-NUMBER = 6(+)2(+)5(+)1(+)9(+)5(+)6 = (`-34) = X TIMES (`-2) = (`-6/8) = `-EQUALED = `-HIS `-ACTUAL and `-VERY `-OWN `-DAY of `-DEATH = JUNE 8th / for ANTHONY MICHAEL BOURDAIN (AMERICAN CELEBRITY CHEF, AUTHOR; and, TRAVEL DOCUMENTARIAN)!!!~'

RUDOLPH ISLEY, PHYLLIS COATES, MARK GODDARD (`-DEATHS in `-ACTION)!!!~'

AMERICAN SINGER & CO-FOUNDER of the "ISLEY BROTHERS" (RUDOLPH "RUDY" BERNARD ISLEY) was `-BORN on (4/1/1939); and, `-DIED on (10/11/2023)!!!~'

`-HE `-DIED at the `-AGE of (`-84) = (8) x (4) = (`-32) = RECIPROCAL = (`-23) = `-DEATH/YEAR!!!~' `-BREAK-DOWN of `-BIRTH/DAY = (4/1/1) = (4) (1+1) = (`-42) x (`-2) = (`-84) = `-AGE of `-DEATH from `-BIRTH/DAY!!!~' `-BREAK-DOWN of `-BIRTH/DAY = (939) = (93) (-) 9) = (`-84) = `-AGE of `-DEATH from `-BIRTH/DAY!!!~' `-PARTIAL `-BIRTH/DAY # `-NUMBER = (4+1+19) = (`-24) x (`-2) - (`-48) = RECIPROCAL = (`-84) = `-HIS `-VERY `-OWN `-AGE of `-DEATH!!!~' `-DEATH/DAY - (10/11) - 10 (+) 11 = (` 21) x (`-4) - (`-84) = `-AGE of `-DEATH from `-HIS `-VERY `-OWN `-DEATH/DAY!!!~' `-DEATH/DAY # `-NUMBER = 10+11+20+23 = (`-64) = (6) x (4) = (`-24) x (`-2) = (`-48) = RECIPROCAL = (`-84) = `-AGE of `-DEATH from `-HIS `-VERY `-OWN `-DEATH/DAY # `-NUMBER!!!~' `-PARTIAL `-DEATH/DAY # `-NUMBER = 10+11+20 = (`-41) = `-EQUALED = `-HIS `-VERY `-OWN `-BIRTH/DAY = (4/1) = APRIL 1st!!!~' `-(DIED) from `-BIRTH-to-DEATH with (`-172) DAYS = (17) x (`-2) = (`-34) = FLIP 3 OVER to AN (`-8) = (`-84) = `-HIS `-VERY `-OWN `-AGE of `-DEATH!!!~' `-BIRTH/YEAR = (1939) = (19) + (39) = (`-58) = `-WAS `-MARRIED to ELAINE JASPER ISLEY in the `-CALENDAR `-YEAR of (`-58)!!!~'

AMERICAN ACTOR MARK GODDARD (BORN: CHARLES HARVEY GODDARD) (PORTRAYED MAJOR DON WEST on the SERIES "LOST in SPACE") was `-BORN on (7/24/1936); and, `-DIED on (10/10/2023)!!!~' HE `-DIED at the `-AGE of (`-87) with a `-BIRTH/DAY of (7/24) = (7) (2x4) = (`-78) = RECIPROCAL = (`-87) =

`-HIS `-VERY `-OWN `-AGE of `-DEATH from `-HIS `-VERY `-OWN `-BIRTH/DAY!!!~' HE `-ALSO `-DIED (`-78) DAYS from `-BIRTH-to-DEATH = RECIPROCAL = (`-87) = `-AGE of `-DEATH!!!~' `-FULL `-CALENDAR `-YEAR (365 (-) 78) = (`-287) = (to) (87) = `-HIS `-VERY `-OWN `-AGE of `-DEATH!!!~' `-DIVORCED SUSAN ANSPACH in (`-78) = `-HIS `-VERY `-OWN `-DAYS from `-BIRTH-to-DEATH = (`-78) = RECIPROCAL = (`-87) = `-ALSO; `-HIS `-VERY `-OWN `-AGE of `-DEATH = (`-87)!!!~' `-FRAGMENTED `-BIRTH/DAY # `-NUMBER = (7+2+4+1+9+3+6) = (`-32) = RECIPROCAL = (`-23) = `-HIS `-VERY `-OWN `-(DEATH/YEAR) from `-HIS `-VERY `-OWN `-FRAGMENTED `-BIRTH/DAY # `-NUMBER!!!~'

AMERICAN ACTRESS PHYLLIS COATES (BORN: GYPSIE ANN EVARTS STELL) (PORTRAYED "LOIS LANE" on the SERIES of "SUPERMAN") was `-BORN on (1/15/1927); and, `-DIED on (10/11/2023)!!!~' SHE `-DIED at the `-AGE of (`-96) with THERE being (`-96) DAYS from `-BIRTH-to-DEATH!!!~' CALENDAR `-YEAR (365 (-) 96) = (`-269) = RECIPROCAL = (`-962) = (96) (too) = (`-96) = `-HER `-VERY `-OWN `-AGE of `-DEATH!!!~' `-BIRTH/YEAR = (1927) = (9) (1-2-7) = (`-96) = `-HER `-VERY `-OWN `-AGE of `-DEATH = (9) x (6) = (`-54) = `-WAS (5' 4") in `-HEIGHT!!!~' `-MARRIED ROBERT NELMS in (`-1950) = (19) + (50) = (`-69) = RECIPROCAL

= (`-96) = `-HER `-VERY `-OWN `-AGE of `-DEATH from `-HER `-VERY `-OWN `-YEAR of `-MARRIAGE!!!~'

`-AMERICAN ACTRESS PIPER LAURIE (BORN: ROSETTA JACOBS) (STARRED in "CHILDREN of a LESSER GOD") was `-BORN on (1/22/1932); and, `-DIED on (10/14/2023)!!!~' `-HER `-BIRTH/YEAR = (`-32) = RECIPROCAL = (`-23) = `-DEATH/YEAR!!!~' `-HER `-BIRTH/YEAR = (`-1932) = RECIPROCAL = (`-2391) = (23) & (91) = `-HER `-DEATH/YEAR; and, `-HER `-VERY `-OWN /|\ `-AGE of `-DEATH = (`-91) (`-AGAIN); from `-HER `-VERY `-OWN `-BIRTH/YEAR!!!~' `-BIRTH/DAY = (1/22) = (1) + (22) = (`-23) = `-HER `-VERY `-OWN `-DEATH/YEAR!!!~'

`-CONCLUSION to `-MY (`-13) BOOKS:

`-ALL of the `-EQUATIONS have been `-PRECISE; and, `-FORTHRIGHT!!!~'

`-WHEN `-WE LOOK to DISCOVER `-ALIENS from ANOTHER PLANET; and, to `-FIND the `-true SENSE of `-OUR `-VERY `-BEGINNINGS; CLEARLY, `-WE; should just `-REALIZE that `-THEY were `-CREATED `-too!!!~'

'-WE'VE been '-EMPOWERED with '-POWERS '-BEYOND '-OUR '-IMAGINATION!!!~' '-CLEARLY, so '-WOULD be the '-SAME for the '-ALIENS!!!~'

'-REALIZE; what '-POWER is '-BEYOND '-ALL '-POWER; and, what '-CONTROL is '-BEYOND '-ALL '-CONTROL!!!~'

READ; to '-SEE -HUNDREDS of '-THESE '-SIMILAR; AND, '-EXACT-' ('-**EQUATIONS**), in '-**MY** ('-**13**) '-**BOOKS**; by **AUTHOR: DWAYNE W. ANDERSON – The '-REAL '-LIVE '-PROPHET of '-DOOM – (DWA)!!!~'**

PATRICK WAYNE SWAYZE was '-MARRIED to LISA NIEMI in ('-75) = RECIPROCAL = ('-57) = '-HIS '-VERY '-OWN '-AGE of '-DEATH!!!~'

THEY were '-MARRIED in (1975) = 19+75 = ('-94) = '-HIS '-VERY '-OWN '-DEATH/DAY was (9/14)!!!~'

JAPANESE FASHION DESIGNER HANAE MORI was '-MARRIED in ('-48) = RECIPROCAL = ('-84) = '-AGE of '-DEATH of '-HER '-VERY '-OWN '-HUSBAND KEN MORI = AGE - ('-84)!!!~'

(48x2) = ('-96) = '-MARRIAGE '-ENDED in ('-96) for WHEN '-HUSBAND KEN MORI died FROM a '-HEART '-ATTACK!!!~'

`-MARRIAGE `-ENDED in (`-96) = `-AGE of `-DEATH for JAPANESE FASHION DESIGNER HANAE MORI = AGE - (`-96)!!!~'

AMERICAN POLITICIAN DIANNE EMIEL FEINSTEIN was `-MARRIED to BERTRAM FEINSTEIN in (`-62) = DIANNE EMIEL FEINSTEIN'S `-BIRTH/DAY = 6/22!!!~'

AMERICAN POLITICIAN DIANNE EMIEL FEINSTEIN `-DIVORCED BERTRAM FEINSTEIN in (1978) = 19+78 = (`-97) = DIANNE EMIEL FEINSTEIN'S `-DEATH/DAY = 9/29 = (9) / (2(-)9) = (`-97)!!!~'

AMERICAN POLITICIAN DIANNE EMIEL FEINSTEIN `-DIVORCED JACK BERMAN in (1959) = 19+59 = (`-78) = `-THE `-VERY `-YEAR that `-SHE had `-DIVORCED BERTRAM FEINSTEIN!!!~'

AMERICAN POLITICIAN DIANNE EMIEL FEINSTEIN `-MARRIED RICHARD C. BLUM in (1980) = (1+9) + (80) = (`-90) = `-The `-VERY `-AGE of `-DEATH for AMERICAN POLITICIAN / DIANNE EMIEL FEINSTEIN!!!~'

`-ONE LAST `-ONE!!!~'

AMERICAN ACTRESS ELIZABETH RUTH GRABLE was `-MARRIED to JACKIE COOGAN in (`-37) = RECIPROCAL = (`-73) = `-HER `-VERY `-OWN

`-DEATH/YEAR = YEAR of (`-73) for BETTY GRABLE'S `-DEATH!!!~'

`-THEY were `-MARRIED in (1937) = 19+37 = (`-56) = `-AGE of `-DEATH for AMERICAN ACTRESS ELIZABETH RUTH GRABLE "BETTY GRABLE"!!!~'

AMERICAN ACTRESS ELIZABETH RUTH GRABLE `-DIVORCED HARRY JAMES in (`-65) = RECIPROCAL = (`-56) = `-AGE of `-DEATH for AMERICAN ACTRESS ELIZABETH RUTH GRABLE "BETTY GRABLE"!!!~'

From `-THEIR `-VERY `-OWN `-MARRIAGES!!!~'

`-ALL of `-YOUR `-marriages are like `-THIS!!!~' I'VE done `-HUNDREDS of `-THESE in `-MY (`-13) BOOKS!!!~' ARE `-you `-MARRIED???

AUTHOR/PROPHET: DWAYNE W. ANDERSON!!!~'

AMERICAN ACTRESS, AUTHOR; and, BUSINESSWOMAN (SUZANNE MARIE SOMERS) (THREE (3)'s COMPANY) died at the AGE of (`-76)!!!~'

SUZANNE MARIE SOMERS `-BIRTH/DAY = 10/16 = 10+16 = (`-26) = FLIP the (`-2) OVER to a (`-7) = (`-76) = `-AGE of `-DEATH for SUZANNE MARIE SOMERS!!!~'

SUZANNE MARIE SOMERS BIRTH/DAY # `-NUMBER = 10+16+19+46 = (`-91)!!!~'

HUSBAND ALAN HAMEL (CANADIAN ENTERTAINER, PRODUCER; and, TELEVISION HOST'S) `-BIRTH/DAY # `-NUMBER = 6+30+19+36 = (`-91)!!!~'

THE `-SAME `-BIRTH/DAY # `-NUMBER (`-91) for `-BOTH `-HUSBAND & WIFE!!!~'

SUZANNE MARIE SOMERS DEATH/DAY # `-NUMBER = 10+15+20+23 = (`-68)!!!~'

(`-68) = 6x8 = (`-48) = RECIPROCAL = (`-84)!!!~'

`-AGE of `-DEATH = (`-76) = 7x6 = (`-42) x (`-2) = (`-84)!!!~'

(84+84) = (`-168) = 1x68 = (`-68) = `-DEATH/DAY # `-NUMBER for SUZANNE MARIE SOMERS!!!~'

(`-SON) BRUCE SOMERS JR. was `-BORN in (1965) = 19+65 = (`-84)!!!~'

(8x4) = (`-32) = RECIPROCAL = (`-23) = `-DEATH/YEAR of `-MOTHER SUZANNE MARIE SOMERS!!!~'

SUZANNE MARIE SOMERS `-BIRTH/DAY was (`-23) DAYS before the `-BIRTH/DAY of (`-SON) BRUCE SOMERS JR.!!!~'

('-SON) BRUCE SOMERS JR. '-BIRTH/YEAR = (1965) = 19(-)65 = ('-46) = '-BIRTH/YEAR of '-MOTHER SUZANNE MARIE SOMERS!!!~'

SUZANNE MARIE SOMERS was '-BORN in 19(46) and was '-MARRIED to ALAN HAMEL /for/ ('-46) '-YEARS!!!~' THEY were '-FIRST '-MARRIED in 19(77); and, SUZANNE MARIE SOMERS died (ONE) (DAY) (SHY) of '-TURNING ('-77) YEARS of '-AGE!!!~'

SUZANNE MARIE SOMERS was '-BORN in (1946) = 19+46 = ('-65) = SHE was '-FIRST '-MARRIED to BRUCE SOMERS in 19('-65)!!!~'

SUZANNE MARIE SOMERS ('-SON) BRUCE SOMERS JR. was '-BORN in 19('-65)!!!~'

('-SON) BRUCE SOMERS JR. '-BIRTH/DAY # '-NUMBER = 11+8+19+65 = ('-103)!!!~'

(65+65) = ('-130) = "SWIPE ('-1) to the '-LEFT" = ('-103) = '-BIRTH/DAY # '-NUMBER!!!~'

('-SON) BRUCE SOMERS JR. '-FRAGMENTED '-BIRTH/DAY # '-NUMBER = 1+1+8+1+9+6+5 = ('-31)!!!~'

(31x2) = ('-62) = RECIPROCAL = ('-26) = FLIP the ('-2) OVER to a ('-7) = ('-76) = '-AGE of '-DEATH of '-MOTHER SUZANNE MARIE SOMERS!!!~'

SUZANNE MARIE SOMERS `-DEATH/DAY # `-NUMBER = 10+15+20+23 = (`-68) = SUZANNE MARIE SOMERS `-DIVORCED BRUCE SOMERS in 19(`-68)!!!~'

`-YEARS `-MARRIED (46) & (3) `-YEARS = 46(-)3 = (`-43) = 20+23 = `-HER `-VERY `-OWN `-DEATH/YEAR for SUZANNE MARIE SOMERS!!!~'

SUZANNE MARIE SOMERS `-FRAGMENTED `-BIRTH/DAY # `-NUMBER = 1+0+1+6+1+9+4+6 = (`-28)!!!~'

HUSBAND ALAN HAMEL (CANADIAN ENTERTAINER, PRODUCER; and, TELEVISION HOST'S `-FRAGMENTED `-BIRTH/DAY # `-NUMBER = 6+3+0+1+9+3+6 = (`-28)!!!~'

(28+28) = (`-56) = 8(x)7 = `-AGE of `-HUSBAND ALAN HAMEL at the `-TIJME of SUZANNE MARIE SOMERS `-TIME of `-DEATH!!!~'

SUZANNE MARIE SOMERS `-FRAGMENTED `-DEATH/DAY # `-NUMBER = 1+0+1+5+2+0+2+3 = (`-14)!!!~'

(14x2) = (`-28) = `-FRAGMENTED `-BIRTH/DAY # `-NUMBER!!!~'

(28+14) = (`-42) = 7(x)6 = `-AGE of `-DEATH for SUZANNE MARIE SOMERS!!!~'

SUZANNE MARIE SOMERS died `-ONE `-DAY `-PRIOR to `-HER `-BIRTH/DAY of `-TURNING (`-77) `-YEARS of `-AGE!!!~'

`-CALENDAR `-YEAR = 365(-)1 = (`-36/4) = (`-ANALYZE `-THIS!!!~') = RECIPROCAL = (`-46/3)-:

(`-36/4) = HUSBAND ALAN HAMEL was `-BORN in (`-36) & SUZANNE MARIE SOMERS (`-46/3) was `-BORN in (`-46)!!!~'

(4/3) = 20+23 = `-DEATH/YEAR of AMERICAN ACTRESS, AUTHOR; and, BUSINESSWOMAN (SUZANNE MARIE SOMERS) (THREE (3)'s COMPANY)!!!~'

THIS is a `-COMMON `-PATTERN in the `-EXISTENCE of `-TIME!!!~' RE-READ (`-ALL) of the `-BOOKS!!!~'

BURT YOUNG (GERALD TOMMASO DELOUISE) – AMERICAN ACTOR ("ROCKY"), AUTHOR; and, PAINTER died at the `-AGE of (`-83)!!!~'

`-BIRTH/YEAR = (1940) = 19+40 = (`-59) = 5x9 = (`-45) = RECIPROCAL = (`-54) = 6x9 = (`-69) = `-YEAR of `-BIRTH for `-DAUGHTER ANNE MOREA & CURRENT `-AGE of `-DAUGHTER ANNE MOREA (`-54) at the `-TIME of `-HER `-FATHER'S `-DEATH!!!~'

'-BIRTH/DAY = 4/30 = 43+0 = ('-43) = 20+23 = '-DEATH/ YEAR for BURT YOUNG!!!~'

'-BIRTH/DAY = 4/30 = 4+30 = ('-34) = RECIPROCAL = ('-43) = 20+23 = '-DEATH/YEAR for BURT YOUNG!!!~'

'-BIRTH/DAY # '-NUMBER = 4+30+19+40 = ('-93)!!!~'

'-DIVORCED GLORIA DELOUISE in (1974) = 19+74 = ('-93)!!!~'

'-DIVORCED in ('-74) = FLIP the ('-7) OVER to a ('-2) = ('-24) = 8x3 = '-AGE of '-DEATH for BURT YOUNG!!!~'

'-DEATH/DAY = 10/8 = 10x8 = ('-80) / '-DIVIDED by ('-2) = ('-40) = '-BIRTH/YEAR for BURT YOUNG!!!~'

'-DEATH/DAY # '-NUMBER = 10+8+20+23 = ('-61)!!!~'

'-DIED ('-161) DAYS from '-BIRTH-to-DEATH!!!~'

'-WAS '-FIRST '-MARRIED to GLORIA DELOUISE in ('-61)!!!~'

'-FIRST '-MARRIED in (1961) = 19(-)61 = ('-42) = RECIPROCAL = ('-24) = 8x3 = '-AGE of '-DEATH for BURT YOUNG ('-83)!!!~'

WAS '-MARRIED for ('-13) '-YEARS = 5+8 = (5' 8") in '-HEIGHT for BURT YOUNG!!!~'

(5' 8") in `-HEIGHT = 5x8 = (`-40) = `-BIRTH/YEAR for BURT YOUNG!!!~'

`-DIVORCED GLORIA DELOUISE in (1974) = 1(-)9 / 7(-)4 = (`-83) = `-AGE of `-DEATH for BURT YOUNG (GERALD TOMMASO DELOUISE) – AMERICAN ACTOR ("ROCKY"), AUTHOR; and, PAINTER (`-83)!!!~'

PATRICK WAYNE SWAYZE (AMERICAN ACTOR, DANCER; and, SINGER-SONGWRITER) died at the `-AGE of (`-57)!!!~'

`-BIRTH/DAY # `-NUMBER = 8+18+19+52 = (`-97)!!!~'

(97x2) = (`-194) = "SWIPE (`-1) to the `-LEFT" = (`-9/14) = `-HIS `-VERY `-OWN `-DEATH/DAY for PATRICK WAYNE SWAYZE!!!~'

`-DEATH/DAY # `-NUMBER = 9+14+20+09 = (`-52) = `-BIRTH/YEAR of PATRICK WAYNE SWAYZE!!!~'

`-BIRTH/YEAR = 52 = FLIP the (`-2) OVER to a (`-7) = (`-57) = `-AGE of `-DEATH for PATRICK WAYNE SWAYZE!!!~'

`-WAS `-MARRIED to LISA NIEMI in (`-75) = RECIPROCAL = (`-57) = `-AGE of `-DEATH for PATRICK WAYNE SWAYZE!!!~'

`-DEATH/DAY = 9/14 = RECIPROCAL = 41/9 = 41+9 = (`-50) = 5x10 = (5' 10") in `-HEIGHT for PATRICK WAYNE SWAYZE!!!~'

`-MARRIAGE `-YEAR = (1975) = 19+75 = (`-94) = `-DEATH/DAY for PATRICK WAYNE SWAYZE = (9/14) = 9 / 1x4 = (`-94)!!!~'

`-FRAGMENTED `-BIRTH/DAY # `-NUMBER = 8+1+8+1+9+5+2 = (`-34) = `-WAS `-MARRIED to LISA NIEMI for (`-34) `-YEARS!!!~'

`-FRAGMENTED `-DEATH/DAY # `-NUMBER = 9+1+4+2+0+0+9 = (`-25) = RECIPROCAL = (`-52) = `-BIRTH/YEAR for PATRICK WAYNE SWAYZE (AMERICAN ACTOR, DANCER; and, SINGER-SONGWRITER)!!!~'

PATRICK WAYNE SWAYZE `-WAS `-BORN in the `-MONTH of (`-8); and, `-DIED in the `-MONTH of (`-9) = (8/9) = 8x9 = (`-72) = "PEOPLE MAGAZINE NAMED `-HIM the "SEXIEST MAN ALIVE" in (1991)" = 19(-)91 = (`-72)!!!~'

`-BIRTH/DAY = 8/18 = 8 / 1+8 = (`-89) = PATRICK WAYNE SWAYZE `-WAS `-BORN in the `-MONTH of (`-8); and, `-DIED in the `-MONTH of (`-9) = (8/9)!!!~'

`-COMMON `-PATTERN: LAURA ANN BRANIGAN (AMERICAN SINGER) was `-BORN in the `-CALENDAR

`-YEAR of (`-52); and, `-DIED at the `-AGE of (`-52)!!!~' REVIEW the `-FIRST `-PART of `-THIS `-BOOK for `-like `-TIME `-CONSTRUCTS!!!~'

BURT FREEMAN BACHARACH (AMERICAN COMPOSER, SONGWRITER, RECORD PRODUCER; and, PIANIST) was `-BORN in the `-CALENDAR `-YEAR of (`-28); and, `-DIED on this `-EXACT `-DATE of (2/8) = FEBRUARY 8th!!!~' `-HIS `-FRAGMENTED `-BIRTH/DAY # `-NUMBER was 5+1+2+1+9+2+8 = (`-28) = `-HIS `-VERY `-OWN `-DEATH/DAY of (2/8) = FEBRUARY 8th = from `-HIS `-VERY `-OWN `-FRAGMENTED `-BIRTH/DAY # `-NUMBER!!!~' `-WAS `-BORN in the `-MONTH of (`-5); and, `-DIED in the `-MONTH of (`-2) = (`-52) = `-BIRTH/DAY = 5/12 = 5(ONE)2!!!~'

`-BURT FREEMAN BACHARACH `-PERFORMED `-WITH the `-FOLLOWING:

`-STAGE `-NAME / "DUSTY SPRINGFIELD" (MARY ISOBEL CATHERINE BERNADETTE O'BRIEN) died at the `-AGE of (`-59)!!!~'

`-FROM `-BIRTH-to-DEATH there are (`-45) `-DAYS = (5x9) = (`-59) = `-AGE of `-DEATH for "DUSTY SPRINGFIELD"!!!~'

`-BIRTH/YEAR = (1939) = (1(-)9(-)3) (9) = (`-59) = `-HER `-VERY `-OWN `-AGE of `-DEATH from `-HER `-VERY `-OWN `-BIRTH/YEAR!!!~'

`-BIRTH/YEAR = (1939) = 2(9's) /|\ `-DEATH/YEAR = (1999) = 3(9's)

`-WHAT'S `-LEFT = (1+3+1) = (`-5) (`-99999) = (`-59) = `-AGE of `-DEATH for `-STAGE `-NAME / "DUSTY SPRINGFIELD" (MARY ISOBEL CATHERINE BERNADETTE O'BRIEN) (`-59)!!!~'

2(9's) (+) 3(9's) = 5(9's) = (`-59) = `-AGE of `-DEATH for `-STAGE `-NAME / "DUSTY SPRINGFIELD" (MARY ISOBEL CATHERINE BERNADETTE O'BRIEN) (`-59)!!!~'

`-BIRTH/YEAR = (`-39) = 3(9's) = (999) = `-DEATH/ YEAR = 1(999)!!!~'

`-BIRTH/YEAR = (`-39) = 3(9's) = (999) = (9x9x9) = (`-729) = 7(-)2 / 9 = (`-59) = `-AGE of `-DEATH for `-STAGE `-NAME / "DUSTY SPRINGFIELD" (MARY ISOBEL CATHERINE BERNADETTE O'BRIEN) (`-59)!!!~'

"DUSTY SPRINGFIELD" `-FRAGMENTED `-BIRTH/ DAY # `-NUMBER = 4+1+6+1+9+3+9 = (`-33) = `-FRAGMENTED `-DEATH/DAY # `-NUMBER!!!~'

"DUSTY SPRINGFIELD" `-FRAGMENTED `-DEATH/DAY # `-NUMBER = 3+2+1+9+9+9 = (`-33) = `-FRAGMENTED `-BIRTH/DAY # `-NUMBER!!!~'

(`-33) `-TWICE & `-DIED on the `-DAY `-PRIOR of (`-3/2) for "DUSTY SPRINGFIELD"!!!~'

`-WAS `-BORN in the `-MONTH of (`-4); and, `-DIED in the `-MONTH of (`-3) = (`-43) = 4(3's) = (`-33/33)!!!~'

`-WAS `-BORN in the `-MONTH of (`-4); and, `-DIED in the `-MONTH of (`-3) = (`-43) = RECIPROCAL = (`-34) = 3(4's) = (4/4/4) = 4x4x4 = (`-64) = RECIPROCAL = (`-46) = `-BIRTH/DAY = (4/16)!!!~'

`-BIRTH/DAY = (4/16) = (4+1) (6) = (`-56) = "FLIP the (`-6) OVER to a (`-9)" = (`-59) = `-AGE of `-DEATH for `-STAGE `-NAME / "DUSTY SPRINGFIELD" (MARY ISOBEL CATHERINE BERNADETTE O'BRIEN) (`-59)!!!~'

`-BIRTH/DAY = (4/16) = RECIPROCAL = (61/4) = 61+4 = (`-65) = RECIPROCAL = (`-56) = "FLIP the (`-6) OVER to a (`-9)" = (`-59) = `-AGE of `-DEATH for `-STAGE `-NAME / "DUSTY SPRINGFIELD" (MARY ISOBEL CATHERINE BERNADETTE O'BRIEN) (`-59)!!!~'

`-BIRTH/DAY = (4/16) = 4x16 = (`-64) / `-DIVIDED by (`-2) = (`-32) = (3/2) = `-DEATH/DAY for `-STAGE `-NAME / "DUSTY SPRINGFIELD" (MARY ISOBEL CATHERINE BERNADETTE O'BRIEN)!!!~'

"DUSTY SPRINGFIELD" `-PARTIAL `-BIRTH/DAY # `-NUMBER = 4+16+19 = (`-39) = `-BIRTH/YEAR = (`-39)!!!~'

"DUSTY SPRINGFIELD" `-BIRTH/DAY # `-NUMBER = 4+16+19+39 = (`-78) = RECIPROCAL = (`-87) = "FLIP the (`-8) OVER to a (`-3)"; "FLIP the (`-7) OVER to a (`-2)" =

(`-32) = (3/2) = `-HER `-VERY `-OWN `-DEATH/DAY for `-DUSTY `-SPRINGFIELD from `-HER `-VERY `-OWN `-BIRTH/DAY # `-NUMBER = RECIPROCAL = (`-23)!!!~'

"DUSTY SPRINGFIELD" `-DEATH/DAY # `-NUMBER = 3+2+19+99 = (`-123)!!!~'

AMERICAN SINGER & DRUMMER (KAREN ANNE CARPENTER) had a `-BIRTH/DAY of (3/2)!!!~' SHE was BORN in the MONTH of (3) & DIED in the MONTH of (2); while, `-DYING at the AGE of (32)!!!~'

AMERICAN ACTOR MARK GODDARD (BORN: CHARLES HARVEY GODDARD) (PORTRAYED MAJOR DON WEST on the SERIES "LOST in SPACE") was `-BORN on (7/24/1936); and, `-DIED on (10/10/2023)!!!~' HE `-DIED at the `-AGE of (`-87) with a`-FRAGMENTED `-BIRTH/DAY # `-NUMBER = (7+2+4+1+9+3+6) = (`-32) = FLIP the 3 OVER to an (`-8); FLIP the 2 OVER to a (`-7) = (`-87) = `-HIS `-VERY `-OWN `-AGE of `-DEATH from `-HIS `-FRAGMENTED `-BIRTH/DAY # `-NUMBER = RECIPROCAL = (`-23) = `-HIS `-VERY `-OWN `-(DEATH/YEAR) from `-HIS `-VERY `-OWN `-FRAGMENTED `-BIRTH/DAY # `-NUMBER!!!~'

BENJAMIN KEOUGH (ELVIS AARON PRESLEY'S DAUGHTER - LISA MARIE PRESLEY'S SON) `-DIED at the `-AGE of (`-27) = 2(7's) = (`-77) = `-YEAR `-HIS `-GRANDFATHER ELVIS AARON PRESLEY `-DIED!!!~'

(ELVIS AARON PRESLEY) FRAGMENTED BIRTHDAY # `-NUMBER = JANUARY 8, 1935 = (1 + 8 + 1 + 9 + 3 + 5) = (`- 27) = `-AGE of `-DEATH of `-GRANDSON (BENJAMIN KEOUGH) = (`-27) = 2(7's) = (`-77) = ELVIS AARON PRESLEY'S `-DEATH/YEAR from `-HIS `-VERY `-OWN `-FRAGMENTED `-BIRTH/ DAY # `-NUMBER!!!~'

GEORGE HERMAN "BABE" RUTH died at the AGE of (`-53) and YOU can CALCULATE it FROM his `-VERY `-OWN `-BIRTH/DAY # `-NUMBER = (2/6/18/95)!!!~' WHAT'S in the MIDDLE of `-his `-BIRTH/DAY # `-NUMBER = (6/18) = RECIPROCAL = (8/16) = `-EQUALS = `-HIS `-ACTUAL `-DAY of `-DEATH!!!~' HE `-ACTUALLY `-DIED on (8/16)!!!~' From `-HIS BIRTH/DAY # `-NUMBER (&) `-HIS `-DEATH/DAY # `-NUMBER = 6/18 = 61(-)8 = (`- 53) = `-HIS `-ACTUAL `-AGE of `-DEATH from `-HIS `-VERY `-OWN `-BIRTH/ DAY # `-NUMBER for GEORGE HERMAN "BABE" RUTH!!!~' `-CAREER in `-BASEBALL `-ENDED in (`-35) = RECIPROCAL = (`-53) = `-HIS `-ACTUAL `-AGE of `-DEATH for GEORGE HERMAN "BABE" RUTH!!!~' `-DIED in (1948) = 19(-)48 = (`-29) = `-MARRIAGE `-BEGAN with CLAIRE MERRITT RUTH in (`-29); and, `-ENDED with `-HELEN `-RUTH in (`-29); just as

`-WELL!!!~' (29+29) = (`-58) = "FLIP the (`-8) OVER to a (`-3)" = (`-53) = `-HIS `-ACTUAL `-AGE of `-DEATH for GEORGE HERMAN "BABE" RUTH!!!~'

JULIA RUTH STEVENS (BABE RUTH'S DAUGHTER) was `-BORN in (1916) = 19+16 = (`-35) = RECIPROCAL = (`-53) = `-AGE of `-DEATH of `-HER `-VERY `-OWN `-FATHER / "BABE" RUTH!!!~' SHE `-died in (2019) = 20+19 = (`-39) = `-DEATH/DAY = (3/9)!!!~' `-SISTER / DOROTHY HELEN RUTH PIRONE, died in the `-CALENDAR `-YEAR of (`-89) = "FLIP the (`-8) OVER to a (`-3)" = (`-39)!!!~' `-AGAIN; `-FATHER'S `-BIRTH/ DAY # `-NUMBER = (2/**6/18**/95)!!!~' (2(-)95) = (`-93) = RECIPROCAL = (`-39)!!!~' JULIA RUTH STEVENS `-DEATH/DAY # `-NUMBER = 3+9+20+19 = (`-51) x (`-2) = (`-102) = `-ACTUAL `-AGE of `-DEATH = `-EQUALS = JULIA RUTH STEVENS `-LIVED to be (`-102) `-YEARS of `-AGE = "FLIP the (`-2) OVER to a (`-7)" = (`-107) = "SEE `-IMMEDIATELY `-HEREAFTER"!!!~' JULIA RUTH STEVENS `-BIRTH/YEAR = (1916) = (91+16) = (`-107) / `-DIVIDED by (`-2) = (`-53.5) = `-ACTUAL `-AGE of `-DEATH for `-HER `-FATHER / "BABE" RUTH!!!~'

GEORGE HERMAN "BABE" RUTH `-BIRTH/YEAR = (`-1895) = `-SEPARATE (`-89) = `-DEATH/YEAR for `-DAUGHTER / DOROTHY HELEN RUTH PIRONE!!!~' (`-1895) = `-SEPARATE (`-15) = RECIPROCAL = (`-51) = `-DEATH/DAY # `-NUMBER for `-DAUGHTER / JULIA RUTH STEVENS!!!~' (`-1895) = 18(-)95 = (`-77) = (7/7) = `-BIRTH/DAY of `-DAUGHTER / JULIA RUTH

STEVENS!!!~' `-HIS `-BIRTH/YEAR `-EQUALED the `-BIRTH/DAY of `-ONE `-DAUGHTER; and, `-HIS `-DEATH/YEAR `-EQUALED the `-BIRTH/DAY of the `-OTHER `-DAUGHTER!!!~' `-AGE of `-DEATH for JULIA RUTH STEVENS (`-102) = (-) MINUS (-) = `-AGE of `-DEATH for DOROTHY HELEN RUTH PIRONE (`-67) = (`-35) = RECIPROCAL = (`-53) = `-AGE of `-DEATH for `-THEIR `-FATHER / GEORGE HERMAN "BABE" RUTH!!!~'

DOROTHY HELEN RUTH PIRONE (BIOLOGICAL DAUGHTER of "BABE" RUTH & MISTRESS JUANITA JENNINGS) / `-BIRTH/DAY # `-NUMBER = 6+7+19+21 = (`-53) = `-ACTUAL `-AGE of `-DEATH of `-HER `-VERY `-OWN `-FATHER / "BABE" RUTH!!!~' `-DEATH/DAY = (5/18) = "FLIP the (`-8) OVER to a (`-3)" = (5/13) = "SEE `-IMMEDIATELY `-BEFORE"!!!~' `-DEATH/DAY = (5/18) = (5) (1+8) = (`-59) = RECIPROCAL = (`-95) = `-FATHER'S / "BABE" RUTH / `-BIRTH/YEAR!!!~' `-DEATH/DAY = (5/18) = RECIPROCAL = (81/5) = 81(-)5 = (`-76) = RECIPROCAL = (`-67) = (6/7) = `-BIRTH/DAY of `-DOROTHY RUTH PIRONE!!!~' DOROTHY HELEN RUTH PIRONE was `-BORN on (`-6/7); and, `-DIED at the `-AGE of (`-67)!!!~' FATHER'S ("BABE" RUTH) `-DEATH/YEAR = (1948) = 19+48 = (`-67) = "SEE the `-DETAILS `-BEFORE-'"!!!~'

RICHARD WAYNE PENNIMAN / AMERICAN MUSICIAN / LITTLE RICHARD'S `-BIRTHDAY = (12/5/19/32) = `-AN `-ACTUAL `-PART of `-HIS `-BIRTH/

DAY # `-NUMBER (RIGHT in the `-MIDDLE) = (5/19) = (5) (1x9) = (`-59) = (5/9) = `-HIS `-ACTUAL `-DAY of `-DEATH = (MAY 9th)!!!~' (5/19) = (5) x (19) = (`-95) = RECIPROCAL = (`-59) = (5/9) = `-HIS `-ACTUAL `-DAY of `-DEATH = (MAY 9th)!!!~' `-HE was `-MARRIED to ERNESTINE CAMPBELL from {`-19(59) to `-19(63)}!!!~' (MARRIED) in (`-59); and, `-DIED on the `-DAY of (5/9)!!!~' `-WHAT'S `-LEFT???-' YOU can `-CALCULATE `-it FROM `-HIS `-ACTUAL `-BIRTH/DAY # `-NUMBER!!!~' `-AGAIN; BIRTH/DAY # `-NUMBER = (*12*/*5*/*19*/*32*) = {1+2+1+32} = (`-36) = RECIPROCAL = (`-63) = `-HIS `-MARRIAGE `-ENDED on this `-DATE of `-YEAR = (`-63)!!!~' `-HIS `-ACTUAL `-BIRTH/DAY # `-NUMBER had told `-HIS `-ACTUAL `-DATE of `-MARRIAGE, `-HIS `-ACTUAL `-DATE of `-DIVORCE; and, `-HIS `-ACTUAL `-DATE / for `-DAY of `-DEATH!!!~' `-WHAT `-ELSE does `-HIS `-FRAGMENTED `-BIRTH/DAY # `-NUMBER tell `-US??? (=) (1+2+5+1+9+3+2) = (`-23) = RECIPROCAL = (`-32) = `-HIS `-BIRTH/YEAR = (`-32) = "FLIP the (`-3) OVER to an (`-8)"; "FLIP the (`-2) OVER to a (`-7)" = (`-87) = `-EQUALS = `-HIS `-ACTUAL `-AGE of `-DEATH for RICHARD WAYNE PENNIMAN (LITTLE RICHARD) from `-HIS `-VERY `-OWN `-BIRTH/DAY # `-NUMBER!!!~'

RICHARD PHILIP LEWIS (AMERICAN STAND-UP COMEDIAN, ACTOR; and, WRITER) died at the `-AGE of (`-76)!!!~'

`-FRAGMENTED `-BIRTH/DAY # `-NUMBER = 6+2+9+1+9+4+7 = (`-38) x (`-2) = (`-76) = `-ACTUAL `-AGE of `-DEATH from `-ACTUAL `-FRAGMENTED `-BIRTH/DAY # `-NUMBER!!!~'

`-FRAGMENTED `-DEATH/DAY # `-NUMBER = 2+2+7+2+0+2+4 = (`-19) = `-WAS `-MARRIED to JOYCE LAPINSKY for (`-19) `-YEARS / (2005-to-2024)!!!~'

`-FRAGMENTED `-DEATH/DAY # `-NUMBER = 2+2+7+2+0+2+4 = (`-19) x (`-2) = (`-38) = `-FRAGMENTED `-BIRTH/DAY # `-NUMBER!!!~'

`-FRAGMENTED `-DEATH/DAY # `-NUMBER = 2+2+7+2+0+2+4 = (`-19) x (`-2) = (`-38) x (`-2) = (`-76) = `-ACTUAL `-AGE of `-DEATH from `-ACTUAL `-FRAGMENTED `-DEATH/DAY # `-NUMBER!!!~'

`-BIRTH/YEAR = (`-47) = "FLIP the (`-7) OVER to a (`-2)" = (`-42) = 7x6 = (`-76) = `-ACTUAL `-AGE of `-DEATH from `-ACTUAL `-BIRTH/YEAR!!!~'

`-BIRTH/YEAR = (`-47) = "FLIP the (`-7) OVER to a (`-2)" = (`-42) = RECIPROCAL = (`-24) = `-ACTUAL `-DEATH/YEAR from `-ACTUAL `-BIRTH/YEAR!!!~'

`-BIRTH/YEAR = (`-47) = `-DEATH/DAY = (2/27) = (2+2) (7) = (`-47)!!!~'

`-DEATH/DAY = (2/27) = RECIPROCAL = (72/2) = 72+2 = (`-74) = RECIPROCAL = (`-47) = `-BIRTH/YEAR!!!~'

(47+47) = (`-94) = "SEE `-IMMEDIATELY `-BELOW"!!!~'

`-BIRTH/DAY = (6/29) = RECIPROCAL = (92/6) = 92+6 = (`-98) / `-DIVIDED by (`-2) = (`-49) = RECIPROCAL = (`-94)!!!~'

`-FRAGMENTED `-DEATH/DAY # `-NUMBER = 2+2+7+2+0+2+4 = (`-19) x (`-4) = (`-76) = `-ACTUAL `-AGE of `-DEATH from `-ACTUAL `-FRAGMENTED `-DEATH/DAY # `-NUMBER!!!~'

`-PARTIAL `-DEATH/DAY # `-NUMBER = 2+27+20 = (`-49) = RECIPROCAL = (`-94) / `-DIVIDED by (`-2) = (`-47) = `-BIRTH/YEAR!!!~'

`-BIRTH/DAY # `-NUMBER = 6+29+19+47 = (`-101)!!!~'

`-DEATH/DAY # `-NUMBER = 2+27+20+24 = (`-73)!!!~'

`-BIRTH/DAY = (6/29) = 6x29 = (`-174) = 1(-)74 = (`-73) = `-DEATH/DAY # `-NUMBER!!!~'

(101+73) = (`-174) = 1x74 = (`-74) = RECIPROCAL = (`-47) = `-BIRTH/YEAR!!!~'

(101(-)73) = (`-28) = 19(-)47 = `-BIRTH/YEAR!!!~'

`-BIRTH/DAY = (6/29) = 6x29 = (`-174) = `-BIRTH/ DAY # `-NUMBER & `-DEATH/DAY # `-NUMBER / `-ADDED `-UP `-TOGETHER / = (`-174) = 1x74 = (`-74) = RECIPROCAL = (`-47) = `-BIRTH/YEAR!!!~'

`-AGE of `-DEATH = (`-76) = 7x6 = (`-42) = RECIPROCAL = (`-24) = `-DEATH/YEAR!!!~'

`-BIRTH/DAY = (6/29) = 6(-)29 = (`-23)!!!~'

`-DIED (`-123) `-DAYS from `-BIRTH-to-DEATH!!!~'

`-WAS `-BORN in the `-MONTH of (`-6); and, `-DIED in the `-MONTH of (`-2) = (`-62) = "FLIP the (`-2) OVER to a (`-7)" = (`-67) = RECIPROCAL = (`-76) = `-AGE of `-DEATH for RICHARD PHILIP LEWIS (AMERICAN STAND-UP COMEDIAN, ACTOR; and, WRITER) (`-76)!!!~'

LANCE REDDICK (AMERICAN ACTOR & MUSICIAN) died at the `-AGE of (`-60)!!!~'

`-BIRTH/YEAR = (1962) = 19(-)62 = (`-43) = 20+23 = `-DEATH/YEAR!!!~'

`-PARTIAL `-BIRTH/DAY # `-NUMBER = 6+7+19 = (`-32) = RECIPROCAL = (`-23) = `-DEATH/YEAR for LANCE REDDICK (AMERICAN ACTOR & MUSICIAN)!!!~'

`-PARTIAL FRAGMENTED `-BIRTH/DAY # `-NUMBER = 6+7+1+9 = (`-23) = `-DEATH/YEAR for LANCE REDDICK (AMERICAN ACTOR & MUSICIAN)!!!~'

`-REVERSE `-LOOKUP on `-BIRTH/DAY # `-NUMBER = 62(-)19(-)7(-)6 = (`-30) x (`-2) = (`-60) = `-AGE of `-DEATH for LANCE REDDICK (AMERICAN ACTOR & MUSICIAN)!!!~'

`-BIRTH/DAY # `-NUMBER = 6+7+19+62 = (`-94)!!!~'

(`-94) = 9x4 = (`-36) = RECIPROCAL = (`-63) = `-DEATH/DAY # `-NUMBER!!!~'

`-DEATH/DAY # `-NUMBER = 3+17+20+23 = (`-63)!!!~'

LANCE REDDICK was `-BORN in the `-MONTH of (`-6); and, `-DIED in the `-MONTH of (`-3) = (`-63) = `-HIS `-VERY `-OWN `-DEATH/DAY # `-NUMBER!!!~'

`-DEATH/DAY = 3/17 = RECIPROCAL = 71/3 = 71(-)3 = (`-68) = FLIP 8 to 3 = (`-63)!!!~'

`-DEATH/DAY = 3/17 = 3 / 1(-)7 = (`-36) = RECIPROCAL = (`-63) = LANCE REDDICK was `-BORN in the `-MONTH of (`-6); and, `-DIED in the `-MONTH of (`-3) = (`-63)!!!~'

FRAGMENTED `-BIRTH/DAY # `-NUMBER = 6+7+1+9+6+2 = (`-31) = "FIRST `-PART of `-DEATH/DAY"!!!~'

`-WAS `-MARRIED to STEPHANIE REDDICK in (2011) = 20+11 = (`-31)!!!~'

FRAGMENTED `-DEATH/DAY # `-NUMBER = 3+1+7+2+0+2+3 = (`-18) = FLIP 8 to 3 = (`-13) =

RECIPROCAL = (`-31) = FRAGMENTED `-BIRTH/DAY # `-NUMBER!!!~'

FRAGMENTED `-DEATH/DAY # `-NUMBER = 3+1+7+2+0+2+3 = (`-18) = FLIP 8 to 3 = (`-13) = 6+7 = `-BIRTH/DAY of LANCE REDDICK (AMERICAN ACTOR & MUSICIAN)!!!~'

`-PARTIAL FRAGMENTED `-DEATH/DAY # `-NUMBER = 3+1+7+2 = (`-13) = 6+7 = `-BIRTH/DAY of LANCE REDDICK (AMERICAN ACTOR & MUSICIAN)!!!~'

FRAGMENTED `-DEATH/DAY # `-NUMBER = 3+1+7+2+0+2+3 = (`-18) = RECIPROCAL = (`-81) = 19+62 = `-BIRTH/YEAR for LANCE REDDICK (AMERICAN ACTOR & MUSICIAN)!!!~'

MATTHEW LANGFORD PERRY (AMERICAN/ CANADIAN ACTOR) died at the `-AGE of (`-54)!!!~'

`-BIRTH/YEAR = (`-69) = 6x9 = (`-54) = `-AGE of `-DEATH for MATTHEW LANGFORD PERRY!!!~'

(`-54) x (`-2) = (`-108) = 10/8 = RECIPROCAL = (8/10) = "SEE `-BELOW"!!!~'

`-DEATH/DAY = 10/28 = 10(to)8 = RECIPROCAL = 8(to)10 = MATTHEW LANGFORD PERRY was `-BORN in the `-MONTH of (`-8); and, `-DIED in the `-MONTH of (`-10) = (8/10) = "SEE `-ABOVE"!!!~'

`-BIRTH/DAY = 8/19 = 8 / 1+9 = (8/10) = "SEE `-RIGHT `-ABOVE"!!!~'

`-BIRTH/DAY # `-NUMBER = 8+19+19+69 = (`-115)!!!~'

(`-115) x 2 = (`-230) = 23+0 = (`-23) = `-DEATH/YEAR!!!~'

`-DEATH/DAY # `-NUMBER = 10+28+20+23 = (`-81) = "SEE `-ABOVE"!!!~'

FRAGMENTED `-BIRTH/DAY # `-NUMBER = 8+1+9+1+9+6+9 = (`-43) = 20+23 = `-DEATH/YEAR!!!~'

FRAGMENTED `-DEATH/DAY # `-NUMBER = 1+0+2+8+2+0+2+3 = (`-18) = RECIPROCAL = (`-81) = "SEE `-ABOVE"!!!~'

`-BIRTH/DAY = 8/19 = RECIPROCAL = 91/8 = 91(+)8 = (`-99) = 9x9 = (`-81) = "SEE `-ABOVE"!!!~'

`-REVERSE `-LOOKUP on `-BIRTH/DAY # `-NUMBER = 69(-)19(-)19(-)8 = (`-23) = `-DEATH/YEAR!!!~'

RICHARD ARNOLD ROUNDTREE (AMERICAN ACTOR "SHAFT" & MODEL) died at the `-AGE of (`-81)!!!~'

`-BIRTH/DAY # `-NUMBER = 7+9+19+42 = (`-77)!!!~'

`-DEATH/DAY # `-NUMBER = 10+24+20+23 = (`-77)!!!~'

`-BIRTH/DAY # `-NUMBER = (`-77) = `-DEATH/DAY # `=NUMBER = (`-77)!!!~'

`-DEATH/DAY = 10/24 = HALF RECIPROCAL = 10/42 = 10(-)42 = (`-32) = "SEE `-BELOW"!!!~'

FRAGMENTED `-BIRTH/DAY # `-NUMBER = 7+9+1+9+4+2 = (`-32) = RECIPROCAL = (`-23) = `-DEATH/YEAR!!!~'

FRAGMENTED `-DEATH/DAY # `-NUMBER = 1+0+2+4+2+0+2+3 = (`-14)!!!~'

FRAGMENTED `-BIRTH/DAY # `-NUMBER = (`-32) = (-) MINUS (-) = (`-14) = `-FRAGMENTED `-DEATH/DAY # `-NUMBER = (`-18) = RECIPROCAL = (`-81) = `-AGE of `-DEATH for RICHARD ARNOLD ROUNDTREE (AMERICAN ACTOR "SHAFT" & MODEL) (`-81)!!!~'

`-BIRTH/DAY = 7/9 = 7x9 = (`-63) = `-WAS FIRST `-MARRIED in 19(63) to MARY JANE GRANT!!!~'

`-DIVORCED MARY JANE GRANT in (1973) = 19+73 = (`-92) = 9x2 = (`-18) = RECIPROCAL = (`-81) = `-AGE of `-DEATH for RICHARD ARNOLD ROUNDTREE (AMERICAN ACTOR "SHAFT" & MODEL) (`-81)!!!~'

'-BIRTH/YEAR = (1942) = 19(-)42 = ('-23) = '-DEATH/ YEAR!!!~'

FRANK FREDERICK BORMAN II (AMERICAN AERONAUTICAL ENGINEER & ASTRONAUT) died at the '-AGE of ('-95)!!!~'

'-BIRTH/DAY = 3/14 = 34x1 = ('-34) = RECIPROCAL = ('-43) = 20+23 = '-DEATH/YEAR!!!~'

'-WAS '-MARRIED to SUSAN BORMAN in 1950 = 19(-)50 = ('-31) = FRANK FREDERICK BORMAN II was '-BORN in the '-MONTH of ('-3); and, '-DIED in the '-MONTH of ('-11) = (3/11) = 31x1 = ('-31)!!!~'

'-WAS '-MARRIED to SUSAN BORMAN in 1950 = 19+50 = ('-69) = 6x9 = ('-54) = RECIPROCAL = ('-45) = 9x5 = '-AGE of '-DEATH for FRANK FREDERICK BORMAN II (AMERICAN AERONAUTICAL ENGINEER & ASTRONAUT)!!!~'

'-BIRTH/DAY # '-NUMBER = 3+14+19+28 = ('-64)!!!~'

('-64) / '-DIVIDED by ('-2) – ('-32) = RECIPROCAL = ('-23) = '-DEATH/YEAR!!!~'

'-DEATH/DAY # '-NUMBER = 11+7+20+23 = ('-61)!!!~'

FRAGMENTED `-BIRTH/DAY # `-NUMBER = 3+1+4+1+9+2+8 = (`-28) = `-BIRTH/YEAR!!!~'

(`-28) = 2x8 = (`-16) = FRAGMENTED `-DEATH/DAY # `-NUMBER = RECIPROCAL = (`-61) = `-DEATH/DAY # `-NUMBER!!!~'

FRAGMENTED `-DEATH/DAY # `-NUMBER = 1+1+7+2+0+2+3 = (`-16)!!!~'

`-BIRTH/YEAR = (1928) = 19+28 = (`-47) x (`-2) = (`-94) = `-DIED the `-VERY `-NEXT `-YEAR `-AFTERWARD at the `-AGE of (`-95)!!!~'

`-DEATH/DAY # `-NUMBER = (`-61) = + PLUS + = (`-16) = FRAGMENTED `-DEATH/DAY # `-NUMBER = (`-77) = 7x7 = (`-49) = RECIPROCAL = (`-94)!!!~'

`-BIRTH/YEAR = (1928) = (9) (1+2(-)8) = (`-95) = `-AGE of `-DEATH for FRANK FREDERICK BORMAN II (AMERICAN AERONAUTICAL ENGINEER & ASTRONAUT)!!!~'

`-REVERSE `-LOOKUP on `-HIS `-RETIREMENT `-DATE = 70(-)19(-)1(-)7 = (`-43) = 20+23 = `-DEATH/ YEAR!!!~'

`-RETIREMENT `-DATE = (7/1)!!!~'

'-DEATH/DAY = 11/7 = RECIPROCAL = 7/11 = 71x1 = (7/1)!!!~'

AMERICAN ACTRESS / FRANCES HUSSEY STERNHAGEN died at the '-AGE of ('-93)!!!~'

'-BIRTH/YEAR = (1930) = 1x93+0 – ('-93) – '-AGE of '-DEATH for AMERICAN ACTRESS / FRANCES HUSSEY STERNHAGEN!!!~'

'-BIRTH/YEAR = (1930) = 19+30 = ('-49) = RECIPROCAL = ('-94) = '-DIED the '-VERY '-YEAR '-PRIOR at the '-AGE of ('-93)!!!~'

'-DEATH/DAY = 11/27 = 11+27 = ('-38)!!!~'

'-SHE '-DIED from '-BIRTH-to-DEATH with ('-318) '-DAYS between '-THEM = RECIPROCAL = ('-813) = (8+1) (3) = ('-93) = '-AGE of '-DEATH for AMERICAN ACTRESS FRANCES HUSSEY STERNHAGEN!!!~'

('-318) = 38x1 = ('-38) = '-DEATH/DAY!!!~'

'-BIRTH/DAY # '-NUMBER = 1+13+19+30 = ('-63)!!!~'

('-63) = FLIP the ('-6) OVER to a ('-9) = ('-93) = '-AGE of '-DEATH for AMERICAN ACTRESS / FRANCES HUSSEY STERNHAGEN!!!~'

'-DEATH/DAY # '-NUMBER = 11+27+20+23 = ('-81)!!!~'

FRAGMENTED `-BIRTH/DAY # `-NUMBER = 1+1+3+1+9+3+0 = (`-18) = RECIPROCAL = (`-81) = `-DEATH/DAY # `-NUMBER!!!~'

FRAGMENTED `-DEATH/DAY # `-NUMBER = 1+1+2+7+2+0+2+3 = (`-18) = FRAGMENTED `-BIRTH/DAY # `-NUMBER = (`-18) = RECIPROCAL = (`-81) = `-DEATH/DAY # `-NUMBER!!!~'

FRAGMENTED `-BIRTH/DAY # `-NUMBER = (`-18) = + PLUS + = (`-18) = FRAGMENTED `-DEATH/DAY # `-NUMBER = (`-36) = RECIPROCAL = (`-63) = `-BIRTH/DAY # `-NUMBER = FLIP the (`-6) OVER to a (`-9) = (`-93) = `-AGE of `-DEATH for AMERICAN ACTRESS / FRANCES HUSSEY STERNHAGEN!!!~'

`-HUSBAND THOMAS A. CARLIN `-DIED in (1991) = 19(-)91 = (`-72) = RECIPROCAL = (`-27) = 9x3 = (`-93) = `-AGE of `-DEATH for AMERICAN ACTRESS / FRANCES HUSSEY STERNHAGEN!!!~'

`-BIRTH/DAY = 1/13 = HALF RECIPROCAL = 1/31 = 1+31 = (`-32) = RECIPROCAL = (`-23) = `-DEATH/YEAR!!!~'

CHARLES THOMAS MUNGER (AMERICAN BUSINESSMAN, INVESTOR, PHILANTHROPIST; and, ATTORNEY) died at the `-AGE of (`-99)!!!~'

`-BIRTH/DAY # `-NUMBER = 1+1+19+24 = (`-45)!!!~'

(`-45) = RECIPROCAL = (`-54)

`-WAS `-MARRIED to NANCY BARRY from (1956) to (2010) = (`-54) `-YEARS!!!~'

`-WAS `-MARRIED to NANCY HUGGINS in (`-45)!!!~'

(45+54) = (`-99) = `-AGE of `-DEATH for CHARLES THOMAS MUNGER (AMERICAN BUSINESSMAN, INVESTOR, PHILANTHROPIST; and, ATTORNEY) = (`-99)!!!~'

`-DEATH/DAY # `-NUMBER = 11+28+20+23 = (`-82) = RECIPROCAL = (`-28) = 7x4 = (`-74) = FLIP the (`-7) OVER to a (`-2) = (`-24) = `-BIRTH/YEAR!!!~'

FRAGMENTED `-BIRTH/DAY # `-NUMBER = 1+1+1+9+2+4 = (`-18) = RECIPROCAL = (`-81) = 9x9 = (`-99) = `-AGE of `-DEATH for CHARLES THOMAS MUNGER (AMERICAN BUSINESSMAN, INVESTOR, PHILANTHROPIST; and, ATTORNEY) = (`-99)!!!~'

FRAGMENTED `-DEATH/DAY # `-NUMBER = 1+1+2+8+2+0+2+3 = (`-19)!!!~'

FRAGMENTED `-BIRTH/DAY # `-NUMBER = (`-18) = 1+8 = (`-9) /|\

FRAGMENTED `-DEATH/DAY # `-NUMBER = (`-19) = 1x9 = (`-9) = (`-99) = `-AGE of `-DEATH for CHARLES

THOMAS MUNGER (AMERICAN BUSINESSMAN, INVESTOR, PHILANTHROPIST; and, ATTORNEY) = (`-99)!!!~'

FROM `-BIRTH-to-DEATH there are (`-34) `-DAYS = RECIPROCAL = (`-43) = 20+23 = `-DEATH/YEAR!!!~'

`-DIVORCED NANCY HUGGINS in (1953) = 19(-)53 = (`-34) = RECIPROCAL = (`-43) = 20+23 = `-DEATH/ YEAR!!!~'

WILLIAM POWELL LEAR (AMERICAN INVENTOR (BATTERY ELIMINATOR) & BUSINESSMAN (FOUNDER of LEARJET) died at the `-AGE of (`-75)!!!~'

`-AGE of `-DEATH = (`-75) = 7x5 = (`-35) = RECIPROCAL = (`-53) = `-BIRTH/DAY # `-NUMBER!!!~'

`-AGE of `-DEATH = (`-75) = 7x5 = (`-35) = FRAGMENTED `-DEATH/DAY # `-NUMBER!!!~'

`-BIRTH/DAY # `-NUMBER = 6+26+19+02 = (`-53) = RECIPROCAL = (`-35) = FRAGMENTED `-DEATH/ DAY # `-NUMBER!!!~'

`-DEATH/DAY = 5/14 = 5 / 1(-)4 = (`-53) = `-BIRTH/DAY # `-NUMBER!!!~'

`-DEATH/DAY # `-NUMBER = 5+14+19+78 = (`-116)!!!~'

(`-116) x (`-2) = (`-232) = Reciprocal-Sequencing-Numerology-RSN!!!~'

FROM `-BIRTH-to-DEATH there are (`-322) `-DAYS = "SWIPE (`-1) to the (`-LEFT)" = (`-232) = Reciprocal-Sequencing-Numerology-RSN!!!~'

(`-116) = 1+1/6 = (`-26) = FRAGMENTED `-BIRTH/DAY # `-NUMBER!!!~'

FRAGMENTED `-BIRTH/DAY # `-NUMBER = 6+2+6+1+9+0+2 = (`-26)!!!~'

(`-26) = FLIP the (`-2) OVER to a (`-7) = (`-76) = `-DIED the `-VERY `-YEAR `-PRIOR at the `-AGE of (`-75)!!!~'

`-BIRTH/YEAR = (1902) = 19x02 = (`-38) x (`-2) = (`-76) = `-DIED the `-VERY `-YEAR `-PRIOR at the `-AGE of (`-75)!!!~'

FRAGMENTED `-DEATH/DAY # `-NUMBER = 5+1+4+1+9+7+8 = (`-35) = RECIPROCAL = (`-53) = `-BIRTH/DAY # `-NUMBER!!!~'

`-BIRTH/YEAR = (1902) = FLIP the (`-2) OVER to a (`-7) = (1907) /|\

`-DEATH/YEAR = (1978) = 19+78 = (`-97)!!!~'

`-BIRTH/DAY = 6/26 = 6+26 = (`-32) = RECIPROCAL = (`-23) = FLIP the (`-2) OVER to a (`-7); FLIP the (`-3) OVER to an (`-8) = (`-78) = `-DEATH/YEAR!!!~'

`-BIRTH/DAY = 6/26 = HALF RECIPROCAL = 6/62 = 6(-)62 = (`-56) = 7x8 = (`-78) = `-DEATH/YEAR!!!~'

`-MARRIED MOYA LEAR in (1942) = 19(-)42 = (`-23) = FLIP the (`-2) OVER to a (`-7); FLIP the (`-3) OVER to an (`-8) = (`-78) = `-DEATH/YEAR!!!~'

`-DEATH/YEAR = (`-78) = 7x8 = (`-56) = RECIPROCAL = (`-65) = WILLIAM POWELL LEAR (AMERICAN INVENTOR (BATTERY ELIMINATOR) & BUSINESSMAN (FOUNDER of LEARJET) was `-BORN in the `-MONTH of (`-6); and, `-DIED in the `-MONTH of (`-5)!!!~'

CHARLES GOODYEAR (AMERICAN SELF-TAUGHT CHEMIST & MANUFACTURING ENGINEER who DEVELOPED VULCANIZED RUBBER) died at the `-AGE of (`-59)!!!~'

`-BIRTH/DAY = 12/29 = (1+2+2) (9) = (`-59) = `-AGE of `-DEATH for CHARLES GOODYEAR (AMERICAN SELF-TAUGHT CHEMIST & MANUFACTURING ENGINEER who DEVELOPED VULCANIZED RUBBER)!!!~'

`-BIRTH/DAY # `-NUMBER = 12+29+18+00 = (`-59) = `-AGE of `-DEATH for CHARLES GOODYEAR (AMERICAN SELF-TAUGHT CHEMIST &

MANUFACTURING ENGINEER who DEVELOPED VULCANIZED RUBBER)!!!~'

`-BIRTH/DAY = 12/29 = RECIPROCAL = 92/21 = 9(-)2 / 2(-)1 = (`-7/1) = `-DEATH/DAY!!!~'

`-BIRTH/DAY = 12/29 = 12 / 2(-)9 = (12/7) = CHARLES GOODYEAR was `-BORN in the `-MONTH of (`-12); and, `-DIED in the `-MONTH of (`-7)!!!~'

`-DEATH/DAY # `-NUMBER = 7+1+18+60 = (`-86) = FLIP the (`-8) OVER to a (`-3) = (`-36) = `-WAS `-MARRIED to CLARISSA BEECHER GOODYEAR for (`-36) `-YEARS!!!~'

FRAGMENTED `-BIRTH/DAY # `-NUMBER = 1+2+2+9+1+8+0+0 = (`-23)!!!~'

FRAGMENTED `-DEATH/DAY # `-NUMBER = 7+1+1+8+6+0 = (`-23)!!!~'

FRAGMENTED `-BIRTH/DAY # `-NUMBER = (`-23) = FRAGMENTED `-DEATH/DAY # `-NUMBER = (`-23)!!!~'

FROM `-BIRTH-to-DEATH there are (`-184) DAYS = CHARLES GOODYEAR was `-BORN in the `-MONTH of (`-12); and, `-DIED in the `-MONTH of (`-7) = (12x7) = (`-84)!!!~'

FORMER FIRST LADY of the UNITED STATES of AMERICA (WIFE of the 39th PRESIDENT/ JIMMY CARTER) (ELEANOR ROSALYNN CARTER) died at the `-AGE of (`-96)!!!~'

(39th `-PRESIDENT) = RECIPROCAL = (`-93) = ELEANOR ROSALYNN CARTER died from `-BIRTH-to-DEATH with (`-93) `-DAYS!!!~'

(365 (-) 93) = (`-272)!!!~

(`-272) = 27x2 = (`-54) = 9x6 = (`-96) = `-AGE of `-DEATH for FORMER FIRST LADY of the UNITED STATES of AMERICA (WIFE of the 39th PRESIDENT/ JIMMY CARTER) (ELEANOR ROSALYNN CARTER) (`-96)!!!~'

`-BIRTH/YEAR = (`-27) = 2(7's) = (`-77) = `-WAS `-MARRIED to FORMER PRESIDENT JIMMY CARTER for (`-77) `-YEARS!!!~'

`-DEATH/DAY = 11/19 = 11 / 1(-)9 = 11/8 = RECIPROCAL = 8/11 = ELEANOR ROSALYNN CARTER was `-BORN in the `-MONTH of (`-8); and, `-DIED in the `-MONTH of (`-11)!!!~'

ELEANOR ROSALYNN CARTER was `-BORN in the `-MONTH of (`-8); and, `-DIED in the `-MONTH of (`-11) = 8/11 = 8x11 = (`-88) = `-BIRTH/DAY = 8/18 = 8(ONE)8!!!~'

`-BIRTH/DAY # `-NUMBER = 8+18+19+27 = (`-72) = "SEE `-ABOVE"!!!~'

`-DEATH/DAY # `-NUMBER = 11+19+20+23 = (`-73)!!!~'

(72+73) = (`-145) = 1x45 = (`-45) = RECIPROCAL = (`-54) = 9x6 = (`-96) = `-AGE of `-DEATH for FORMER FIRST LADY of the UNITED STATES of AMERICA (WIFE of the 39th PRESIDENT/ JIMMY CARTER) (ELEANOR ROSALYNN CARTER) (`-96)!!!~'

`-PARTIAL FRAGMENTED `-BIRTH/DAY # `-NUMBER = 8+1+8+1+9 = (`-27) = "SEE `-ABOVE"!!!~'

FRAGMENTED `-BIRTH/DAY # `-NUMBER = 8+1+8+1+9+2+7 = (`-36) x (`-2) = (`-72) = "SEE `-ABOVE"!!!~'

FRAGMENTED `-DEATH/DAY # `-NUMBER = 1+1+1+9+2+0+2+3 = (`-19)!!!~'

(19) x (`-5) = (`-95) = `-DIED the `-VERY `-YEAR `-AFTERWARD at the `-AGE of (`-96)!!!~'

BIRTH/DAY = 8/18 = 8+18 = (`-26) = 2(6's) = (`-66) = FLIP the (`-6) OVER to a (`-9) = (`-99) = `-AGE of `-HOSPICE `-CARE for `-HER `-HUSBAND `-FORMER PRESIDENT JIMMY CARTER!!!~'

`-BIRTH/DAY = 8/18 = HALF RECIPROCAL = 8/81 = 8+81 = (`-89) = FLIP the (`-8) OVER to a (`-3) = (`-39) = RECIPROCAL = (`-93) = "SEE at the `-TOP / `-ABOVE"!!!~'

`-DEATH/DAY = 11/19 = HALF RECIPROCAL = 11/91 = (9) (1+1+1) = (`-93) = RECIPROCAL = (`-39) = "SEE `-PREVIOUS & `-ABOVE"!!!~'

`-DEATH/DAY = 11/19 = (1+1+1) (9) = (`-39) = RECIPROCAL = (`-93) = "SEE `-PREVIOUS & `-ABOVE"!!!~'

`-PARTIAL `-BIRTH/DAY # `-NUMBER = 8+18+19 = (`-45) = RECIPROCAL = (`-54) = 9x6 = (`-96) = `-AGE of `-DEATH for FORMER FIRST LADY of the UNITED STATES of AMERICA (WIFE of the 39th PRESIDENT/ JIMMY CARTER) (ELEANOR ROSALYNN CARTER) (`-96)!!!~'

`-MARRIED to JIMMY CARTER in (1946) = 19(-)46 = (`-27) = `-BIRTH/YEAR for FORMER FIRST LADY of the UNITED STATES of AMERICA (WIFE of the 39th PRESIDENT/ JIMMY CARTER) (ELEANOR ROSALYNN CARTER)!!!~'

`-BIRTH/YEAR = (1927) = (9) (1(-)2(-)7) = (`-96) = `-AGE of `-DEATH for FORMER FIRST LADY of the UNITED STATES of AMERICA (WIFE of the 39th PRESIDENT/ JIMMY CARTER) (ELEANOR ROSALYNN CARTER)!!!~'

`-BIRTH/YEAR = (1927) = (1x9) (2+7) = (`-99) = `-AGE of `-HOSPICE `-CARE for `-HER `-HUSBAND FORMER

39ᵗʰ/PRESIDENT of the UNITED STATES of AMERICA (JIMMY CARTER) (`-99)!!!~'

17ᵗʰ/PRESIDENT ANDREW JOHNSON died at the `-AGE of (`-66)!!!~'

`-AGE of `-DEATH = (`-66) = 6x6 = (`-36) = RECIPROCAL = (`-63) = `-AGE of `-DEATH of the `-VERY `-NEXT `-18ᵗʰ/ PRESIDENT / ULYSSES S. GRANT!!!~'

`-BIRTH/YEAR = (1808) = 18+08 = (`-26) = 2(6's) = (`-66) = `-AGE of `-DEATH for the 17ᵗʰ/PRESIDENT ANDREW JOHNSON (`-66)!!!~'

`-BIRTH/DAY # `-NUMBER = 12+29+18+08 = (`-67)!!!~'

(`-67) = 6x7 = (`-42) x (`-2) = (`-84) / `-DIVIDED `-by `-HIS `BIRTH/MONTH (`-12) = (`-7) = `-DEATH/MONTH!!!~'

FRAGMENTED `-BIRTH/DAY # `-NUMBER = 1+2+2+9+1+8+0+8 = (`-31) = `-DEATH/DAY!!!~'

`-DEATH/DAY # `-NUMBER = 7+31+18+75 = (`-131) = 1x31 = (`-31) = FRAGMENTED `-BIRTH/DAY # `-NUMBER!!!~'

FRAGMENTED `-DEATH/DAY # `-NUMBER = 7+3+1+1+8+7+5 = (`-32)!!!~'

(`-32) x (`-2) = (`-64) = RECIPROCAL = (`-46) = "SEE `-BELOW"!!!~'

BECAME `-PRESIDENT on (4/15) = 4 / 1+5 = (`-46)!!!~'

`-WAS `-MARRIED to ELIZA MCCARDLE JOHNSON in (1827) = 18+27 = (`-45) = `-BECAME `-PRESIDENT on (4/15) = 45x1 = (`-45)!!!~'

17th/PRESIDENT ANDREW JOHNSON was `-BORN in the `-MONTH of (`-12); and, `-DIED in the `-MONTH of (`-7) = 12/7 = 12x7 = (`-84)!!!~'

(`-214) = 21x4 = (`-84)!!!~'

(84+84) = (`-168) = 1(-)68 = (`-67) = `-BIRTH/DAY # `-NUMBER!!!~'

`-DIED (`-214) `-DAYS from `-BIRTH-to-DEATH = RECIPROCAL = (`-412) /|\ (41)(`-too)

`-BIRTH/DAY = 12+29 = (`-41)!!!~'

(365 (-) 214) = (`-151) = 1x51 = (`-51)!!!~'

PRESIDENTIAL `-TERM `-ENDED in (1869) = 18(-)69 = (`-51)!!!~'

FRED E. WHITE (AMERICAN MUSICIAN & SONGWRITER of "EARTH, WIND; &, FIRE") died at the `-AGE of (`-67)!!!~'

`-DAY of `-BIRTH = (`-13th) = 6+7 = (`-67) = `-AGE of `-DEATH for FRED E. WHITE (AMERICAN MUSICIAN & SONGWRITER of "EARTH, WIND; &, FIRE")!!!~'

`-DIVIDE / FRED E. WHITE'S `-BIRTH/DAY in `-SEGMENTS = (1/1) (3+1+9+5+5)

(1/1) = `-DEATH/DAY!!!~'

(3+1+9+5+5) = (`-23) = `-DEATH/YEAR!!!~'

`-BIRTH/DAY # `-NUMBER = 1+13+19+55 = (`-88) = 8+8 = (`-16) x (`-2) = (`-32) = RECIPROCAL = (`-23) = `-DEATH/YEAR!!!~'

`-BIRTH/DAY = 1/13 = HALF RECIPROCAL = 1/31 = 1+31 = (`-32) = RECIPROCAL = (`-23) = `-DEATH/YEAR!!!~'

`-DEATH/DAY # `-NUMBER = 1+1+20+23 = (`-45)!!!~'

FRAGMENTED `-BIRTH/DAY # `-NUMBER = 1+1+3+1+9+5+5 = (`-25)!!!~'

FRAGMENTED `-DEATH/DAY # `-NUMBER = 1+1+2+0+2+3 = (`-9) = `-WAS in the `-MUSICAL `-GROUP "EARTH, WIND; & FIRE" for (`-9) `-YEARS!!!~'

(25+9) = (`-34) = `-RECIPROCAL = (`-43) = 20+23 = `-DEATH/YEAR!!!~'

`-BIRTH/YEAR = (1955) = 19+55 = (`-74) = `-BECAME `-PART of the `-MUSICAL `-GROUP "EARTH, WIND; & FIRE" in 19(74)!!!~'

`-REVERSE `-LOOKUP on the `-PARTIAL `-BIRTH/ DAY # `-NUMBER = 55(-)19(-)13) = (`-23) = `-DEATH/ YEAR!!!~'

`-BIRTH/DAY = 1/13 = (1+1) (3) = (`-23) = `-DEATH/ YEAR!!!~'

HENRY ALFRED KISSINGER (FORMER UNITED STATES SECRETARY of STATE & NATIONAL SECURITY ADVISOR) died at the `-AGE of (`-100)!!!~'

`-BIRTH/DAY = 5/27 = FLIP the (`-7) OVER to a (`-2) = 52/2 = HALF RECIPROCAL = 25/2 = 25x2 = (`-50) x (`-2) = (`-100) = `-AGE of `-DEATH for HENRY ALFRED KISSINGER (FORMER UNITED STATES SECRETARY of STATE & NATIONAL SECURITY ADVISOR) = (`-100)!!!~'

`-BIRTH/DAY = 5/27 = 5+27 = (`-32) = RECIPROCAL = (`-23) = `-DEATH/YEAR!!!~'

`-BIRTH/DAY # `-NUMBER = 5+27+19+23 = (`-74)!!!~'

`-WAS `-MARRIED to NANCY KISSINGER in 19(74)!!!~'

(`-1974) = 19(-)74 = (`-55) = HENRY ALFRED KISSINGER was `-BORN in the `-MONTH of (`-5); and, `-DIED in the `-MONTH of (`-11) = 5/11 = 5x11 = (`-55)!!!~'

`-DEATH/DAY # `-NUMBER = 11+29+20+23 = (`-83)!!!~'

`-DIVORCED ANN FLEISCHER in (1964) = 19+64 = (`-83)!!!~'

FRAGMENTED `-BIRTH/DAY # `-NUMBER = 5+2+7+1+9+2+3 = (`-29) = `-DAY of `-DEATH = (`-29th)!!!~'

(`-29) = 2(9's) = (`-99) = `-DIED the `-VERY `-NEXT `-YEAR `-AFTERWARD at the `-AGE of (`-100)!!!~'

FRAGMENTED `-DEATH/DAY # `-NUMBER = 1+1+2+9+2+0+2+3 = (`-20) x (`-5) = (`-100) = `-AGE of `-DEATH for HENRY ALFRED KISSINGER (FORMER UNITED STATES SECRETARY of STATE & NATIONAL SECURITY ADVISOR) = (`-100)!!!~'

FROM `-BIRTH-to=DEATH there are (`-179) `-DAYS!!!~'

(365 (-) 179) = (`-186) = "SEE `-BELOW"!!!~'

`-WAS `-MARRIED to ANN FLEISCHER in (1949) = 19+49 = (`-68) = RECIPROCAL = (`-86)!!!~'

`-MARRIAGE `-ENDED to NANCY KISSINGER in (2023) = 20+23 = (`-43) x (`-2) = (`-86)!!!~'

`-NANCY KISSINGER was `-BORN in (`-34) = RECIPROCAL = (`-43) = 20+23 = `-**DEATH/YEAR** for `-HER `-HUSBAND HENRY ALFRED KISSINGER (FORMER UNITED STATES SECRETARY of STATE & NATIONAL SECURITY ADVISOR)!!!~'

`-WAS `-MARRIED to NANCY KISSINGER for (`-49) `-YEARS!!!~'

`-WAS `-FIRST `-MARRIED to ANN FLEISCHER in 19(49)!!!~'

`-DEATH/DAY = 11/29 = RECIPROCAL = 92/11 = (92+1+1) = (`-94) = RECIPROCAL = (`-49)!!!~'

`-DEATH/DAY = 11/29 = (1+1+2) (9) = (`-49) = "SEE `-ALL of the `-ABOVE"!!!~'

SANDRA DAY O'CONNOR (FORMER ASSOCIATE JUSTICE of the SUPREME COURT of the UNITED STATES of AMERICA) died at the `-AGE of (`-93)!!!~'

`-BIRTH/YEAR = (1930) = 1x93+0 = (`-93) = `-AGE of `-DEATH for SANDRA DAY O'CONNOR (FORMER ASSOCIATE JUSTICE of the SUPREME COURT of the UNITED STATES of AMERICA)!!!~'

`-BIRTH/DAY = 3/26 = 3(-)26 = (`-23) = `-DEATH/ YEAR!!!~'

`-BIRTH/DAY = 3/26 = 3+26 = (`-29) = 20+09 = `-MARRIAGE `-ENDED to JOHN JAY O'CONNOR for `-WHEN `-HE had `-DIED of ALZHEIMER'S DISEASE!!!~'

`-BIRTH/DAY = 3/26 = 3+26 = (`-29) = FLIP the (`-2) OVER to a (`-7) = (`-79) = `-AGE of `-DEATH for `-HUSBAND JOHN JAY O'CONNOR!!!~'

HUSBAND JOHN JAY O'CONNOR was `-BORN in (`-1930) just as `-WELL = 1x93+0 = (`-93) = `-AGE of `-DEATH for `-HIS `-WIFE SANDRA DAY O'CONNOR (FORMER ASSOCIATE JUSTICE of the SUPREME COURT of the UNITED STATES of AMERICA)!!!~'

HUSBAND JOHN JAY O'CONNOR died at the `-AGE of (`-79) = 7x9 = (`-63) = FLIP the (`-6) OVER to a (`-9) = (`-93) = `-AGE of `-DEATH for `-HIS `-WIFE SANDRA DAY O'CONNOR (FORMER ASSOCIATE JUSTICE of the SUPREME COURT of the UNITED STATES of AMERICA)!!!~'

`-BIRTH/DAY # `-NUMBER = 3+26+19+30 = (`-78)!!!~'

`-HUSBAND JOHN JAY O'CONNOR `-died at the `-AGE of (`-79)!!!~'

(`-78) = 7x8 = (`-56) = `-DEATH/DAY # `-NUMBER!!!~'

(`-78) = FLIP the (`-7) OVER to a (`-2); FLIP the (`-8) OVER to a (`-3) = (`-23) = `-DEATH/YEAR!!!~'

`-DEATH/DAY # `-NUMBER = 12+1+20+23 = (`-56)!!!~'

FRAGMENTED `-BIRTH/DAY # `-NUMBER = 3+2+6+1+9+3+0 = (`-24)!!!~'

SANDRA DAY O'CONNOR served on The SUPREME COURT for (`-24) `-YEARS!!!~'

(`-24) = 12+12 = "FIRST `-PART of `-DEATH/DAY # `-NUMBER!!!~'

SANDRA DAY O'CONNOR was the `-FIRST `-WOMAN to SERVE on the SUPREME COURT in (`-192) `-YEARS = 1+92 = (`-93) = `-AGE of `-DEATH for SANDRA DAY O'CONNOR (FORMER ASSOCIATE JUSTICE of the SUPREME COURT of the UNITED STATES of AMERICA)!!!~'

FRAGMENTED `-DEATH/DAY # `-NUMBER = 1+2+1+2+0+2+3 = (`-11)!!!~'

(`-11) = 20(-)09 = `-WHEN `-MARRIAGE `-ENDED due to `-HUSBAND JOHN JAY O'CONNOR'S `-DEATH!!!~'

FROM `-BIRTH-to-DEATH there are (`-115) `-DAYS x (`-2) = (`-230) = 23+0 = (`-23) = `-DEATH/YEAR!!!~'

(365 (-) 115) = (`-250) = 25+0 = (`-25) = RECIPROCAL = (`-52) = `-WAS `-FIRST `-MARRIED to JOHN JAY O'CONNOR in (`-52)!!!~'

('-52) = FLIP the ('-2) OVER to a ('-7) = ('-57) = '-THEY were '-MARRIED for ('-57) '-YEARS!!!~'

'-MARRIAGE of ('-57) '-YEARS = RECIPROCAL = ('-75) = 57+75 = ('-132) = 1x32 = ('-32) = RECIPROCAL = ('-23) = '-DEATH/YEAR for SANDRA DAY O'CONNOR (FORMER ASSOCIATE JUSTICE of the SUPREME COURT of the UNITED STATES of AMERICA)!!!~'

ALEXEI ANATOLYEVICH NAVALNY (RUSSIAN OPPOSITION LEADER, LAWYER, ANTI-CORRUPTION ACTIVIST; and, POLITICAL PRISONER) died at the '-AGE of ('-<u>47</u>)!!!~'

'-BIRTH/DAY # '-NUMBER in '-REVERSE = 76(-)19(-)4(-)6 = ('-<u>47</u>) = '-EQUALS = '-HIS '-VERY '-OWN '-AGE of '-DEATH = ('-<u>47</u>)!!!~' '-HE had this '-BIRTH/DAY # '-NUMBER '-HIS '-ENTIRE '-LIFE!!!~'

'-BIRTH/YEAR = ('-76) = 7x6 = ('-42) = RECIPROCAL = ('-24) = '-HIS '-VERY '-OWN '-DEATH/YEAR!!!~'

'-DEATH/DAY = (2/16) = 2(ONE)6 = '-DIED in the '-MONTH of ('-2); and, '-WAS '-BORN in the '-MONTH of ('-6) = (2/6)!!!~'

'-DEATH/DAY # '-NUMBER = 2+16+20+24 = ('-62) = '-WAS '-BORN in the '-MONTH of ('-6); and, '-DIED in the '-MONTH of ('-2) = ('-6/2)!!!~'

`-BIRTH/MONTH = JUNE (`-6) with (`-30) `-DAYS =

(30 (-) 4) – DAY of `-BIRTH = (`-26) = "SEE `-ABOVE & `-BEFORE" for `-DEATH/DAY = RECIPROCAL = (`-62) = `-DEATH/DAY # `-NUMBER!!!~'

`-DEATH/DAY = (2/16) = 2x16 = (`-32) x (`-2) = (`-64) = (6/4) = `-BIRTH/DAY!!!~'

`-BIRTH/YEAR = (1976) = (1+9(-)6) (7) = (`-47) = `-AGE of `-DEATH from `-HIS `-VERY `-OWN `-BIRTH/YEAR!!!~'

`-MARRIED to YULIA NAVALNAYA from 2000 to 2024 = (`-24) = `-DEATH/YEAR!!!~'

`-DAUGHTER DARIA NAVALNAYA was (`-23) `-YEARS of `-AGE at the `-TIME of `-HER `-FATHER'S `-DEATH!!!~' FATHER'S `-AGE of `-DEATH (`-47) = (-) MINUS (-) = DAUGHTER'S `-AGE (`-23) at `-HER `-FATHER'S `-TIME of `-DEATH = (`-24) = `-FATHER / ALEXEI ANATOLYEVICH NAVALNY (RUSSIAN OPPOSITION LEADER, LAWYER, ANTI-CORRUPTION ACTIVIST; and, POLITICAL PRISONER) / `-DEATH/YEAR = (`-24)!!!~'

`-DEATH/DAY = (2/16) = 2x16 = (`-32) = RECIPROCAL = (`-23) = `-DAUGHTER DARIA NAVALNAYA'S `-AGE at the `-TIME of `-HER / `-VERY `-OWN `-FATHER'S `-DEATH!!!~'

`-BIRTH/YEAR = (`-76) = 7x6 = (`-42) = FLIP the (`-2) OVER to a (`-7) = (`-47) = `-HIS `-VERY `-OWN `-AGE of `-DEATH for ALEXEI ANATOLYEVICH NAVALNY (RUSSIAN OPPOSITION LEADER, LAWYER, ANTI-CORRUPTION ACTIVIST; and, POLITICAL PRISONER) from `-HIS `-VERY `-OWN `-BIRTH/YEAR!!!~'

`-DEATH/DAY = (2/16) = FLIP the (`-2) OVER to a (`-7) = (7/16) = (7) (1x6) = (`-76) = `-BIRTH/YEAR for ALEXEI ANATOLYEVICH NAVALNY (RUSSIAN OPPOSITION LEADER, LAWYER, ANTI-CORRUPTION ACTIVIST; and, POLITICAL PRISONER) from `-HIS `-VERY `-OWN `-DEATH/DAY!!!~'

NORMAN MILTON LEAR (AMERICAN SCREENWRITER, CREATOR; &, PRODUCER) died at the `-AGE of (`-101)!!!~'

`-BIRTH/DAY # `-NUMBER = 7+27+19+22 = (`-75)!!!~'

(`-75) = RECIPROCAL = (`-57) = 5' 7" in `-HEIGHT for NORMAN MILTON LEAR (AMERICAN SCREENWRITER & PRODUCER)!!!~'

`-MARRIED FRANCES LEAR in (1956) = 19+56 = (`-75) = `-BIRTH/DAY # `-NUMBER!!!~'

`-A `-COMMON `-PATTERN!!!~'

`-HEIGHT = 5' 7" = 5x7 = (`-35) = RECIPROCAL = (`-53)!!!~'

`-PARTIAL `-BIRTH/DAY # `-NUMBER = 7+27+19 = (`-53) X TIMES (`-2) = (`-106) = 10x6 = (`-60)!!!~'

`-WAS `-MARRIED to LYN LEAR in (1987) = 19+87 = (`-106) = 10x6 = (`-60)!!!~'

`-DEATH/DAY # `-NUMBER = 12+5+20+23 = (`-60)!!!~'

(60) / `-DIVIDED by (`-2) = (`-30) = FRAGMENTED `-BIRTH/DAY # `-NUMBER!!!~'

FRAGMENTED `-BIRTH/DAY # `-NUMBER = 7+2+7+1+9+2+2 = (`-30)!!!~'

`-WAS `-MARRIED to `-FRANCES `-LEAR for (`-30) `-YEARS (1956-1986)!!!~'

FRAGMENTED `-BIRTH/DAY # `-NUMBER = (`-30) = 5x6 = (`-56) = 8x7 = (`-87) = WAS `-MARRIED to LYN LEARS in 19(87)!!!~'

`-WAS `-MARRIED to `-FRANCES `-LEAR in (`-56)!!!~'

`-BIRTH/DAY = 7/27 = HALF RECIPROCAL = 7/72 = 7(-)72 = (`-65) = RECIPROCAL = (`-56) = "SEE `-IMMEDIATELY `-ABOVE"!!!~'

FRAGMENTED `-DEATH/DAY # `-NUMBER = 1+2+5+2+0+2+3 = (`-15)!!!~'

('-15) X TIMES ('-2) = ('-30) = FRAGMENTED '-BIRTH/
DAY # '-NUMBER!!!~'

'-BIRTH/DAY = 7/27 = 7+27 = ('-34)!!!~'

('-34) = RECIPROCAL = ('-43) = 20+23 = '-DEATH/
YEAR!!!~'

FROM '-BIRTH-to-DEATH there are ('-234) '-DAYS =
PROPHETIC-LINEAR-PROGRESSION-PLP!!!~'

('-131) = 13+1 = ('-14) = RECIPROCAL = ('-41)!!!~'

(365 (-) 234) = ('-131) '-DAYS from '-BIRTH-to-DEATH in
the '-OTHER '-DIRECTION = 1+3 / 1 = ('-41)!!!~'

'-BIRTH/YEAR = (1922) = 19+22 = ('-41)!!!~'

('-41)   X   TIMES   ('-3)   =   ('-123)   =
PROPHETIC-LINEAR-PROGRESSION-PLP!!!~'

'-FORMER '-WIFE FRANCES LEAR was '-BORN in the
'-MONTH of ('-7); and, '-DIED in the '-MONTH of ('-9)
= ('-79) = RECIPROCAL = ('-97)!!!~'

'-BIRTH/DAY = 7/27 = HALF RECIPROCAL = 7/72 =
7+72 = ('-79) = RECIPROCAL = ('-97)!!!~'

'-BIRTH/DAY = 7/27 = 7+2 / 7 = ('-97) = 9x7 = ('-63) =
RECIPROCAL = ('-36) = '-WAS '-MARRIED to LYN
LEAR for ('-36) '-YEARS (1987-2023)!!!~'

`-DIVORCED CHARLOTTE LEAR in (1947) = 19+47 = (`-66) = 6x6 = (`-36)!!!~'

`-WAS `-FIRST `-MARRIED to CHARLOTTE LEAR in 19(43) = (`-43) = 20+23 = `-DEATH/YEAR of NORMAN MILTON LEAR (AMERICAN SCREENWRITER & PRODUCER)!!!~'

`-FORMER `-WIFE FRANCES LEAR'S `-BIRTH/DAY # `-NUMBER = 7+14+19+23 = (`-63) = RECIPROCAL = (`-36)!!!~'

`-FORMER `-WIFE FRANCES LEAR was `-BORN in the `-YEAR of (`-23) = `-DEATH/YEAR (`-23) of `-HER `-FORMER `-HUSBAND NORMAN MILTON LEAR (AMERICAN SCREENWRITER & PRODUCER)!!!~'

NORMAN MILTON LEAR'S `-PARTIAL `-DEATH/ DAY # `-NUMBER = 12+5+20 = (`-37) = RECIPROCAL = (`-73)!!!~'

`-FORMER `-WIFE FRANCES LEAR `-LIVED TO BE (`-73) `-YEARS of `-AGE = FLIP the (`-7) OVER to a (`-2) = (`-23) = `-DEATH/YEAR of `-HER `-FORMER `-HUSBAND NORMAN MILTON LEAR (AMERICAN SCREENWRITER & PRODUCER)!!!~'

`-FORMER `-WIFE FRANCES LEAR `-DEATH/DAY # `-NUMBER = 9+30+19+96 = (`-154)!!!~'

('-154) (-) MINUS (-) ('-63) = BIRTH/DAY # '-NUMBER = ('-91) = RECIPROCAL = ('-19) = NORMAN MILTON LEAR was '-BORN in the '-MONTH of ('-7); and, '-DIED in the '-MONTH of ('-12) = (7/12) = 7+12 = ('-19)!!!~' (HUSBAND & WIVES are '-ALL '-LINKED '-TOGETHER)!!!~' "A COMMON '-PATTERN"!!!~'

(7/12) = 7x12 = ('-84) = 8x4 = ('-32) = RECIPROCAL = ('-23) = '-DEATH/YEAR for NORMAN MILTON LEAR (AMERICAN SCREENWRITER, CREATOR; &, PRODUCER)!!!~'

'-DIVORCED FRANCES LEAR in 19(86)!!!~'

'-DEATH/YEAR = 20+23 = ('-43) X TIMES ('-2) = ('-86)!!!~'

'-MARRIED LYN LEAR in (1987) = 19(-)87 = ('-68) = RECIPROCAL = ('-86)!!!~'

FROM '-BIRTH-to-DEATH there are ('-234) '-DAYS for NORMAN MILTON LEAR = 2x34 = ('-68) = RECIPROCAL = ('-86)!!!~'

AMERICAN ACTOR RYAN O'NEAL died at the '-AGE of ('-82)!!!~'

`-BIRTH/YEAR = (`-41) X TIMES (`-2) = (`-82) = `-AGE of `-DEATH for AMERICAN ACTOR RYAN O'NEAL (`-82)!!!~'

`-DEATH/DAY = 12/8 = RECIPROCAL = 8/21 = 82x1 = (`-82) = `-AGE of `-DEATH for AMERICAN ACTOR RYAN O'NEAL (`-82)!!!~'

`-PARTIAL `-BIRTH/DAY # `-NUMBER = 4+20+19 = (`-43) = 20+23 = `-DEATH/YEAR for AMERICAN ACTOR RYAN O'NEAL!!!~'

`-BIRTH/DAY # `-NUMBER = 4+20+19+41 = (`-84)!!!~'

RYAN O'NEAL was `-BORN in the `-MONTH of (`-4); and, `-DIED in the `-MONTH of (`-12) = (4/12) = 4x12 = (`-48) = RECIPROCAL = (`-84) = `-BIRTH/DAY # `-NUMBER!!!~'

(`-84) = 8x4 = (`-32) = FLIP the (`-3) OVER to an (`-8) = (`-82) = `-AGE of `-DEATH for AMERICAN ACTOR RYAN O'NEAL (`-82)!!!~'

`-DEATH/DAY # `-NUMBER = 12+8+20+23 = (`-63) = "SEE `-BELOW"!!!~'

FRAGMENTED `-BIRTH/DAY # `-NUMBER = 4+2+0+1+9+4+1 = (`-21) = RECIPROCAL = (`-12) = `-DEATH/MONTH!!!~'

FRAGMENTED `-DEATH/DAY # `-NUMBER = 1+2+8+2+0+2+3 = (`-18)!!!~'

FROM `-BIRTH-to-DEATH there are (`-133) `-DAYS = 1(-)3 / 3 = (`-23) = `-DEATH/YEAR for AMERICAN ACTOR RYAN O'NEAL!!!~'

(365 (-) 133) = (`-232) `-DAYS from `-BIRTH-to-DEATH going in the `-OTHER `-DIRECTION = (`-232) = RECIPROCAL-SEQUENCING-NUMEROLOGY-RSN!!!~'

`-WAS `-MARRIED to JOANNA MOORE in (1963) = 19+63 = (`-82) = `-AGE of `-DEATH for AMERICAN ACTOR RYAN O'NEAL (`-82)!!!~'

`-WAS `-MARRIED to LEIGH TAYLOR-YOUNG from (1967-1974) = (`-7) `-YEARS of `-MARRIAGE!!!~'

`-WAS `-MARRIED to JOANNA MOORE from (1963-1967) = (`-4) `-YEARS of `-MARRIAGE!!!~'

`-YEARS of `-MARRIAGES = 7 & 4 = `-DIVORCED LEIGH TAYLOR-YOUNG in 19(74)!!!~'

`-FORMER `-WIFE JOANNA MOORE `-BIRTH/DAY # `-NUMBER = 11+10+19+34 = (`-74) = "SEE `-ABOVE & `-BELOW"!!!~'

'-FORMER '-WIFE JOANNA MOORE '-BIRTH/YEAR = ('-34) = RECIPROCAL = ('-43) = 20+23 = '-DEATH/YEAR for '-HER FORMER HUSBAND RYAN O'NEAL!!!~'

'-MARRIED LEIGH TAYLOR-YOUNG in 19(67) & '-DIVORCED JOANNA MOORE in 19(67)!!!~'

('-1967) = 19(-)67 = ('-48) = RECIPROCAL = ('-84) = '-BIRTH/DAY # '-NUMBER for AMERICAN ACTOR RYAN O'NEAL ('-84)!!!~'

'-MARRIED JOANNA MOORE in 19(63) = ('-63) = '-DEATH/DAY # '-NUMBER for AMERICAN ACTOR RYAN O'NEAL ('-63)!!!~'

'-FORMER '-WIFE JOANNA MOORE '-DEATH/YEAR = ('-97) = 9x7 = ('-63)!!!~'

'-FORMER '-WIFE JOANNA MOORE '-DEATH/YEAR = (1997) = 19(-)97 = ('-78) = FLIP the ('-7) OVER to a ('-2); FLIP the ('-8) OVER to a ('-3) = ('-23) = DEATH/YEAR of '-HER '-FORMER '-HUSBAND / AMERICAN ACTOR RYAN O'NEAL!!!~'

'-DIVORCED LEIGH TAYLOR-YOUNG in (1974) = 19+74 = ('-93) = FLIP the ('-9) OVER to a ('-6) = ('-63) = '-DEATH/DAY # '-NUMBER for AMERICAN ACTOR RYAN O'NEAL ('-63)!!!~'

'-DAUGHTER TATUM O'NEAL was '-BORN in 19(63) = '-BIRTH/YEAR = ('-63) = '-DEATH/DAY # '-NUMBER for `-HER `-FATHER / AMERICAN ACTOR RYAN O'NEAL (`-63)!!!~'

`-DAUGHTER TATUM O'NEAL was `-BORN in (1963) = 19+63 = (`-82) = `-AGE of `-DEATH for `-HER `-FATHER / AMERICAN ACTOR RYAN O'NEAL (`-82)!!!~'

`-DAUGHTER TATUM O'NEAL `-REVERSE `-LOOKUP on `-HER `-BIRTH/DAY # `-NUMBER = 63(-)19(-)5(-)11 = (`-28) = RECIPROCAL = (`-82) = `-AGE of `-DEATH for `-HER `-FATHER / AMERICAN ACTOR RYAN O'NEAL (`-82)!!!~'

AMERICAN ACTOR ANDRE KEITH BRAUGHER died at the `-AGE of (`-61)!!!~'

`-BIRTH/YEAR = (1962) = 19(-)62 = (`-43) = 20+23 = `-DEATH/YEAR!!!~'

`-BIRTH/YEAR = (`-62) = `-DIED the `-VERY `-YEAR `-PRIOR at the `-AGE of (`-61)!!!~'

`-DEATH/DAY = 12/11 = 12+11 = (`-23) = `-DEATH/YEAR!!!~'

`-BIRTH/DAY # `-NUMBER = 7+1+19+62 = (`-89)!!!~'

(89 (-) 66) = (`-23) = `-DEATH/YEAR for AMERICAN ACTOR ANDRE KEITH BRAUGHER!!!~'

`-DEATH/DAY # `-NUMBER = 12+11+20+23 = (`-66)!!!~'

(`-66) = 6x6 = (`-36) = FLIP the (`-3) OVER to an (`-8); FLIP the (`-6) OVER to a (`-9) = (`-89) = `-BIRTH/DAY # `-NUMBER!!!~'

FRAGMENTED `-BIRTH/DAY # `-NUMBER = 7+1+1+9+6+2 = (`-26) = RECIPROCAL = (`-62) = `-BIRTH/ YEAR!!!~'

FRAGMENTED `-DEATH/DAY # `-NUMBER = 1+2+1+1+2+0+2+3 = (`-12) = 6x2 = (`-62) = `-BIRTH/ YEAR!!!~'

FROM `-BIRTH-to-DEATH there are (`-202) `-DAYS!!!~'

(365 (-) 202) = (`-163) = RECIPROCAL = (`-361) = "THREE (`-3) `-TIMES for `-EMPHASIS on (`-61)" = `-AGE of `-DEATH for AMERICAN ACTOR ANDRE KEITH BRAUGHER!!!~'

(365 (-) 202) = (`-163) = (16x3) = (`-48) = RECIPROCAL = (`-84) = 7x12 = AMERICAN ACTOR ANDRE KEITH BRAUGHER was `-BORN in the `-MONTH of (`-7); and, `-DIED in the `-MONTH of (`-12)!!!~'

`-MARRIED AMI BRABSON in (`-91) = FLIP the (`-9) OVER to a (`-6) = (`-61) = `-AGE of `-DEATH for AMERICAN ACTOR ANDRE KEITH BRAUGHER (`-61)!!!~'

'-MARRIED to AMI BRABSON for ('-32) '-YEARS = RECIPROCAL = ('-23) = '-DEATH/YEAR for AMERICAN ACTOR ANDRE KEITH BRAUGHER!!!~'

'-SON JOHN WESLEY BRAUGHER was '-BORN in (2003) = 20+03 = ('-23) = '-DEATH/YEAR of '-HIS '-FATHER / AMERICAN ACTOR ANDRE KEITH BRAUGHER!!!~'

'-SON MICHAEL BRAUGHER was '-BORN in (1992) = 19(-)92 = ('-73) = FLIP the ('-7) OVER to a ('-2) = ('-23) = '-DEATH/YEAR of '-HIS '-FATHER / AMERICAN ACTOR ANDRE KEITH BRAUGHER!!!~'

'-SON ISAIAH BRAUGHER was '-BORN in (1996) = 19+96 = ('-115) x ('-2) = ('-230) = 23+0 = ('-23) = '-DEATH/ YEAR of '-HIS '-FATHER / AMERICAN ACTOR ANDRE KEITH BRAUGHER!!!~'

'-AGES at '-TIME of '-DEATH of their '-FATHER / ANDRE KEITH BRAUGHER = '-SON JOHN WESLEY BRAUGHER ('-20), '-SON MICHAEL BRAUGHER ('-31); and, '-SON ISAIAH BRAUGHER ('-27)!!!~'

(20+31+27) = ('-78) = FLIP the ('-7) OVER to a ('-2); FLIP the ('-8) OVER to a ('-3) = ('-23) = DEATH/YEAR of '-THEIR '-FATHER / AMERICAN ACTOR ANDRE KEITH BRAUGHER!!!~'

AMERICAN ACTOR ANDRE KEITH BRAUGHER was '-BORN in the '-MONTH of ('-7); and, '-DIED in the

`-MONTH of (`-12) = (7/12) = 7x12 = (`-84) = 8x4 = (`-32) = RECIPROCAL = (`-23) = `-DEATH/YEAR!!!~'

AMERICAN ACTOR ANDRE KEITH BRAUGHER was `-BORN in the `-MONTH of (`-7); and, `-DIED in the `-MONTH of (`-12) = (7/12) = 7x12 = (`-84) = {84 (-) MINUS (-) 61 - AGE of `-DEATH} = (`-23) = `-DEATH/YEAR!!!~'

AMERICAN BAPTIST MINISTER AND ACTIVIST MARTIN LUTHER KING JR. died at the AGE of 39!!!~'

DEATH/YEAR = 19/68 = (19 + 68) = 87 = RECIPROCAL = 78 = AGE of DEATH for WIFE AMERICAN AUTHOR, ACTIVIST, CIVIL RIGHTS LEADER CORETTA SCOTT KING!!!~'

BIRTH/YEAR = 19/29 = (19 + 29) = 48 = (4 x 8) = (`-32) = `-HIS / FRAGMENTED DEATH/DAY # `-NUMBER!!!~'

BIRTHDAY # `-NUMBER = 1/15/19/29 = 1 + 15 + 19 + 29 = 64

(`-64 / `-DIVIDED by (`-2)) = (`-32) = `-HIS / FRAGMENTED DEATH/DAY # `-NUMBER!!!~'

DEATHDAY # `-NUMBER = 4/4/19/68 = 4 + 4 + 19 + 68 = 95

(64/95) = (6 – 9) (4 + 5) = 39 = AGE of DEATH for AMERICAN BAPTIST MINISTER AND ACTIVIST MARTIN LUTHER KING JR.!!!~'

(64 + 95) = 159 = (1 x 59) = 59 = RECIPROCAL = 95 = DEATH/DAY # '-NUMBER!!!~'

(95 (-) 64) = 31 = WIFE'S DEATH/DAY = (1/30) = (1 + 30) = ('-31) = & = SON / DEXTER KING'S '-BIRTH/DAY = (1/30) = 1+30 = ('-31)!!!~'

FRAGMENTED DEATHDAY # '-NUMBER for MARTIN LUTHER KING, JR. = 4 + 4 + 1 + 9 + 6 + 8 = ('-32)!!!~'

DEATH/MONTH for MARTIN LUTHER KING JR. = APRIL = 30 DAYS!!!~'

(30 (-) 4) – (DAY of DEATH) = ('-26) = RECIPROCAL = ('-62) = '-AGE of '-DEATH for '-SON / DEXTER KING!!!~'

DEATH/MONTH for MARTIN LUTHER KING JR. = APRIL = 30 DAYS!!!~'

(30 (-) 4) – (DAY of DEATH) = 26 = "FLIP EVERY ('-6) OVER to a ('-9)" = 29 = BIRTH/YEAR for MARTIN LUTHER KING JR.!!!~'

WAS '-MARRIED to CORETTA SCOTT KING from 1953 to 1968 = 15 YEARS = BIRTH/DAY for MARTIN LUTHER KING JR. = 1/15 = (1 x 15) = 15!!!~'

`-MARRIED in (19/53) = (19 + 53) = 72 = RECIPROCAL = 27 = (3 X 9) = AGE of DEATH for AMERICAN BAPTIST MINISTER AND ACTIVIST MARTIN LUTHER KING JR.!!!~'

`-MARRIED in (19/53) = (19 + 53) = 72 = RECIPROCAL = 27 = "SEE `-RIGHT `-BELOW"!!!~'

AMERICAN AUTHOR, ACTIVIST, CIVIL RIGHTS LEADER; AND, WIFE of MARTIN LUTHER KING JR. CORETTA SCOTT KING died at the AGE of 78!!!~'

`-DAY of `-BIRTH (`-27$^{th}$) = YEAR of `-BIRTH = (`-27)!!!~'

FROM BIRTH-TO-DEATH there are 79 DAYS for MARTIN LUTHER KING JR. = WIFE CORETTA SCOTT KING `-DIED within `-HER (79th) YEAR of EXISTENCE!!!~'

(365 (-) 79) = 286 = (2 x 86) = 172 = (1 x 72) = 72 = RECIPROCAL = 27 = (3 X 9) = AGE of DEATH for AMERICAN BAPTIST MINISTER AND ACTIVIST MARTIN LUTHER KING JR. = & = `-ALSO, SEE `-JUST `-RIGHT `-ABOVE"!!!~'

BIRTH/YEAR = 19/29 = (1 + 2) (99) = (3) (99) = AGE of DEATH for AMERICAN BAPTIST MINISTER AND ACTIVIST MARTIN LUTHER KING JR.!!!~'

BIRTH/YEAR = 19/29 = (9) (1 + 2 + 9) = (9) (12) = (9) (1 + 2) = (`-93) = RECIPROCAL = (`-39) = AGE of DEATH for AMERICAN BAPTIST MINISTER AND ACTIVIST MARTIN LUTHER KING JR.!!!~'

`-BIRTH/YEAR = (`-29) = RECIPROCAL = (`-92) = FLIP the (`-9) over to a (`-6) = (`-62) = `-AGE of `-DEATH for `-SON / DEXTER KING!!!~'

DEATH/YEAR = 19/68 = (19 – 68) = 49 = (4 x 9) = 36 = "FLIP EVERY (`-6) OVER to a (`-9)" = 39 = AGE of DEATH for AMERICAN BAPTIST MINISTER AND ACTIVIST MARTIN LUTHER KING JR.!!!~'

DEATH/YEAR for MARTIN LUTHER KING JR. = 19/68 = (19 + 68) = 87 = RECIPROCAL = 78 = AGE of DEATH for WIFE AMERICAN AUTHOR, ACTIVIST, CIVIL RIGHTS LEADER CORETTA SCOTT KING!!!~'

AMERICAN AUTHOR, ACTIVIST, CIVIL RIGHTS LEADER; AND, WIFE of MARTIN LUTHER KING JR. CORETTA SCOTT KING died at the AGE of 78!!!~'

`-DAY of `-BIRTH (`-27th) = YEAR of `-BIRTH = (`-27)!!!~'

BIRTH/DAY = 4/27 (+) DEATH/DAY = 1/30 /|\ (4 + 27 + 1 + 30) = 62 = RECIPROCAL = 26 = DEATH/YEAR = (20 + 06) = (`-26) = RECIPROCAL = (`-62) = "SEE `-RIGHT `-BELOW"!!!~'

BIRTH/DAY = 4/27 (+) DEATH/DAY = 1/30 /|\ (4 + 27 + 1 + 30) = 62 = `-AGE of `-DEATH for `-HER `-VERY `-OWN `-SON / DEXTER KING!!!~' CORETTA SCOTT KING died on `-HER `-SON / DEXTER KING'S `-BIRTH/DAY = (1/30)!!!~'

CORETTA SCOTT KING'S `-BIRTH/DAY = 4/27 = HALF RECIPROCAL = 4/72 = 4(-)72 = (`-68) = `-YEAR of `-DEATH for `-HER `-VERY `-OWN `-HUSBAND / MARTIN LUTHER KING JR.!!!~'

BIRTHDAY # `-NUMBER = 4/27/19/27 = 4 + 27 + 19 + 27 = 77

BIRTHDAY # `-NUMBER = 77 = (7 x 7) = 49 = (19 – 68) = DEATH/YEAR of `-HER `-VERY `-OWN `-HUSBAND AMERICAN BAPTIST MINISTER AND ACTIVIST MARTIN LUTHER KING JR.!!!~'

SON / DEXTER KING `-DIED (`-8) DAYS `-AWAY from `-TURNING (`-63) = (`-8) = 6+2 = (`-62) = `-AGE of `-DEATH for `-SON / DEXTER KING!!!~'

(`-63) = RECIPROCAL = (`-36) = FLIP the (`-6) OVER to a (`-9) = (`-39) = `-AGE of `-DEATH for `-HIS `-VERY `-OWN `-FATHER / MARTIN LUTHER KING JR.!!!~'

SON / DEXTER KING `-DIED (`-357) DAYS from `-BIRTH-to-DEATH!!!~'

DEATHDAY # `-NUMBER for CORETTA SCOTT KING = 1/30/20/06 = 1 + 30 + 20 + 06 = 57

(77 + 57) = 134 = (1 + 34) = 35 = RECIPROCAL = 53 = WAS `-MARRIED in (`-53)!!!~'

BIRTH/DAY for CORETTA SCOTT KING = 4/27 = (4 + 27) = 31 = DEATH/DAY = 1/30 = (1 + 30) = 31 = SON / DEXTER KING'S `-BIRTH/DAY = (1/30) = 1+30 = (`-31)!!!~'

(31 + 31) = (`-62) = `-AGE of `-DEATH for `-SON / DEXTER KING!!!~'

SON / DEXTER KING'S FRAGMENTED `-DEATH/ DAY # `-NUMBER = 1+2+2+2+0+2+4 = (`-13) = `-WAS `-MARRIED to LEAH WEBER in the `-CALENDAR `-YEAR of (`-13) = RECIPROCAL = (`-31) = 1+30 = `-HIS `-VERY `-OWN `-BIRTH/DAY!!!~'

(31 + 31) = (`-62) = `-AGE of `-DEATH for `-SON / DEXTER KING!!!~'

BIRTH/MONTH for CORETTA SCOTT KING = APRIL = 30 DAYS!!!~'

(30 (-) 27) – (DAY of BIRTH) = 3 = DEATH/DAY = 1/30 = (1 x 3 + 0) = 3

FRAGMENTED BIRTHDAY # `-NUMBER = 4 + 2 + 7 + 1 + 9 + 2 + 7 = (`-32)

FRAGMENTED BIRTH/DAY # `-NUMBER = (`-32) = RECIPROCAL = (`-23) = "FLIP EVERY (`-2) OVER to a (`-7)"; "FLIP EVERY (`-3) OVER to an (`-8)" = (`-78) = `-HER `-VERY `-OWN `-AGE of DEATH for AMERICAN AUTHOR, ACTIVIST, CIVIL RIGHTS LEADER; AND, WIFE of MARTIN LUTHER KING JR. CORETTA SCOTT KING from `-HER `-VERY `-OWN `-FRAGMENTED `-BIRTH/DAY # `-NUMBER!!!~'

FRAGMENTED BIRTH/DAY # `-NUMBER = (`-32) = FRAGMENTED `-DEATH/DAY # `-NUMBER = (`-32) = of `-HER `-VERY `-OWN `-HUSBAND AMERICAN BAPTIST MINISTER AND ACTIVIST MARTIN LUTHER KING JR.!!!~'

(`-32) = RECIPROCAL = (`-23)!!!~'

SON / DEXTER KING `-LIVED (`-23) `-YEARS `-LONGER than `-HIS `-FATHER / MARTIN LUTHER KING JR.!!!~'

SON / DEXTER KING'S `-DEATH/DAY = 1/22 = 1+22 = (`-23)!!!~'

SON / DEXTER KING `-DIED (`-16) `-YEARS `-YOUNGER than `-HIS `-MOTHER!!!~'

(`-16) = 4x4 = (`-4/4) = `-DEATH/DAY of `-HIS `-VERY `-OWN `-FATHER / MARTIN LUTHER KING JR.!!!~'

(`-16) = RECIPROCAL = (`-61) = SON / DEXTER KING'S `-BIRTH/YEAR!!!~'

FRAGMENTED DEATHDAY # `-NUMBER for CORETTA SCOTT KING = 1 + 3 + 0 + 2 + 0 + 0 + 6 = 12

FRAGMENTED DEATH/DAY # `-NUMBER = 12 = (3 + 9) = AGE of DEATH for `-HER `-VERY `-OWN `-HUSBAND AMERICAN BAPTIST MINISTER AND ACTIVIST MARTIN LUTHER KING JR.!!!~'

(32 + 12) = 4/4 = DEATH/DAY of `-HER `-VERY `-OWN ` HUSBAND AMERICAN BAPTIST MINISTER AND ACTIVIST MARTIN LUTHER KING JR.!!!~'

(32 + 12) = (3 + 2) (1 + 2) = 53 = YEAR of `-MARRIAGE (`-53)!!!~'

WAS `-MARRIED to MARTIN LUTHER KING JR. from 1953 to 1968 = 15 YEARS = BIRTH/DAY of HUSBAND = 1/15 = (1 x 15) = 15!!!~'

`-MARRIED in (19/53) = (19 + 53) = 72 = RECIPROCAL = 27 = (3 X 9) = AGE of DEATH for HUSBAND AMERICAN BAPTIST MINISTER AND ACTIVIST MARTIN LUTHER KING JR.!!!~'

FROM BIRTH-TO-DEATH there are (`-87) DAYS for CORETTA SCOTT KING = RECIPROCAL = (`-78) = AGE of DEATH for AMERICAN AUTHOR, ACTIVIST, CIVIL RIGHTS LEADER; AND, WIFE of MARTIN LUTHER KING JR. CORETTA SCOTT KING!!!~'

(365 (-) 87) = 2(78) = (27 + 8) = 35 = RECIPROCAL = 53
= WAS `-MARRIED in (`-53)!!!~'

SON / DEXTER KING was `-BORN in (1961) = 19(-)61 =
(`-42) = RECIPROCAL = (`-24) = `-HIS `-VERY `-OWN
`-DEATH/YEAR!!!~'

SON / DEXTER KING'S FRAGMENTED `-BIRTH/
DAY # `-NUMBER = 1+3+0+1+9+6+1 = (`-21) = X TIMES
(`-2) = (`-42) = RECIPROCAL = (`-24) = `-HIS `-VERY
`-OWN `-DEATH/YEAR!!!~'

SON / DEXTER KING'S `-DEATH/DAY # `-NUMBER =
1+22+20+24 = (`-67) = FLIP the (`-7) OVER to (`-2) = (`-62)
= `-HIS `-VERY `-OWN `-AGE of `-DEATH!!!~'

SON / DEXTER KING'S `-BIRTH/YEAR = (1961) = (6)
(1+9+1) = (6) (11) = (6) (1+1) = (`-62) = `-HIS `-VERY `-OWN
`-AGE of `-DEATH!!!~'

(`-ALL of this `-FAMILY is `-INTERTWINED as `-ALL the
`-REST of `-US are with `-ABSOLUTE `-CERTAINTY-)!!!~'

(SEE `-ONE of `-MY other (`-13) `-BOOKS `-ENTITLED =
"DO YOU `-BELIEVE in `-GOD??? IS DESTINY REAL???"
for `-FURTHER `-LAYOUTS on the `-FAMILIES)!!!~'

AMERICAN ACTOR, DIRECTOR; and, AMERICAN
FOOTBALL LINEBACKER (CARL WEATHERS)

(ROCKY/PREDATOR/STAR WARS) died AT the AGE of (`-76)!!!~'

(`-76) = 7x6 = (`-42) = RECIPROCAL = (`-24) = `-HIS `-VERY `-OWN `-DEATH/YEAR!!!~'

`-BIRTH/YEAR = (`-48) / `-DIVIDED by (`-2) = (`-24) = `-HIS `-VERY `-OWN `-DEATH/YEAR!!!~'

`-BIRTH/YEAR = (`-48) = RECIPROCAL = (`-84) = `-WAS `-MARRIED to RHONA UNSELL in the `-CALENDAR `-YEAR of (`-84)!!!~'

`-BIRTH/DAY = 1/14 = RECIPROCAL = 41/1 = 41+1 = (`-42) = 7x6 = (`-76) = `-HIS `-VERY `-OWN `-AGE of `-DEATH for AMERICAN ACTOR, DIRECTOR; and, AMERICAN FOOTBALL LINEBACKER (CARL WEATHERS)!!!~'

`-DIVORCED RHONA UNSELL in (2006) = 20+06 = (`-26) = FLIP the (`-2) OVER to a (`-7) = (`-76) = `-HIS `-VERY `-OWN `-AGE of `-DEATH for AMERICAN ACTOR, DIRECTOR; and, AMERICAN FOOTBALL LINEBACKER (CARL WEATHERS)!!!~'

`-HEIGHT = 6' 2" = FLIP the (`-2) OVER to a (`-7) = (`-67) = 19+48 = `-HIS `-VERY `-OWN `-BIRTH/YEAR!!!~'

`-HEIGHT = 6' 2" = FLIP the (`-2) OVER to a (`-7) = (`-67) = RECIPROCAL = (`-76) = `-HIS `-VERY `-OWN `-AGE of `-DEATH for AMERICAN ACTOR, DIRECTOR;

and, AMERICAN FOOTBALL LINEBACKER (CARL WEATHERS)!!!~'

`-BIRTH/YEAR = (1948) = 19+48 = (`-67) = RECIPROCAL = (`-76) = `-HIS `-VERY `-OWN `-AGE of `-DEATH for AMERICAN ACTOR, DIRECTOR; and, AMERICAN FOOTBALL LINEBACKER (CARL WEATHERS)!!!~'

`-BIRTH/DAY = 1/14 = RECIPROCAL = 41/1 = 41+1 = (`-42) = RECIPROCAL = (`-24) = `-HIS `-VERY `-OWN `-DEATH/YEAR!!!~'

`-BIRTH/DAY = 1/14 = 1(-)14 = (`-13) = 7+6 = (`-76) = `-HIS `-VERY `-OWN `-AGE of `-DEATH for AMERICAN ACTOR, DIRECTOR; and, AMERICAN FOOTBALL LINEBACKER (CARL WEATHERS)!!!~'

`-DIED in the `-MONTH of (`-2); and, `-WAS `-BORN in the `-MONTH of (`-1) = `-DEATH/DAY = 2/1 / (!!!~')

`-BIRTH/DAY # `-NUMBER = 1 + 14 + 19 + 48 = (`-82)!!!~'

FRAGMENTED `-BIRTH/DAY # `-NUMBER = 1 + 1 + 4 + 1 + 9 + 4 + 8 = (`-28)!!!~'

(82 (-) 28) = (`-54) = 19(-)73 = `-YEAR `-FIRST `-MARRIED to MARY ANN CASTLE!!!~'

`-DIVORCED MARY ANN CASTLE in (`-83) = 8x3 = (`-24) = `-DEATH/YEAR for AMERICAN

ACTOR, DIRECTOR; and, AMERICAN FOOTBALL LINEBACKER (CARL WEATHERS)!!!~'

'-DIVORCED MARY ANN CASTLE in (1983) = 19(-)83 = ('-64) = 6x4 = ('-24) = '-DEATH/YEAR for AMERICAN ACTOR, DIRECTOR; and, AMERICAN FOOTBALL LINEBACKER (CARL WEATHERS)!!!~'

'-DEATH/DAY # '-NUMBER = 2 + 1 + 20 + 24 = ('-47) = 4x7 – ('-28) = '-FRAGMENTED '-BIRTH/DAY # '-NUMBER = ('-28) = RECIPROCAL = ('-82) = '-HIS '-VERY '-OWN '-BIRTH/DAY # '-NUMBER!!!~'

'-DEATH/DAY # '-NUMBER = 2 + 1 + 20 + 24 = ('-47) x ('-2) = ('-94) = (-) MINUS (-) = ('-76) '-AGE of '-DEATH = ('-18) = '-DAYS from '-BIRTH to '-DEATH!!!~'

FRAGMENTED '-DEATH/DAY # '-NUMBER = 2 + 1 + 2 + 0 + 2 + 4 = ('-11)!!!~'

(47 + 11) = ('-58) = 5+8 = ('-13) = 7+6 = ('-76) = '-HIS '-VERY '-OWN '-AGE of '-DEATH for AMERICAN ACTOR, DIRECTOR; and, AMERICAN FOOTBALL LINEBACKER (CARL WEATHERS)!!!~'

'-WAS '-MARRIED to JENNIFER PETERSON from (2007) TO (2009) = (20+07) + (20+09) = ('-27) + ('-29) = ('-56) = RECIPROCAL = ('-65) = 19(-)84 = '-MARRIED to RHONA UNSELL!!!~'

'-FROM '-BIRTH-to-DEATH there are ('-18) '-DAYS = 2x9 = ('-29) = 20+09 = '-YEAR '-MARRIAGE '-ENDED with JENNIFER PETERSON!!!~'

'-DEATH/DAY = 2/1 = 21 (x) 4 = ('-84) = '-YEAR '-MARRIED to RHONA UNSELL = RECIPROCAL = ('-48) = '-HIS '-VERY '-OWN '-BIRTH/YEAR for AMERICAN ACTOR, DIRECTOR; and, AMERICAN FOOTBALL LINEBACKER (CARL WEATHERS) (ROCKY/PREDATOR/STAR WARS)!!!~'

'-PARTIAL '-BIRTH/DAY # '-NUMBER = 1 + 14 + 19 = ('-34) = '-HAD ('-34) '-YEARS of '-MARRIAGE / for AMERICAN ACTOR, DIRECTOR; and, AMERICAN FOOTBALL LINEBACKER (CARL WEATHERS) (ROCKY/PREDATOR/STAR WARS)!!!~'

'-DEATH/YEAR = ('-24) x ('-2) = ('-48) = '-BIRTH/ YEAR!!!~'

JOHN PIERPONT MORGAN (AMERICAN FINANCIER & INVESTMENT BANKER) died at the '-AGE of ('-75)!!!~'

J. P. MORGAN SR. / '-DAY of '-BIRTH = ('-17th) = '-DIED ('-17) '-DAYS from '-BIRTH-to-DEATH for J. P. MORGAN SR.!!!~'

J. P. MORGAN SR. = `-BIRTH/DAY = 4/17 = RECIPROCAL = 71/4 = 71+4 = (`-75) = `-AGE of `-DEATH for JOHN PIERPONT MORGAN SR. (AMERICAN FINANCIER & INVESTMENT BANKER) (`-75); and, `-SON/ JOHN PIERPONT MORGAN JR. `-AGE of `-DEATH = (`-75); `-JUST as `-WELL!!!~'

J. P. MORGAN SR. = `-BIRTH/DAY = 4/17 = HALF RECIPROCAL = 4/71 = 4+71 = (`-75) = `-AGE of `-DEATH for JOHN PIERPONT MORGAN SR. (AMERICAN FINANCIER & INVESTMENT BANKER) (`-75); and, `-SON/ JOHN PIERPONT MORGAN JR. `-AGE of `-DEATH = (`-75); `-JUST as `-WELL!!!~'

SR. `-MARRIED FRANCES TRACY MORGAN in (1865) = 18(-)65 = (`-47) = (4) (1x7) = `-BIRTH/DAY of J. P. MORGAN SR. (4/17)!!!~'

SR. DAUGHTER-IN-LAW / JANE NORTON GREW'S `-DEATH/DAY = (8/14) = (8(-)1) (4) = (`-74) = RECIPROCAL = (`-47) = (4) (1x7) = `-BIRTH/DAY of `-FATHER-IN-LAW / J. P. MORGAN SR. = (4/17)!!!~'

SR. `-MARRIED AMELIA STURGES in (1861) = 18(-)61 = (`-43) = J. P. MORGAN SR. was `-BORN in the `-MONTH of (`-4); and, `-DIED in the `-MONTH of (`-3)!!!~'

SR. `-WAS `-MARRIED to FRANCES TRACY MORGAN from (1865-1913) for (`-48) `-YEARS = (`-48) = (4) (1+7) = `-BIRTH/DAY (4/17) for J. P. MORGAN SR.!!!~'

SR. `-WAS `-MARRIED to FRANCES TRACY MORGAN from (1865-1913) for (`-48) `-YEARS = 4x8 = (`-32) = 19+13 = `-DEATH/YEAR for J. P. MORGAN SR.!!!~'

J. P. MORGAN SR. FRAGMENTED `-BIRTH/DAY # `-NUMBER = 4+1+7+1+8+3+7 = (`-31) = RECIPROCAL = (`-**13**) = `-**HIS** `-**DEATH/YEAR** for JOHN PIERPONT MORGAN SR. (AMERICAN FINANCIER & INVESTMENT BANKER) from `-HIS `-VERY `-OWN FRAGMENTED `-BIRTH/DAY # `-NUMBER = (`-31)!!!~'

SR. `-DEATH/DAY = 3/31 = (3) (3+1) = (`-34) = `-DIED in the `-MONTH of (`-3); and, WAS `-BORN in the `-MONTH of (`-4) for J. P. MORGAN SR.!!!~'

SR. `-DEATH/DAY = 3/31 = 3+31 = (`-34) = `-DIED in the `-MONTH of (`-3); and, WAS `-BORN in the `-MONTH of (`-4) for J. P. MORGAN SR.!!!~'

`-SON / JOHN PIERPONT MORGAN JR. `-PARTIAL `-BIRTH/DAY # `-NUMBER = 9+7+18 = (`-34) = "SEE `-DIRECTLY `-ABOVE"!!!~'

J. P. MORGAN SR. `-DEATH/YEAR = (1913) = 19+13 = (`-32) = FLIP the (`-2) OVER to a (`-7) = (`-37) = `-BIRTH/YEAR for J. P. MORGAN SR.!!!~'

`-SON / JOHN PIERPONT MORGAN JR. `-DEATH/DAY = 3/(13) = RECIPROCAL = FATHER'S DEATH/DAY = 3/(31)!!!~'

SR. J. P. MORGAN '-DEATH/DAY = (3/31) = 3x31 = ('-93) = '-SON / JOHN PIERPONT MORGAN JR. was '-BORN in the '-MONTH of ('-9); and, '-DIED in the '-MONTH of ('-3) = ('-**9/3**)!!!~'

JR. J. P. MORGAN'S WIFE / JANE NORTON GREW'S '-BIRTH/DAY = (**9/3**0) = 9+30 = ('-39) = RECIPROCAL = ('-**93**)!!!~'

SR. J. P. MORGAN '-PARTIAL '-BIRTH/DAY # '-NUMBER = 4+17+18 = ('-39) = RECIPROCAL = ('-**93**)!!!~'

JR. J. P. MORGAN '-DEATH/DAY = (3/13) = 3x13 = ('-39) = RECIPROCAL = ('-**93**) = "SEE '-DIRECTLY '-ABOVE"!!!~'

'-SON / JOHN PIERPONT MORGAN JR. '-REVERSE '-LOOKUP on '-HIS '-BIRTH/DAY # '-NUMBER = 67(-)18(-)7(-)9 = ('-**33**) = '-HIS '-DEATH/DAY = **3(ONE)3**!!!~'

JOHN PIERPONT MORGAN SR. '-MARRIED AMELIA STURGES in (1861) = 18(-)61 = ('-43) = J. P. MORGAN SR. was '-BORN in the '-MONTH of ('-4); and, '-DIED in the '-MONTH of ('-3) = (**4/3**)!!!~'

JOHN PIERPONT MORGAN SR.'s / 2nd '-WIFE / FRANCES TRACY MORGAN'S / '-DEATH/YEAR = (1924) = 19+24 = ('-**43**)!!!~'

'-SON / JOHN PIERPONT MORGAN JR. died in the '-CALENDAR '-YEAR of ('-**43**) = 3/13/19**43**!!!~'

`-SON / JOHN PIERPONT MORGAN JR.'s WIFE / JANE NORTON GREW'S `-BIRTH/YEAR = (1868) = 18+68 = (`-86) / `-DIVIDED by (`-2) = (`-**43**) = `-HUSBAND'S / J. P. MORGAN JR.'s `-DEATH/YEAR = (`-**43**)!!!~'

`-SON / JOHN PIERPONT MORGAN JR. `-DEATH/YEAR = (1943) = 19+43 = (`-62) = FLIP the (`-2) OVER to a (`-7) = (`-67) = `-HIS `-VERY `-OWN `-BIRTH/YEAR for JOHN PIERPONT MORGAN JR.!!!~'

JOHN PIERPONT MORGAN SR. `-died at the `-AGE of (`-75); and, `-HIS `-SON / JOHN PIERPONT MORGAN JR. `-died at the `-AGE of (`-75), `-TOO!!!~'

JOHN PIERPONT MORGAN SR. `-BIRTH/DAY # `-NUMBER = 4+17+18+37 = (`-76) = RECIPROCAL = (`-67) = `-SON / JOHN PIERPONT MORGAN JR. was `-BORN in the `-CALENDAR `-YEAR of (`-67)!!!~'

`-SON / JOHN PIERPONT MORGAN JR. `-BIRTH/YEAR = (`-67) = 6+7 = (`-13) = `-FATHER'S / JOHN PIERPONT MORGAN SENIOR'S `-DEATH/YEAR = (`-13)!!!~'

`-SON / JOHN PIERPONT MORGAN JR.'s `-WIFE / JANE NORTON GREW / died in the `-CALENDAR `-YEAR of (`-25) = FLIP the (`-2) OVER to a (`-7) = (`-75) = `-AGE of `-DEATH for `-HER `-FORMER `-HUSBAND J. P. MORGAN JR.!!!~'

J. P. MORGAN JR.'s `-PARTIAL FRAGMENTED `-BIRTH/DAY # `-NUMBER = 9+7+1+8 = (`-25) = `-HIS `-VERY `-OWN `-WIFE'S / JANE NORTON GREW'S `-DEATH/YEAR = 19(25)!!!~'

J. P. MORGAN JR.'s WIFE / JANE NORTON GREW'S `-BIRTH/DAY # `-NUMBER = 9+30+18+68 = (`-125) = 1x25 = (`-25) = `-HER `-VERY `-OWN `-DEATH/YEAR = 19(25)!!!~'

JANE NORTON GREW'S `-PARTIAL `-BIRTH/DAY # `-NUMBER = 9+30+18 = (`-57) = RECIPROCAL = (`-75) = `-AGE of `-DEATH for `-HER `-HUSBAND / J. P. MORGAN JR. = (`-75)!!!~'

`-SON / JOHN PIERPONT MORGAN JR. was `-BORN in the `-MONTH of (`-9); and, `-DIED in the `-MONTH of (`-3) = (`-9/3) = 9x3 = (`-27) = RECIPROCAL = (`-72) = `-MARRIED in (1890) to JANE NORTON GREW = 18(-)90 = (`-72)!!!~'

`-SON / JOHN PIERPONT MORGAN JR. was `-MARRIED to JANE NORTON GREW for (`-35) `-YEARS = (`-35) = 7x5 = (`-75) = `-AGE of `-DEATH for J. P. MORGAN JR. = (`-75)!!!~'

J. P. MORGAN SR.'s `-PARTIAL `-DEATH/DAY # `-NUMBER = 3+31+19 = (`-53) = RECIPROCAL = (`-35) = 7x5 = `-AGES of `-DEATH for `-FATHER & `-SON / J. P. MORGAN!!!~'

J. P. MORGAN JR.'s `-PARTIAL `-DEATH/DAY # `-NUMBER = 3+13+19 = (`-35) = 7x5 = `-AGES of `-DEATH for `-FATHER & `-SON / J. P. MORGAN!!!~'

`-SON / JOHN PIERPONT MORGAN JR.'s `-WIFE / JANE NORTON GREW'S FRAGMENTED `-BIRTH/DAY # `-NUMBER = 9+3+0+1+8+6+8 = (`-35) = `-SHE `-WAS `-MARRIED for (`-35) `-YEARS to J. P. MORGAN JR. = & = "SEE the `-PREVIOUS `-LINKS to `-HUSBAND & FATHER-IN-LAW / J. P. MORGAN'S / `-AGES of `-DEATH"!!!~'

`-SON / JOHN PIERPONT MORGAN JR. died (`-178) `-DAYS from `-BIRTH-to-DEATH = 1x78 = (`-78)!!!~'

`-SON / JOHN PIERPONT MORGAN JR. `-DEATH/DAY # `-NUMBER = 3+13+19+43 = (`-78) = RECIPROCAL = (`-87)!!!~'

(365 (-) 178) = (`-187)!!!~'

J. P. MORGAN JR.'s FRAGMENTED `-BIRTH/DAY # `-NUMBER = 9+7+1+8+6+7 = (`-38)!!!~'

(`-38) x (`-2) = (`-76) = J. P. MORGAN SR.'s `-BIRTH/DAY # `-NUMBER = (`-76) = RECIPROCAL = (`-67) = J. P. MORGAN JR.'s `-BIRTH/YEAR = (`-67)!!!~'

J. P. MORGAN JR.'s `-BIRTH/YEAR = (1867) = 18(-)67 = (`-49) = `-HIS `-FATHER J. P. MORGAN SR. was `-MARRIED for (`-49) `-YEARS `-TOTAL!!!~' (`-48)

`-YEARS to `-HIS / J. P. MORGAN JR.'s `-MOTHER / (FRANCES TRACY MORGAN); and, (`-1) `-YEAR to / AMELIA STURGES!!!~'

J. P. MORGAN JR.'s `-BIRTH/DAY = (9/7) = RECIPROCAL = (7/9) = `-AGE of `-DEATH for `-HIS `-VERY `-OWN `-MOTHER / FRANCES TRACY MORGAN = (`-79)!!!~'

J. P. MORGAN JR.'s FRAGMENTED `-DEATH/DAY # `-NUMBER = 3+1+3+1+9+4+3 = (`-24) = `-HIS `-VERY `-OWN `-MOTHER'S / FRANCES TRACY MORGAN'S / `-DEATH/YEAR = (`-24)!!!~'

J. P. MORGAN JR.'s FRAGMENTED `-DEATH/DAY # `-NUMBER = 3+1+3+1+9+4+3 = (`-24) = RECIPROCAL = (`-42) = 6x7 = (`-67) = `-BIRTH/YEAR for J. P. MORGAN JR.!!!~'

J. P. MORGAN JR.'s / `-PARENTS were `-MARRIED in 18(**65**) = (`-**65**) = RECIPROCAL = (`-**56**) = J. P. MORGAN JR.'s `-WIFE / JANE NORTON GREW / died at the `-AGE of (`-**56**)!!!~'

J. P. MORGAN JR.'s / `-WIFE / JANE NORTON GREW'S `-FRAGMENTED `-DEATH/DAY # `-NUMBER = 8+1+4+1+9+2+5 = (`-30) = 5x6 = (`-**56**) = `-HER `-VERY `-OWN `-AGE of `-DEATH = (`-**56**)!!!~'

`-WIFE of J. P. MORGAN JR. / JANE NORTON GREW was `-BORN in the `-MONTH of (`-9); and, `-DIED in the `-MONTH of (`-8) = (9/8) = RECIPROCAL = (8/9)

= `-WAS `-MARRIED to J. P. MORGAN JR. in (1890) = (1x8) (9+0) = (`-89)!!!~'

J. P. MORGAN SR.'s `-DEATH/DAY # `-NUMBER = 3+31+19+13 = (`-66)!!!~'

J. P, MORGAN SR. / DAUGHTER-IN-LAW / JANE NORTON GREW'S `-DEATH/DAY # `-NUMBER = 8+14+19+25 = (`-66)!!!~'

(66(+)66) = (`-132) = 1x32 = (`-32) = 19+13 = `-DEATH/ YEAR for J. P. MORGAN SR.!!!~'

J. P. MORGAN SR.'s / FIRST WIFE / AMELIA STURGES `-DEATH/DAY # `-NUMBER = 2+17+18+62 = (`-99) = FLIP EVERY (`-9) OVER to a (`-6) = (`-66) = `-MATCHES `-HER `-HUSBAND'S `-DEATH/DAY # `-NUMBER = (`-66)!!!~'

`-REVERSE `-LOOKUP on AMELIA STURGES `-DEATH/DAY # `-NUMBER = 62(-)18(-)17(-)2 = (`-25) = FLIP EVERY (`-2) OVER to a (`-7) = (`-75) = `-AGE of `-DEATH for `-HER `-FORMER `-HUSBAND / J. P. MORGAN SR. = (`-75)!!!~'

`-FORMER `-WIFE AMELIA STURGES was `-BORN in 18(35) = (`-35) = 7x5 = (`-75) = `-AGE of `-DEATH for `-HER `-FORMER `-HUSBAND / J. P. MORGAN SR. = (`-75)!!!~'

(`-1835) = 18+35 = (`-53) = RECIPROCAL = (`-35) = 7x5 = (`-75) = `-AGE of `-DEATH for `-HER `-FORMER `-HUSBAND / J. P. MORGAN SR. = (`-75)!!!~'

`-FORMER `-WIFE AMELIA STURGES `-BIRTH/DAY = (2/17) = (2) (1x7) = (`-27) = `-HER `-VERY `-OWN `-AGE of `-DEATH from `-HER `-VERY `-OWN `-BIRTH/DAY!!!~'

J. P. MORGAN SR. / `-MARRIED / FRANCES TRACY MORGAN / in (1865) = 18+65 = (`-83) = "SEE `-IMMEDIATELY `-BELOW"!!!~'

J. P. MORGAN SR.'s / 2nd `-WIFE / FRANCES TRACY MORGAN'S `-BIRTH/DAY # `-NUMBER = 5+15+18+45 = (`-83) = 8x3 = (`-24) = `-HER `-VERY `-OWN `-DEATH/ YEAR = (`-24) = from `-HER `-VERY `-OWN `-BIRTH/ DAY # `-NUMBER!!!~'

J. P. MORGAN JR.'s FRAGMENTED `-BIRTH/DAY # `-NUMBER = 9+7+1+8+6+7 = (`-38) = RECIPROCAL = (`-83) = `-MOTHER'S / FRANCES TRACY MORGAN'S / `-BIRTH/DAY # `-NUMBER = (`-83)!!!~'

J. P. MORGAN SR.'s / 2nd `-WIFE / FRANCES TRACY MORGAN'S `-PARTIAL `-BIRTH/DAY # `-NUMBER = 5+15+18 = (`-38) = `-SON / J. P. MORGAN JR.'s / FRAGMENTED `-BIRTH/DAY # `-NUMBER = (`-38)!!!~'

J. P. MORGAN SR.'s / 2nd `-WIFE / FRANCES TRACY MORGAN'S `-BIRTH/DAY = 5/15 = (5x15) = (`-75) = `- AGE of `-DEATH for `-FORMER `-HUSBAND / J. P.

MORGAN SR.; and, `-AGE of `-DEATH for `-SON / J. P. MORGAN JR. = (`-75)!!!~'

J. P. MORGAN SR.'s / 2nd `-WIFE / FRANCES TRACY MORGAN'S `-DEATH/DAY # `-NUMBER = 11+16+19+24 = (`-70) / `-DIVIDED by (`-2) = (`-35) = 7x5 = (`-75) = `-AGE of `-DEATH for `-FORMER `-HUSBAND / J. P. MORGAN SR.; and, `-AGE of `-DEATH for `-SON / J. P. MORGAN JR. = (`-75)!!!~'

J. P. MORGAN SR.'s / 2nd `-WIFE / FRANCES TRACY MORGAN'S FRAGMENTED `-DEATH/DAY # `-NUMBER = 1+1+1+6+1+9+2+4 = (`-25) = FLIP EVERY (`-2) OVER to a (`-7) = (`-75) = `-AGE of `-DEATH for `-FORMER `-HUSBAND / J. P. MORGAN SR.; and, `-AGE of `-DEATH for `-SON / J. P. MORGAN JR. = (`-75)!!!~'

THROUGHOUT the `-UNIVERSE; `-GOD can have an `-ENGAGING `-CONVERSATION with `-EACH of `-HIS `-VARIED `-CREATIONS, `-SIMULTANEOUSLY/`-CONCURRENTLY!!!~' `-HE can IN FACT `-CREATE an entire `-UNIVERSE for `-EACH of `-HIS `-OWN `-VARIED `-CREATIONS; if, `-HE so `-DESIRED!!!~'

`-MY `-NEXT `-BOOK of the `-PROPHET will be `-ENTITLED: "The `-SECRETS of `-GOD"; but

`-WAIT, I'VE already / just GIVEN `-YOU / `-ALL / of these `-SECRETS in `-MY previous (`-13) `-BOOKS!!!~' CLEARLY, our `-WORLD, OUR solar SYSTEM, OUR GALAXIES, OUR `-UNIVERSE, the COSMOS, are `-ALL OF `-*SUPER* `-DIVINE `-order; AND, are `-ALL of `-*SUPER* `-DIVINE `-ARRANGEMENTS!!!~'

ECCLESIASTES 3:2 / From the ` BIBLE!!!~'

VERSE / 2) a time to be born, and a time to die; a time to plant, and a time to pluck up that which is planted; (-English Revised Edition-1885)…

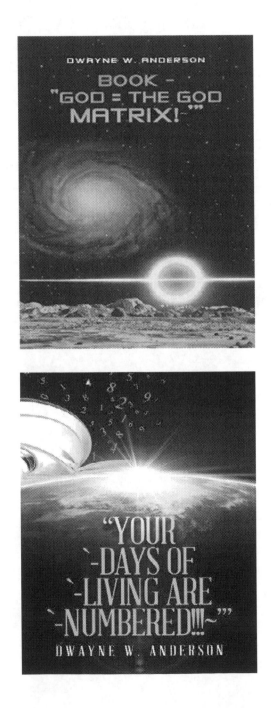

Printed in the United States
by Baker & Taylor Publisher Services